How to Get U.S. Government Contracts and Classified Work

A Contractor's Guide to Bidding on Classified Work and Building a Compliant Security Program to Win Federal Contracts

How to Get U.S. Government Contracts and Classified Work

A Contractor's Guide to Bidding on Classified Work and Building a Compliant Security Program to Win Federal Contracts

Jeffrey W. Bennett, ISOC, ISP, SAPPC, SFPC

How to Get U.S. Government Contracts and Classified Work
A Contractor's Guide to Bidding on Classified Work and Building a Compliant
Security Program to Win Federal Contracts

Published by: Red Bike Publishing

Copyright © 2020 by Red Bike Publishing, Huntsville, Alabama
Published in the United States of America
https://www.redbikepublishing.com

Library of Congress Control Number: 2020941004
ISBN: 978-1-936800-26-1

ABOUT THE AUTHOR

Jeffrey W. Bennett, ISOC, ISP, SAPPC, SFPC, has a plenty of government, contractor and security experience. Plus he is board certified to protect classified information. He is a former Army officer who has served in military intelligence, logistics and speaks three languages. He has an MBA from Columbia College and a Masters Degree in Acquisitions and Procurement Management from Webster University. Jeff is a featured speaker in many venues including a presenter at the University of Alabama in Huntsville.

To find out more about the author, visit:
https://www.redbikepublishing.com

ABOUT RED BIKE PUBLISHING...

Mission:

Red Bike Publishing exists to create value for our partners, shareholders and customers by building a business to last. This is what we are dedicated to. As the foremost niche publishing organization, we offer what other publishers cannot; focused delivery of industry publications to enhance the professional's skill levels. We do this by writing and publishing superior fiction, nonfiction, traditional and e-book and providing empowering training resources at affordable prices.

Vision:
Red Bike Publishing will be valued for its one of a kind niche publishing and ability to positively impact our customers.

See more at
https://www.redbikepublishing.com

NOTE TO THE READER

You know how there are many opportunities to work with the government but the guidance is disparate? Well I wrote this book to help defense contractors bid, perform on classified contracts and develop security programs to protect classified information.

Congratulations on buying this book. You have just taken the first step to improving your understanding of how to become a cleared defense contractor and win classified contracts. Inside you'll discover techniques and methodologies you need to develop programs to protect classified information. In fact, I want you to read the first two chapters today so that you can get a good foundation that you will be able to apply immediately.

This book goes beyond just winning the bid. It covers information from Presidential Executive Orders and the National Industrial Security Program Operating Manual that you need to know to plan for performing on classified contracts. Being technically proficient is great, but building an award winning program gets you noticed. Business owners and defense contractors will understand what it takes to get security clearances and move to the next step of protecting classified information.

For those who desire to perform on classified contracts, this book will show you how to do so. It unravels the web of requirements to lead you to a smooth transition to that of a cleared defense contractor.

In small companies the roles one employee may have are many. For larger companies, NISPOM responsibilities and positions are accomplished by a team of cleared employees focused on one mission. However, with small companies these roles are held by a single employee performing many tasks. This book can show you how to assign and share critical tasks without becoming overwhelmed.

DEDICATION

This book is dedicated to the men and women of all vocations and walks of life who defend our country and protect our Nation's secrets.

ACKNOWLEDGEMENTS

None of this would have been possible without the loving support of my family. You have so willingly provided encouragement while understanding my need to write this book. The time involved in writing and editing meant burning a lot of midnight oil. Kathleen, Patrick, Claire and Molly, I love you all.

Appreciation to Joe Farkas, Stan Koryta and countless other Facility Security Officers (FSO) who choose to remain nameless, but have provided excellent technical editing for this project.

I would like to thank Shama Patel for her social media support and editing services. You can reach her at Evening Light Designs, LLC https://www.eveninglightdesigns.com

If you want more information about security clearances, check out our video and training.
https://www.redbikepublishing.com/security/

Intent

I want to provide Cleared Defense Contractors and employees with insight into the National Industrial Security Program. My intention is to walk the reader step by step through getting a facility security clearance (FCL) personnel security clearances (PCL) bidding on and performing on classified contracts.

This book is meant to compliment the federal regulations and executive orders bringing about the National Industrial Security Program. It is also designed to help the reader draw from experience and suggests ways to establish a working environment fit for classified contracts. Those who are new to the field can use this as a guide, but any security and compliance related issues that an organization may face should be pursued with the Cognizant Security Agency (CSA), Government Contracting Activity (GCA) or other Federal agencies and legal activities.

I have made every effort to make this book as accurate and complete as possible. As the author, I am certified by the DoD to protect classified information. It has been reviewed and edited by some of the most experienced Facility Security Officers (FSO), defense contractors and Industrial Security Professionals (ISP) in the business. It is reviewed often and revised to keep current.

Not every defense contractor is the same. Classified contracts further differentiate requirements. Each contractor may have a unique mission based on skill sets and core competencies. Each contract has unique requirements based on product and service needs. Defense contractors working on classified contracts will have further defined roles based on requirements listed in the Contract Security Classification Specification (DD Form 254) and contract clauses and language. Specifically, cleared contractors have unique security requirements based on the DD Form 254 identifying the clearance level and classified storage level. The following are two examples out of many possible scenarios:

Example 1: A defense contractor is required to have a Facility

Security Clearance (FCL) of TOP SECRET while having a classified storage level of TOP SECRET. In this case they can expect to have employees with TOP SECRET security clearances supporting contracts on site with TOP SECRET work and TOP SECRET information. In the course of their work they will store tens of thousands of classified items. Their security requirements are complex depending on the amount of classified items, level of classified information, amount of international contracts, and etc.

Example 2: In another example a contractor has a SECRET FCL and no authorization to store or perform classified work on site. They require the SECRET FCL for the sole purpose of providing employees with security clearances to perform work off site at a customer location. They will have no requirement for security containers or in-depth security to protect classified information on site.

The purpose of this book is not to provide exact solutions for each of thousands of possible scenarios. There are too many variables to be contained in any one book. It is written to inform and provide resources that the defense contractor can use to either seek additional expert help from the CSA, GCA, Prime Contractor or competent consultant. This book is written to reflect guidance from the National Industrial Security Program Operating Manual (NISPOM), but is not written to be used instead of the NISPOM. Additionally, there is guidance in the NISPOM not covered in this book.

After each chapter you will find a section called "Resources" that will identify key NISPOM points and where in the NISPOM to find the relevant information. You can take my word for it, or follow along with your own NISPOM copy. Download your copy of NISPOM from the DCSA website, or grab your print version from

https://www.redbikepublishing.com/nispom/

This book is written to familiarize and inform defense contractors of NISPOM requirements. This book covers general areas most cleared contractors may encounter. It is meant to help the reader determine which parts of NISPOM apply, direct the reader to available resources and suggest general ways of implementing the NISPOM. The reader should always consult NISPOM, GCA, Prime Contractor and the CSO concerning policy and contract requirements.

For a step by step and chapter by chapter walk through of the NISPOM visit:
https://www.bennettinstitute.com

Table of Contents

CHAPTER 1 WHY CLASSIFIED CONTRACTS

INTRODUCTION

Thanks again for buying this book. I am so glad you did and wish you well in your journey as a Cleared Defense Contractor (CDC). CDCs and cleared employees who desire to perform on classified contracts do not always know where to go to find information on what might be expected of them. Some might purposefully bid for classified contracts while others find that contracts beginning as unclassified may become classified at a later time, leaving them with a steep learning curve. The leadership of companies not experienced in working with classified contracts may not know where to look for information or gain access to training or possible expenses until after the Government grants their security clearances.

There are numerous locations with opportunities to learn this information within government and professional organizations. However, other than government regulations, there are few published books addressing the subject. This book is intended to provide answers that help those who would like to know more about what it takes to get Facility security Clearances (FCL) and Personnel security Clearances (PCL) and prepare for work on classified contracts. The following chapters will teach about Original Classification Authorities (OCA), the qualifications and reasons for classification, how to get security clearances and how to protect classified information.

A defense contractor is a business entity that has registered to bid on government contracts. A CDC is a defense contractor that has been granted a FCL, authorizing them to perform on classified contracts. This book's purpose is to equip the defense contractor with some knowledge of what it takes to work on classified contracts and protect classified material. The reader will also learn about resources available to help them protect our nation's secrets and become value added employees in their organizations. The cleared contractor's designated Facility Security Officer (FSO) is the front line in any enterprise working with classified materials and is responsible for security awareness training and prevention of unauthorized disclosure of Government secrets.

A National Level View of Protecting the Nation's Secrets

Under the National Industrial Security Program (NISP), the Department of Defense, Department of Energy, Director of National Intelligence, the Nuclear Regulatory Commission and their cleared contractors are charged with protecting classified information. Classified information is US Government material, documents, software, hardware, or any other official information in any other format that requires protection from unauthorized disclosure. Unauthorized disclosure could cause damage to national security.

Each of the above mentioned government agencies are also known as Cognizant Security Agencies (CSA) and each has established guidelines for protecting classified information and ensuring compliance. Though each agency has its own written guidelines, the NISP ensures that each follows a national standard. The CSAs have Cognizant Security Offices (CSO) that take care of administrative functions. The CSAs and their CSOs assisted you with your security clearance, both FCL and PCL. They will also work with you to ensure that the classified information in your possession is protected. They are listed below:

- CSA: Department of Defense
  - CSO: Defense Counterintelligence and Security Agency (DCSA)
- CSA: Department of Energy
  - CSO: Department of Energy Field Offices Safeguards and

Security Divisions
- CSA: Central Intelligence Agency
  - CSO: Contract Officer's Security Representative (COSR)
- CSA: Nuclear Regulatory Commission
  - CSO: US Nuclear Regulatory Commission

This book addresses protection of classified information in the Department of Defense (DoD) and their contractors. The DoD is a CSA and DCSA is the CSO. Guidelines for protecting classified information are found in the National Industrial Security Program Operating Manual (NISPOM). The NISPOM provides guidance for protecting classified information and ensures that holders of classified information should be able to produce the classified information within a reasonable amount of time [1]. The loss, compromise or suspected compromise of classified information should be investigated and reported. Loss, compromise or suspected compromise could occur without control, accountability, and documentation of classified information.

Original Classification Authority (OCA)

An original classification authority (OCA) follows a six step process that determines sensitivity, demonstrates the level of damage to national security and communicates that classification level. The OCA assigns classification to qualifying equipment, documents, tools, pictures, software, and other items that need protection against unauthorized disclosure. For the purposes of this book, we will refer to classified items of all configurations and media as classified information.

Facility Security Officer (FSO)

Because this book is about performing on classified projects, the emphasis is on the FSO since they are a large part of the process at CDCs. CDCs are required to appoint an FSO during the establishment of a FCL. The FSO processes employee security clearance requests, answers questions about security clearances and leads the continuous evaluation process. Security clearances and FSOs go hand in hand.

Cleared contractors falling under the NISPOM are required to appoint a FSO to design and implement a security program to protect classified information. DCSA provides mandatory training and offers other helpful topical training for the FSO. Training punctuates the serious implications of losing accountability. In cases of security incidents involving classified information, FSOs initiate a targeted preliminary inquiry to determine whether or not a loss, compromise or suspected compromise occurred. When loss, compromise or suspected compromise cannot be ruled out, the FSO reports it to DCSA. Loss, compromise or suspected compromise of classified information can cause damage to national security, lead to reduced company profits or loss of the contract and or criminal penalties.

Appointed FSOs can be a current cleared employee with additional responsibilities or a cleared employee hired for the exclusive security work. The FSO must complete mandatory training either designed for working in possessing or non-possessing facilities. A possessing facility is approved for storing classified information on site. A non-possessing facility is not authorized to store classified information on site and work is usually performed at other approved locations. In either case, the FSO establishes and continuously ensures classified information is protected by identifying, handling, transmitting, and destroying it and ensuring cleared employees receive required training.

This book addresses situations where designated FSOs are full time security employees or are designated responsibilities in addition to their regular job description. In many cases human resources personnel, executive assistants, engineers, business developers, owners, presidents, contracts managers or other cleared employees perform FSO functions as an additional duty. They may not have the luxury of dedicating as much time to managing classified information as does a full time FSO.

Threat to National Security

For over 18 years John A. Walker, Jr. had sold secrets during and after his career in the Navy. Though entrusted with a security clearance and a "need-to know", he began to violate the trustworthiness his thorough background investigation deemed him worthy. He took advantage of his position and responsibilities to smuggle classified information to his Russian connections.

During the investigation into his arrest, authorities discovered a complex spy ring consisting of family members and other recruited operatives. Walker had influenced some family members to help commit one of the most notorious of all espionage cases. As a result of his crimes, he received a two life terms plus 10 year, his son received 25 years and the damage to the US national security was tremendous [2].

The ignored indicators of espionage activities as in the case of Walker and others are enlightening. Properly trained and alert cleared employees should be part of the countermeasures implemented to help identify attempts of espionage. The safeguarding procedures, security awareness training and documentation required by the NISP should be applied to protect assets and recognize and prevent future instances of costly espionage.

Executive Order 12829

The US Government awards contracts, grants and licenses to defense contractors in the course of providing a product or service. The contracts, grants and licenses may be classified in nature. The NISP is designed to protect classified government information that is released to cleared contractors. The result is a partnership between the government and the cleared contractor to protect the classified information at the level the government has determined it to be.

Executive Order (EO) 12829 establishes the NISP. The NISP gives guidance, training and directives that those in industrial security should use to better protect classified materials. It also creates agencies that have oversight of contractors performing on classified contracts.

The NISP's purpose is to safeguard classified information that has been or may be released to "...current, prospective, or former contractors, licensees, or grantees of United States agencies". It is also designed to provide for the protection of classified material as outlined in EO 12356 and the Atomic Energy Act of 1954, as Amended [3].

The implementing and monitoring of the NISP is granted to the Director of the Information Security Oversight Office (ISOO), under the guidance of the National Security Council (NSC). While the NSC provides policy and direction, the ISOO is the operations unit. As such, the Director of ISOO provides guidelines to industry for how classified information is designated and classification markings.

EO 12829 also provides guidance for safeguarding classified information, required security education topics and training programs. The ISOO monitors NISP compliance and gives contractors guidance for self-inspection programs. The director has many other responsibilities while working with other agencies to develop directives for implementation; reviewing and modifying regulations; overseeing compliance; inspecting and conducting on-site review of cleared contractors who have access to or store classified information; reporting violations to heads of agencies or the senior official designated; addressing issues and complaints concerning the NISP and report annually to the President through the NSC [4].

The NISP also establishes the National Industrial Security Program Policy Advisory Committee (NISPPAC). This NISPPAC is designed to represent the departments and agencies affected by the NISP and is chaired by the Director of ISOO. Together they work to advise departments and the President on matters concerning the NISP, recommend changes to policies identified in the executive orders and discuss policy issues in dispute.

The NISPOM

The members of the NISPPAC are both government and contractor representatives. The Administrator of General Services supports the committee with resources to include facilities and staff. The EO requires that the Secretary of Defense work with the Secretary of Energy, the Nuclear Regulatory Commission and the Director of Central Intelligence to issue and maintain the NISPOM [5].

Other non DoD agencies provide material for NISPOM guidance. For example, the Secretary of Energy and the Nuclear Regulatory Commission (NRC) will have the lead in detailing requirements for protecting classified information identified in the Atomic Energy Act of 1954. The Director of National Intelligence (DNI) will provide a section for intelligence sources and methods, to include Sensitive Compartmented Information (SCI). However, in this coordination each agency maintains its authority.

The NISPOM applies to authorized users of classified information and equips those working on classified contracts with critical instruction on how to implement the NISP within their organizations. It is up to the cleared contractor and DCSA to work together in providing accurate interpretation of the NISPOM to the specific classified contract requirements. It is this interpretation that DCSA will use while conducting annual security reviews.

Defense contractors should apply the concept of risk management while implementing the NISPOM. There are three factors necessary in determining risk. The first is the damage to national security that could be reasonably expected to result from unauthorized disclosure of classified material. This book will discuss the levels of classification that are used to designate and recognize the severity of damage. At this point it is important to know that the NISPOM provides explicit guidance to users on how to identify and protect classified items at all levels.

The second factor is the existing or anticipated threat to disclosure of information. The third factor is the short and long term costs of the requirements, restrictions, and other safeguards. The second and third factors aren't spelled out in the NISPOM, but are recognized as legitimate concerns that the FSO and DCSA should be prepared to address.

The Secretary of Defense inspects, monitors, and determines who has access to classified material. The Director of Central Intelligence serves the same purpose for matters of intelligence and has oversight. The Secretary of Energy and the NRC have similar oversight roles concerning energy. The Director of Central Intelligence, the Secretary of Energy and the NRC can enter into written agreements giving the

Secretary of Defense authorization to inspect or monitor programs or facilities (Figure 1-1) [5]. Otherwise the areas are carved out and not inspected or monitored by the Secretary of Defense.

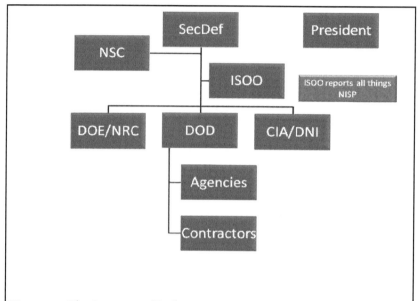

Figure 1-1 - The Secretary of Defense, DoE/NRC and CIA/DNI provide input to and issue the National Industrial Security Program Operating Manual.

As the executive agent, the Secretary of Defense can work with the other agencies to standardize procedures to help promote and implement the NISP. Without this standardization, the implementation of the NISP would prove difficult. EO 12829 directs the Secretary of Defense and agencies involved to document and account for all costs associate with the program. These costs will be reported through the Director of ISOO to the President.

How the US Government Oversees Classification Management

How do classified items receive their designations? Who is responsible for assigning classification levels? What recourse do security managers have after discovering a classification error? Can anything be assigned a classification level by anyone? These are questions that may be asked by those new to the NISP. Although there is guidance to demonstrate control, accountability, documentation, storage, dissemination and destruction of classified material, new industrial security specialists and FSOs may not understand the fundamentals.

Classification

The Government has designed policy to ensure that classified material is protected at the level designated to prevent unauthorized disclosure. The President has designated the authority to assign a classification level. EO 13526 defines an accountability process to ensure classification is assigned at the appropriate level and protection is adequate. The person holding the appointed position of OCA has both the duty and responsibility to classify information properly.

Classified information is marked with CONFIDENTIAL, SECRET or TOP SECRET and must be afforded protection at the appropriate level. TOP SECRET has more restrictions than SECRET and SECRET has more restrictions than CONFIDENTIAL. Each must be protected according to the classification markings. For example, unauthorized disclosure of CONFIDENTIAL information could reasonably be expected to cause damage; SECRET could reasonably be expected to cause serious damage; and TOP SECRET could reasonably be expected to cause exceptionally grave damage to national security.

When the classification level is determined, the OCA places the markings. The markings indicate the level of classification, identify the exact information to be protected, provide guidance on downgrading and declassification, give reasons for classification and sources of classification, and warn of special access, control or safeguarding requirements. According to a report from the Chairman of the House

National Security Subcommittee, 10% of secrets should have never been classified and that nearly 90% of classified information has been assigned a classification level higher than required. For example, classified information marked as TOP SECRET should have been marked CONFIDENTIAL or SECRET. In another report provided by DCSA in 2003, nearly $6.5 billion was spent to classify information [6].

How The Government Assigns Classification

To prevent system abuse, EO 13526 provides guidance to train and prevent OCAs from arbitrarily assigning a classification level. The information has to meet certain criteria before the level can be designated. The EO also ensures that delegation of OCA is not haphazard. Specific job positions are reserved for the responsibility. The OCAs attends extensive training in preparation of the responsibilities ahead of them.

As over-classification results in unnecessary costs, under classification can lead to possible compromise of classified information. In cases where items may be assigned an original classification, four conditions must be met [7]:

- A designated OCA is applying the classification level
- The information is owned by, produced for, or is controlled by the US Government
- Information meets one of eight categories
- The OCA determines unauthorized disclosure could cause damage to national security to include transnational terrorism and they can identify or describe the damage.

National security is the defense of our nation or foreign relations of the United States.

1. Original Classification Authority

How is information classified or who designates the level of classification? A review of EO 13526 provides the answer. OCA is practiced by designated officials. These individuals are selected to assign a classification level based on specific guidelines and whether or not the information meets certain criteria. These safeguards are in place for many reasons, including preventing unnecessary classification which may become a burden to the NISP.

The President and in certain circumstances the Vice President, agency heads designated by the President in the Federal Register, and appointed US Government Officials can serve as OCA [7.] Agency heads are responsible for ensuring that only the minimum amount of subordinate officials are delegated OCA. It is these Government checks and balances that ensure responsibility and accountability. Classified information should be identified and protected accordingly throughout its existence.

The President, Vice President, agency heads, and officials designated by the President can delegate TOP SECRET OCA. SECRET and CONFIDENTIAL OCA also may be given to senior agency officials who are designated by agency heads in writing. The authority may not be automatically re-delegated [7.]

The OCAs attend annual training covering how to identify classified information, how to determine classification level, safeguarding of classified information and the criminal, civil, and administrative penalties charged against those who fail to protect it from unauthorized disclosure.

2. The Information is Owned by, Produced for or Under the Control of the US Government

An OCA cannot assign a classification level to anything that is not owned by, produced for or under the control of the US Government. The work is based on a legitimate US Government requirement. For example, a Government Contracting Agency (GCA) contracts a CDC company to provide classified goods and services. The CDC should protect the products according to the NISP. As part of the contract, the GCA requires that the company construct and assemble items that must be safeguarded at the SECRET level of classification. The GCA will also provide direction and means for production and security.

The contractor then agrees to protect the classified information in the course of the contract.

3. Information meets one of eight categories

Classification levels are assigned to classified materials and information only if they fall into one of eight categories designated in EO paragraph 1.4.

3a. Military plans, weapons systems or operations

The US Government provides instructions for protecting weapons and plans. If plans and operations were released to the wrong hands, the information could damage national security and adversely affect the nation's ability to defend itself. Cleared contractors with the responsibility of providing for the construction, modification, repair or other service of weapons is charged with protecting these items at the highest level required.

3b. Foreign Government Information

Foreign government information includes classified documents or products provided by a foreign country in the fulfillment of a Government to Government contract or as collaboration. It is worth mentioning that in many instances and depending on the contract, a company may find itself safeguarding Foreign Government Information (FGI) or information classified by a foreign country. This information has been entrusted to the United States Government and is expected to be protected at the indicated equivalent level or higher. Appropriate agencies describe procedures for companies possessing FGI to include, but are not limited to separate storage and documentation.

3c. Intelligence activities, sources, methods or cryptology

Sources of classified information must be protected. One can imagine what damage could take place if any intelligence gathering sources, methods or activities were compromised. The suspecting adversary could become aware of the threat and cease their activity or design countermeasures designed to thwart future collection efforts.

3d. Foreign relations or activities of the United States including confidential sources

This information includes US foreign policy activities and sources friendly to US efforts and US organizations. Such is protected to ensure the safety of the relations and success of the activities. Compromise of any sources could cause damage to National Security.

3e. Scientific, technological, or economic matters relating to national security, including defense against transnational terrorism

Unauthorized access to national security related US scientific, technological, and economic data could compromise plans, production, and strategies and leave certain vulnerabilities. Furthermore, foreign adversaries could gain the advantages of expensive US research and development without sacrifice.

A more realistic example concerns Noshir S. Gowadia; an Indian-born engineer was indicted on 21 counts of exports violations, espionage and other charges. While working in Hawaii he had allegedly provided information to a Chinese agent and missile technicians. Through covert email messages he gave information for the purpose of building a radar evading cruise missile. This information gave the Chinese the capability to build a missile to evade anti-missile technology [8].

3f. US programs for safeguarding nuclear materials or facilities

Risk managers assess their material and facilities. They then identify threats, how to prevent the threats, the impact of the threat and how to reduce that impact. Good security managers work with their companies and government customers to provide operations security (OPSEC) and support strategies to protect nuclear materials or facilities. Vulnerabilities and strengths are assessed to ensure the best possible measures are in place to protect these items. Plans, strategies and programs are only effective if enforced and access is limited. An adversary could use the programs to gain advantage, steal, damage, or destroy nuclear materials or facilities.

3g. Vulnerabilities of systems, installations, infrastructures, projects, plans or protection services related to national security including terrorism

Government and civilian organizations constantly develop procedures for safeguarding classified information and are usually resilient and well thought out. However, the people the system are designed to protect and help are often the biggest threat. We may agree that the insider provides the most probability with the highest impact as the following event illustrates:

In 2001, the Federal Bureau of Investigation (FBI) arrested FBI Agent Robert Phillip Hanssen on charges of espionage. From 1985 until 2001, Agent Hanssen had worked closely with the Russians, providing highly classified intelligence information. Some of his charges included revealing information about intelligence collection efforts, double agents and critical research on the KGB [9]. This information revealed weaknesses in security that had since caused considerable and irreparable damage to national security. The activity also resulted in prison sentences for and executions of Russian citizens abroad. In 2007 Hollywood turned this famous case into the movie *Breech*. The case also provides a training model for many security awareness programs and counter-intelligence lessons.

3h. Weapons of Mass Destruction

Information fitting this category is classified to prevent unauthorized disclosure. Such unauthorized disclosure could make the US vulnerable to adversaries. Looking back in history, we can learn from the events leading to the bombing of Japan using nuclear weapons. The development of such technical data had been kept secret throughout the life cycle. Many of the nation's top scientists worked in absolute secrecy in the construction and testing phases. The US was in a race to produce the first nuclear bomb. If technical and classified information had not been protected, the US citizens could quite have possibly been on the receiving end of a nuclear strike.

4. Unauthorized disclosure could cause damage to national security to include transnational terrorism and they can identify or describe the damage

This is the fourth and final requirement that must be met before an OCA can assign a classification level. Classification levels are designed to identify the sensitivity and required level of protection. To complete the picture, the consequence of unauthorized disclosure must also be addressed. Where the OCA identifies what should be protected, the other side of risk management is for the OCA to also identify the level of damage coinciding with the level of protection.

The OCA Six Step Process

To determine whether or not information is classified, the OCA goes through a six step process. As a review, the OCA is an appointed position. The person holding that position may not actually conduct this review. More likely, it will be conducted by government employees responsible for the program. If classification is determined, the program will produce a SCG for the OCA's approval.

1. Determine if the information is official government information

The US Government must own, have an interest or control the information. During the review, the OCA determines not only whether or not the information should be classified, but also whether or not the information has already been classified by another agency. If so, then the prior determination is used.

2. Determine if the information is eligible to be classified

This determination is made based on guidance provided in EO 13526. The EO lists the four conditions that must be met prior to classifying information.

3. Determine if there is potential for damage to national security if unauthorized release occurs

The OCA should be able to determine whether or not the unauthorized release of information will cause damage to national security and be able to describe the damage.

4. Assign a level of classification

The impact of disclosure is categorized from reasonably causing "damage" for CONFIDENTIAL information, "serious damage" for SECRET information and "seriously grave damage" for TOP SECRET information. The impact of loss or compromise of the information must be at one of the three defined levels in order to be assigned a classification. Also, the classifier should be able to describe or identify the damage to national security. This measure informs the user that the information is to be safeguarded and also to prevent the OCA from assigning a classification level needlessly.

5. Make a decision about classification duration

Once the classification authority assigns a classification level; they still have another task to fulfill; assigning a duration or time period. After the end date, the information should be automatically declassified based on the sensitivity level. This assists in the control of the classified information as well as ensuring items do not maintain an unnecessary classification.

The OCA's are trained to declassify information when classification is no longer necessary. Anyone who has extensive experience in the NISP may remember a time when duration was not always assigned a specific date or event. The EO 13526 designed parameters to ensure that information is only classified as necessary and for only as long as needed.

The OCAs should assign a date or event for declassification based on the national security sensitivity, but should not exceed 25 years. When the OCA is unable to determine an earlier date or event then they will assign a declassification date for 10 years from the original decision date (date of classification). When national security sensitivity requires more time, this date can be set not to exceed 25 years from the date of the decision [10]. Information that no longer meets the requirements for classification under EO 13526 or has reached the threshold of the declassification date should be declassified immediately. The defense contractor should contact the OCA or GCA before declassifying or downgrading.

6. Communicate the decision

The OCA communicates the classification level through a SCG and classification markings.

Security Classification Guide (SCG)

The SCG communicates classification instructions issued by the OCA. CDCs should ensure that an FSO is on site for each classified contract or as determined in the DD Form 254.

Classification Markings

Classified information should be conspicuously marked and immediately apparent. These important markings serve to alert holders to the presence of classified information; identify the exact information to be protected and the level of protection required; provide guidance on information sharing; warn holders of special access, dissemination control, or safeguarding requirements and provide guidance on downgrading and declassification.

The display of classified markings will be covered in later chapters, but this introduction is necessary to demonstrate how material is identified and labeled. All classified information should be marked and protected.

Classified information should be marked to identify the classification level, the classification authority, the agency and office of classification authority, declassification instructions, and a specific reason for the classification. Furthermore, the classification should identify which pages, paragraphs and portions are classified and unclassified. There can be no doubt of which part of the media is or is not classified as it will notify the user of how to derive data for inclusion into new media.

Classification Limits

There are restrictions in determining classification levels. For example, a classification authority cannot assign a classification for personal or political gain. It is only to be designed to further national security and offer the protection. A classification cannot be assigned to hide legal violations, inefficiencies or mistakes. Nor can the OCAs assign a classification just to prevent embarrassment, prevent or restrict competition or delay the release of information that hasn't previously required such a level of protection [11.]

Compilation

A cleared contractor may find that while working with unclassified information they create a classified product after the introduction or compilation of new unclassified information. In the course of work requirements, they may assemble individually unclassified product into a collection. This collection of independently (or individually) unclassified information may become a classified product per the associated SCG. This is not a random event, as there are tools to help the user identify the probability of such events occurring.

Challenges to Classification

Holders of classified information could discover that the assigned classification level may be inappropriate or unnecessary. These holders have a duty to report their findings. The NISPOM requires the reporting of such discovery to the ISOO. However, such reports can be handled with the GCA or program channels and reviewed for a decision. Typically such challenges are handled through the government program channels. In other words, the defense contractor can notify their government program manager or comparable technical point of contact.

For example, two similar contract efforts might have different levels of classification. One government contract might be unclassified while the other is SECRET. The contractor could challenge the classification effort through their program manager or government industrial security specialist. The agency heads or senior officials are required to ensure there is no retribution for the report as well as notifying the individuals that they have a right to appeal the agency decisions to the Interagency Security Classification Appeals Panel [12.]

Derivative Classification

CDCs do not have OCA. OCA is delegated to government positions to effectively and responsibly assign a classification level. However, holders of classified material may be contractually authorized to paraphrase, quote, extract, summarize classified information or label classified material according to source material or the SCG. CDCs conducting derivative classification are required to conduct Derivative Classifier Training. Training is available at the DCSA website and at: *https://www.bennettinstitute.com.*

Creating classified material as compilation or derived from other classified information requires the user to follow OCA classification designations. Derivative classification markings also include the transfer of the declassification requirements identified on the original classified information source that possesses the longest duration of classification and a listing of the original sources.

For example, a user is creating a report from two different classified sources. The first source is classified as CONFIDENTIAL and has a declassification date of 31 December 2037. The second source is classified CONFIDENTIAL and has a declassification date 31 December 2029. The new compilation will have a derivative classification of CONFIDENTIAL with a declassification date of 31 December 2037.

Protection of Classified Information

Access to classified information requires authorization based on a security clearance and need to know of the information. Security clearances are awarded based on favorable information gathered from a properly executed investigation. This process can take over 12 months to complete. After the access is granted and prior to gaining access to the classified information, the individual signs a Classified Information Non Disclosure Agreement (SF 312). Cleared employees with access to classified information are trained on at a minimum, safeguarding procedures and sanctions imposed on those who fail to protect it from unauthorized disclosure.

Classified information should remain under the control of the originating agency. If classified information is necessary at another agency, then written authority is required from the originating agency. Classified information cannot be automatically transferred interagency without the necessary approval. Each originating agency provides instructions on the protection, use, storage, transmission and destruction of the information. One important implied task for users of classified information is to thoroughly document its status, manage receipts, and anything else necessary to allow retrieval of the classified information within a reasonable amount of time. In future chapters we will demonstrate how to document and catalog not only classified information, but the associated receipts that transmission, reproduction, and destruction require. Learning how to protect, document and account for classified information will help identify and prevent instances of espionage, theft and other events of unauthorized disclosure.

This book will demonstrate how to protect classified information throughout its life cycle and provide more specific examples of the proper methods of protecting, documenting and accounting for classified material. This chapter has provided a glimpse into the national level policy of how information is designated with a level of classification and the protection expected by the OCA. Future chapters will help determine how cleared contractors and employees operate under the standards of the NISP.

Summary

Executive Order 12829 created the NISP. The purpose of the program is to protect Government classified information at CDC facilities from unauthorized disclosure. The NISPOM was created to provide guidance on protecting classified information. Presidential Executive Order 13526 provides classified national security protection information. It delivers a cohesive method for the assignment of a classification, protecting and declassifying national security information. The executive order describes the authority to classify information and provides strict requirements.

Classified information should always be marked to indicate the classification level. These markings notify the user how to protect the information from unauthorized disclosure. If information has been found to be classified improperly, the person discovering the error should challenge the classification through the government program. Users of classified material may compile classified information into a new document in a process called derivative classification.

Before employees are provided the opportunity to perform on a classified project, they must possess a security clearance, have a need to know and sign the SF312. Security clearances are issued upon a favorable determination of a properly executed investigation.

PROBLEMS

1. You are the FSO for a defense contractor which is authorized to possess classified information at the SECRET level. Some of the material involves nuclear capabilities and intelligence sources. Which three agencies have oversight of the classified material?

2. As a guest speaker at your professional organization you are speaking on the topic of the NISP. Which executive order will you refer to and when was it signed?

3. As FSO, you are working with your management on a plan to win classified contracts. Explain the purpose of the NISP and your company's requirements to protected classified information.

4. Through whom does the Secretary of Defense report costs associate with the NISP?

5. As a security leader, one of your jobs is to provide annual training to your company. You want to introduce them to the NISP and you conduct a search for NISPOM using your favorite search engine. Report on the various hits with information on who originated the information and the topic of the hit.

6. As the FSO, you are continuing to build a great security education program. As part of the program, you want to help your company understand how classified information is designated. Describe the eight qualifications and four conditions that information must meet before it can be classified.

7. According to Executive Order 13526 there are some reasons that an OCA cannot use to assign a classification. What are some of those reasons?

8. You are providing guidance to an engineer who is deriving a classified product from three different sources. The first source is classified at the CONFIDENTIAL level with a declassification date of 31 December 2032, the second source is classified SECRET with a declassification date of 2024 and the third is also SECRET with a declassification date of

2039. Based on this information, what is the highest level of classification of the final product and what is the duration?

9. What are the two things must a person possess before you can allow them to have access to the classified information?

References

1. DoD 5220.22-M *National Industrial Security Program Operating Manual (NISPOM)*, 1-303. Reports of Loss, Compromise or Suspected Compromise, Under Secretary of Defense for Intelligence, 2006

2. O'Connor, John, *TV View; American Spies In Pursuit Of The American Dream*, New York Times, NY, 1990 http://query.nytimes.com/gst/fullpage.html?res=9C0CE6DA133BF937A35751C0A966958260, Feb 4, 2008

3. The President, Executive Order 12829—*National Industrial Security Program*, Section 101 (a) (Federal Register, Jan 1993)

4. The President, Executive Order 12829—*National Industrial Security Program*, Section 102 (Federal Register, Jan 1993)

5. The President, Executive Order 12829—*National Industrial Security Program*, Section 201 (a) (Federal Register, Jan 1993)

6. *Too Many Secrets: Overclassification As A Barrier To Critical Information Sharing*, (Hearing Before The Subcommittee On National Security, Emerging Threats And International Relations Of The Committee On Government Reform House Of Representatives One Hundred Eighth Congress Second Session August 24, 2004) Serial No. 108-263, Available Via The World Wide Web: http://frwebgate.access.gpo.gov/cgi-bin/getdoc.cgi?dbname=108_house_hearings&docid=f:98291.pdf.

7. The President, Executive Order 13526, *Classified National Security Information—National Industrial Security Program*, Section 1.3, (Federal Register, Dec 2009)

8. *Engineer Indicted on Spying*, Washington Times, Nov 23,2006, http://www.washingtontimes.com/news/2006/nov/23/20061123-122450-1979r/

9. *United States of America v. Phillip Robert Hanssen*, Affidavit In

Support Of Criminal Complaint, Arrest Warrant And Search Warrants, http://www.fas.org/irp/ops/ci/hanssen_affidavit.html, Downloaded Feb 2008

10. The President, Executive Order 13526, *Classified National Security Information—National Industrial Security Program*, Section 1.5, (Federal Register, Dec 2009)

11. The President, Executive Order 13526, *Classified National Security Information—National Industrial Security Program*, Section 1.7, (Federal Register, Dec 2009)

12. The President, Executive Order 13526, *Classified National Security Information—National Industrial Security Program*, Section 1.8b, (Federal Register, Dec 2009)

CHAPTER 2 OVERSIGHT, COMPLIANCE AND THE FSO

INTRODUCTION

Once a defense contractor wins a bid on a classified contract, they should prepare to become a Cleared Defense Contractors (CDC). Once they become a CDC, they are required to appoint a Facility Security Officer (FSO) [1.] The FSO should be a US citizen with a security clearance at the same level as the CDC Facility Security Clearance (FCL). This chapter provides suggestions of who to appoint as FSO and their potential duties and responsibilities.

THE FACILITY SECURITY OFFICER AND SECURITY CLEARANCES

The FSO has a tremendous scope of responsibility in the direction and implementation of a security program designed to protect classified information. They are also a vital link between the government contractor, DCSA and the GCA for the execution of work on classified contracts. A CDC may not necessarily need to hire a new employee to serve as an FSO, but may simply appoint an existing cleared employee to serve in the role. Sometimes, the owner, an assistant, engineer, program manager, human resources specialist or other cleared employees can assume the additional responsibility. On the other hand, some cleared contractors may have the funding and work to hire additional personnel dedicated entirely to industrial security functions (Figure 2-1).

A FCL is awarded to defense contractor facilities that have a need to perform on classified contracts. The Personnel security Clearance (PCL) is also awarded based on the contractual need. Both the CDC and the FSO must be US entities and have a history of integrity and conduct that prevents or limits exploitation or coercion to release classified material in an unauthorized manner.

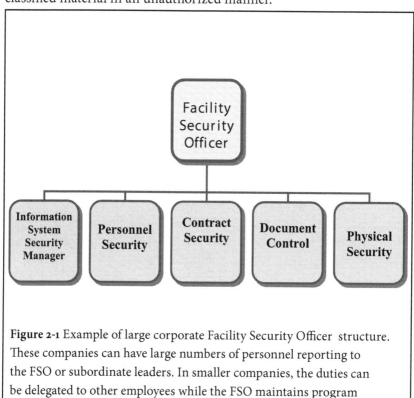

Figure 2-1 Example of large corporate Facility Security Officer structure. These companies can have large numbers of personnel reporting to the FSO or subordinate leaders. In smaller companies, the duties can be delegated to other employees while the FSO maintains program accountability.

The appointed FSO implements and directs security measures to protect classified information as required by NISPOM. Guidance includes but is not limited to requesting security clearances, coordinating for the approval of closed areas, classified information system processing, and the storage of classified information. Implied tasks include anticipating the level of security effort, infrastructure, supplies and personnel necessary to meet the security requirements.

The FSO works in the CDC, but the government has oversight of the security program. Any unauthorized disclosure can cause problems such as: loss of reputation, loss of contracts, jail time, fines or disciplinary actions against the employee, and loss of security clearance for the employee and the business.

The FSO's security program success depends on building trust with employees, managers and executives, training all cleared employees on the security program and required NISPOM topics, and understanding how NISPOM applies to the CDC and employees. This allows the implementation of NISPOM requirements into company policies, security awareness training, volunteer employee reporting of security infractions or change of status, and the coordination for the protection of classified information. Any of the above mentioned success milestones are difficult to obtain in a changing employee and contract environment. However, it can be simplified through employee and executive buy-in.

They should develop the security plan in concert with other company business units including contracts, engineers, program managers or other relevant departments to ensure all aspects of business are captured to insert the security plan into company culture.[2] The NISPOM requires the guides the CDC to provide input to the DD Form 254 and how it to apply guidance at the CDC facility. The FSO should review the DD Form 254 with affected cleared employees to ensure it is accurate, clear and that everyone performing on the contract understands the security requirements. Additionally, the FSO should ensure they receive the classification guidance.

It is the cleared contractor's responsibility to ensure the organization understands and applies the security requirements provided and the CSO will inspect the CDC based on how well they apply NISPOM guidance to the classified contract.

FSO responsibilities include providing a good assessment of any security product and service costs necessary to meet requirements. While the government pays for the security clearance process, provides the classified material, and government funded equipment, the CDC incurs the costs required to protecting the classified information. For example, the defense contractor agrees to abide by the NISPOM and is expected to bring their facilities up to the level necessary to protect the classified information. The CDC should consider costs required to implement the NISPOM. These costs include alarms, GSA Approved Security Containers, staff, dedicated facility space, and office equipment required to mail, document, destroy or otherwise handle the disposition of classified material.

CREATING A SECURITY CONSCIOUS ENTERPRISE

A key trait an FSO should demonstrate is the ability to work within organizational structures to gain executive, manager and work force cooperation. This is critical for integrating the security plan into all business units and company operations. For example, one cause of security violations is the improper introduction or removal of classified material into or from a cleared facility. An FSO can train and write policy but without the enterprise's full cooperation, will find it difficult to enforce (Figure 2-2).

A well integrated security plan ensures that all business units within an enterprise notify the FSO of any change in disposition of cleared employees or classified contracts. This integrated system will trigger the contracts, program manager, business development and other units to coordinate with and keep the FSO informed of expired, current, and future contract opportunities and responsibilities. The coordination allows the FSO to be proactive and able to better support the classified contracts. Having a security program integrated into all aspects of the company produces desired situations and dramatically reduces security violations.

An important task that an FSO faces is the successful implementation of the security program while supporting the company's primary mission; to make money while successfully performing on classified contracts. Security efforts should be risk based and focused while meeting NISPOM requirements. The FSO can direct an award winning program while remaining fiscally responsible.

Figure 2-2 The FSO should incorporate every employee and business unit into the security program.

Companies are investing more in personnel and are able to effectively communicate and realize a return on investment. An FSO with business competency and know how is highly desired. For small contractors, this could mean selecting the most competent employee for the appointed duty. For large organizations, a thorough job description and performance requirements should capture the best candidates. The appointed FSO should be able to safeguard classified material while implementing cost reducing procedures and conducting operations as well as any other professional. As such, each employee has the responsibility of identifying new methods, processes and tools to increase efficiency, reduce waste and maintain compliance with budget in mind and without increasing the risk to national security.

PERSONNEL SECURITY CLEARANCE REQUEST

Employee:

Title: Business Unit:

Clearance Level Requested

CONFIDENTIAL   SECRET   TOP SECRET

Contract Number:

Justification: (The following questions are not speculative but are based on actual performance requirements.)

DEFINITIONS:

Classified Contract: Requires access to classified information by a contractor or employees in performance of contract.

Classified Information: Official Government information determined to require protection. Common markings include: CONFIDENTIAL, SECRET, TOP SECRET

1. Is individual required to transport classified equipment/information?
2. Is individual required to document, transpose or write classified procedures?
3. Is individual required to sign out, work with, and return classified material?
4. Is individual required to use classified blueprints to make classified material?
5. Is individual required to attend classified meetings?
6. If the answer to any of the above questions is yes, then process the person for a clearance. If no, to all the above, then a clearance is not necessary.

Other Access Required:

NATO	_____	Intelligence Information	_____
Courier Authorization	_____	COMSEC	_____
CNWDI	_____	NATO	_____
STU-II	_____		

Supervisor Request   Date

Dept. Mgr/VP Validation   Date

Date received by FSO/initials

Figure 2-3 Security Clearance Request and Justification.

The constantly evolving world situation creates an ever changing security environment. Some changes may result in new government policies and guidance. These guidance and policy implementations may provide a changing environment through which the FSO and security staff must be able to negotiate. For the FSO, DCSA communicates changes to the NISPOM through Industrial Security Letters (ISL). When changes are identified, the FSO should take advantage of an integrated security plan to notify affected programs and employees to reach a feasible solution.

Reporting Structure

In a best case scenario, the FSO reports to a senior executive. The FSO should foster a credible reputation with management and stakeholders to enable a reporting process and improve the state of security. The senior officers of the company drive the business and could possibly affect classified contracts. The FSO should possess good communication skills and the know how to present information with clarity, reliability and authority.

Large defense contractors may need a structure composed of an FSO with supporting security staff; each employee having a unique discipline. Supporting security staff would focus on one of or a combination of various security descriptions such as: classified contracts, security clearances, physical security, exports compliance, classified computer processing, shipping and receiving and document accountability. In smaller organizations, the FSO could handle all tasks in conjunction with other duties (Figure 2-1).

DD Form 254

Work on classified contracts should be executed as specified in the Contract Security Classification Specification (DD Form 254). The FSO works with contracts, engineers, program managers or other departments to ensure that the company understands the customer's security requirements. The DD Form 254 specifies what type of work, how and where the classified work is to be performed. The FSO should review requirements and provide feedback into the completeness, accuracy and clarity of DD Form 254 and how it is applied.

Also important is determining whether or not the FSO implements a plan at a possessing or non-possessing facility. In a possessing facility, classified work is conducted and safeguarded on site. In a non-possessing facility, employees are cleared, but classified work and safeguarding of classified information are conducted at another cleared location. The DD Form 254 will indicate where classified work is to be performed.

Managing Classified Information

Contractors should maintain the minimum number of cleared employees necessary to accomplish the mission [3]. The organizations should also provide personnel clearance justification based on the classified contract. There are many ways to document justification, but an example can be found in figure 2-3. In this case, the manager recommends that an employee receive a security clearance based on a classified contract need. The request is signed by the first executive in their rating chain. Once signed, the request is sent to the FSO. The FSO starts the clearance request process with the justification on file.

Cleared contractors working with classified information in a possessing facility might be required to receive, store, copy, disseminate, destroy, and process classified material according to the specifications of the contract. In many cases the FSO performs control of status and documentation of classified information. In a large organization, the FSO and supporting staff can focus on full time industrial security requirements. Small contractors may be just as complex, but again, these tasks might only be performed by one appointed employee.

The FSO develops physical security measures either identified in the classified contract or as deemed necessary by the customer or based on an organization's risk assessment. Alarms, access control, storage and closed area or Sensitive Compartmented Information Facility (SCIF) are required for protecting SECRET and TOP SECRET information in certain environments. Otherwise when these security measures are not required the may still be considered based on a risk assessment.

For example, the NISPOM requires that classified information at the SECRET level to be stored in a GSA approved security container, with no alarms or supplemental controls. However, open bin storage of the same level of classification requires alarms and monitoring. These efforts are expensive and may not be necessary in most situations. In the case of SECRET information, the storage in a GSA approved security container may be adequate according to NISPOM. However, in certain circumstances, such as a high crime area, environmental instability, civil unrest, or other high risk situations, a risk assessment may lead the FSO to apply additional security measures. Assessment tools can help FSOs make such decisions as unnecessary systems are expensive and cost could be prohibitive for a small company.

In cases where a cleared contractor involves a one-person operation, that person serves as the FSO for that entity. The single employee FSO is as critical as any other FSO. The main difference is that the single employee FSO is the only one who has access to safe or vault combinations and access control and alarm codes. If the employee dies or is incapacitated a backup plan is necessary to better protect the classified material. In cases of sole employees, the FSO will give the combinations to DCSA or the home office if part of a larger organization [4.]

How to Conduct the Risk Assessment

The FSO should apply the NISPOM in conjunction with a risk assessment. This helps determine how to safeguard classified information outside of its protected environment. Tools for the risk assessment include police reports, crime statistics and knowledge of threat. This assessment could be conducted in addition to issues affecting life and safety of all employees or simply to provide an extra layer of protection. Either way, the risk assessment is to determine whether or not to provide protection of classified information above and beyond that required by NISPOM.

This protection may also be driven by needs to protect employees and unclassified information and products. The risk assessment should help determine what is needed to protect classified information in all possible situations. In the first step, the FSO should determine what should be protected (classified items by classification level), the second step is identify threat to classified information, the third step is assessing the probability of occurrence, fourth, assess the impact if threat occurs and fifth requires making mitigation and countermeasure decisions.

In addition to the five steps, the reader should also keep in mind environmental variables that may produce different results. For example, an FSO in a facility located in a high crime area will have different risks than facility in a low crime area. An FSO in a non-possessing facility will have different concerns as there may be no threat to classified information. Also, more established CDCs will have different considerations than would a brand new cleared contractor with limited experience protecting classified information. Each risk assessment should be tailored to the environment.

Identifying what needs to be protected

Consider a possessing facility with a contract to perform on and protect classified information at the SECRET level. For the example, the classified information is required to be kept in a GSA container approved for the storage of classified material. The contractor keeps the GSA approved container in a room where classified work is conducted. Classified information is often removed and brought to cleared employee offices. The defense contractor is on a tight budget and the facility does not have alarms or enhanced security measures other than a key and lock system. The appointed FSO determines that the classified information is at risk when removed from the security container.

Identifying the Risk

Next, the FSO lists risks to classified information. She might consider threats such as break in, severe weather, fire, employee workplace violence, forgetfulness and espionage. Each threat will have an individual assessment into how real the threat can be.

Assessing Probability of Occurrence

Once the threats are listed, the FSO can check the probability of occurrence by using a rating of 1 through 5. Level 1 could represent a slight risk and level 5 can be significant risk. The identified threats from the above paragraph are provided in the example:

Break in-The FSO pulls police reports based on the facility zip code, she might discover there have been no break-ins or theft in the current and surrounding zip codes. Such research can be conducted by contacting local law enforcement or using a search engine. Additionally, the protective measures offered by the GSA container are adequate for preventing theft and list the probability as 1.

Severe Weather-The facility is in an area where severe weather is a reoccurring event. Employees often have to seek shelter against high winds and tornados. In this case, the probability is a 4.

Fire- The safety officer practices fire drills and does a great job at keeping the risk of fire low. However, in the event of a fire or fire drill, an employee may have classified information in their possession. The FSO assigns probability at level 2. Though the risk of fire is low, employees with classified information during an event will have to be addressed.

Employee Workplace Violence-Though a life safety application, such a risk can impact the protection of classified information. When unexpected violence breaks out, the first priority is protection of life. As people react, classified information might be left unprotected and possibly compromised. Violence is not likely, it will be assigned a level 2 for probability.

Employee forgetfulness-The FSO has identified security incidents where classified information has been left unattended during bathroom breaks and over lunch periods. Though further investigation has determined no compromise of classified information, the incidents are severe enough and probable enough to warrant a level of 4. The impact will have to be addressed later.

Espionage-Classified information is protected against espionage. The probability of someone targeting the classified information and breaking in to steal it is a level 1. However, an employee providing unauthorized access is a greater possibility. The FSO gives an overall probability rating of 3.

Assessing Impact of Threat to Classified Information

Once the threats are assessed, the FSO can check the impact by using a rating of 1 through 5. Level 1 represents a low impact and level 5 a significant impact. Let's continue to use the identified threats from the above scenario as an example:

Break in-The probability of occurrence was rated at level 1. Stolen classified information could pose a threat to national security as well as problems for the contractor. The FSO assigns a level of 5 for impact. Multiply the probability by impact for an overall rating of 5.

Severe Weather-In our example, the cleared facility is in an area where severe weather is a reoccurring event. Employees often have to seek shelter against high winds and tornados. As such, the risk level is 4. If severe weather occurs when classified information is outside of the security container, the impact could be significant as it could be disclosed after being transported in all direction by wind, floods and other environmental factors. The FSO might assign the impact level at 5. Multiply the occurrence by the impact for an overall rating of 20.

Fire-The FSO assigns probability at level 2. If a fire or fire drill occurs when classified information is outside of the security container, it could be compromised by emergency responders or uncleared employees. This would not be as severe as a complete loss of classified information so the FSO might assign the impact level at 4. Multiply the occurrence by the impact for an overall rating of 8.

Employee Workplace Violence-The FSO assigns a level 2 for probability. If violence occurs when classified information is outside of the security container, it could be compromised by emergency responders or uncleared employees. The FSO assigns the impact level at 4. Multiply the occurrence by the impact for an overall rating of 8.

Employee forgetfulness-the FSO has assigned a probability level of 4. If employees forget that they have classified information in their possession, it could be compromised by uncleared persons. The FSO assigns the impact level at 4. Multiply the occurrence by the impact for an overall rating of 16.

Espionage-The overall probability rating is 3. If espionage occurs classified information would be compromised by a foreign government. This would be severe so the FSO might assign the impact level at 5. Multiply the occurrence by the impact for an overall rating of 15.

Make a Determination

The risk assessment determines the level of risk from lowest to highest. It is the high ratings that should get the FSO's attention. In our example the risks are from highest to lowest: severe weather, employee forgetfulness, espionage, fire, workplace violence and theft (Figure 2-4). The FSO will then build a security program with security measures supporting NISPOM, but tailored to the facility. They will begin by developing countermeasures to meet the significant threat.

In our example, since break in is the least impacting threat, alarms and closed circuit television may not be warranted in the protection of classified information. The protection of classified information alone would not be a justification for such expenses as there is no NISPOM based requirement. If there are other issues such as life safety considerations, they would need to be assessed separately.

From our example, it appears our FSO would spend more time and resources in developing training to address procedures for protecting classified information during severe weather, fire and other emergencies. The countermeasures could also involve rehearsals and other inexpensive solutions.

Employee forgetfulness and espionage countermeasures are almost similar as the cleared employees provide an insider threat. These risky insiders have clearance and access, but because of carelessness or intent to commit espionage they are not trustworthy. Combating such threats include employee security awareness training specific to the problem, posting reminders to cleared employees, conducting random checks of offices and employees as they enter and exit buildings, using a keyword search to check e-mail and computer generated documents to ensure classified information is not leaving through unauthorized channels, conducting robust classified document accountability, etc.

Asset	Risk	Probability (1-5) Lowest to Highest	Impact (1-5) Lowest to Highest	Total Score (Higher Scores Are Greater Risks)	Priority of Focus
Classified Information	Break-in	2	4	8	4th
	Severe Weather	4	5	20	1st
	Fire	2	4	8	4th
	Violence	2	4	8	4th
	Forgetfulness	4	4	16	2nd
	Espionage	3	5	15	3d

Figure 2-4 Sample Risk Analysis Matrix

FOCUSED EFFORT BASED ON NISPOM STRUCTURE

The FSO can focus security efforts and better streamline the security program by determining which parts of the NISPOM apply. The FSO should also understand that the NISPOM is guidance, but there are waivers available for NISPOM requirements. The NISPOM is a large manual that encompasses many areas and many cleared contractors will apply only some parts of the NISPOM while few may have to comply with all chapters. DCSA can help FSOs determine how best to apply the NISPOM within the specific cleared facility.

The risk assessment helps FSOs focus countermeasures to protect classified information from actual identifiable threats by probability. The matrix in figure 2-4 helps the FSO determine how to protect the classified information above and beyond the NISPOM guidance. The same approach should be used in determining which parts of the NISPOM apply to an FSO's facility. For example, a non-possessing facility with cleared employees performing classified work at another facility should not focus security efforts on protecting classified processing. However, they should focus their efforts on NISPOM chapters 1, 2, 3 and 6, parts of chapter 5 and Appendices A and C; the parts of NISPOM that apply to ALL cleared contractors. The following describes the parts of NISPOM that apply to all CDCs.

The first chapter is dedicated to general industrial security concerns. The chapter is divided into three sections which provide the introduction, general and reporting requirements. Coverage in this chapter includes information concerning the NISPOM's purpose, how the NISPOM is put together, annual reviews, waivers, reporting and other topics. It also describes the FSO position and implementation of the Insider Threat Plan and required reports.

Chapter two is divided into sections that cover facility clearances, personnel clearances and Foreign Ownership Control and Influence (FOCI) information. In this chapter FSOs can find instructions on how facility clearances are awarded and learn reasons to process personnel clearances and when to do so. Finally, it discusses the factors and procedures to apply when a company is partially or fully under foreign control.

Chapter three instructs how to conduct security training and briefings. It gives detail to what type of training is required and the necessary topics to train.

Chapter five gives methods of safeguarding classified information. It provides general safeguarding practices such as oral communication, perimeter controls and emergency procedures.

Chapter six distinguishes between classified visits and meetings and provides information how each is conducted.

Appendix A. Cognizant Security Office Information-lists contact information for the CSOs for the four CSAs under the NISP.

Appendix C. Definitions Provides an alphabetical list of key industrial security definitions. Some terms and phrases have a unique meaning in the context of the NISP.

FSOs can use a simple question and answer session to determine which additional chapters apply to their cleared facilities. These questions are based on the cleared contractor's DD Forms 254. If the answer to any of the following is yes, the FSO can refer to the corresponding NISPOM chapter or section.

Does the cleared facility provide classification markings? See NISPOM chapter 4.

Does the cleared facility store, disseminate, or destroy classified information? See NISPOM chapter 5.

Is the cleared facility a prime contractor with classified subcontracts? See NISPOM chapter 7.

Does the cleared contractor process classified information using an information system? See NISPOM chapter 8.

Does the cleared facility have contracts that involve special handling such as Restricted Data (RD), Formerly Restricted Data (FRD), Critical Nuclear Weapon Design Information (CNWDI), Intelligence information or Communications Security (COMSEC) information? See NISPOM chapter 9.

Do cleared employees perform international operations, store Foreign Government information or transfer classified information to foreign entities? See NISPOM chapter 10 .

Does the cleared facility have contracts that include TEMPEST, Defense Technical Information Center (DTIC) or involved in Independent Research and Development (IR&D) efforts that involve classified information? See NISPOM chapter 11.

FSOs should become familiar with the NISPOM. However, trying to implement parts of NISPOM that do not apply to the types of classified contracts involved may waste effort and resources. Leading purposeful and efficient security begins with an assessment of both risk and identifying applicable parts of the NISPOM.

SUMMARY

In this chapter we covered the role of the Facility Security Officer as related to the NISP. A Department of Defense cleared contractor must appoint an FSO. The role of the FSO is to direct and implement security procedures to protect classified material as identified in the NISPOM.

PROBLEMS

1. Your company president has just informed you that the company has won a classified contract and she wants to appoint you as the new FSO. What are the minimum qualifications that you need to fill the position?
2. According to NISPOM, what are the qualifications an employee must have before being appointed as an FSO?

REFERENCES

1. Department of Defense, DoD 5220.22-M, *National Industrial Security Operating Manual*, section 1-201, February 2016
2. Bennett, Jeffrey W., *Insider's Guide to Security Clearances*, Huntsville, AL, Red Bike Publishing
3. Executive Order 12968—*Access to Classified Information*, section 2-1 (b), Federal Register, August 1995
4. Department of Defense, DoD 5220.22-M, *National Industrial Security Operating Manual*, section 1-204, February 2016

CHAPTER 3 SECURITY CLEARANCES

INTRODUCTION

There are two types of security clearances that should be in place prior to performing classified work and those are the Facility security Clearance (FCL) and the Personnel security Clearance (PCL).

The FCL is a security clearance for business entities. A company does not need an FCL to bid on classified contracts. However, they must be able to obtain one to perform on the contract. The first step is registering as a defense contractor. Both cleared and uncleared defense contractors may bid on classified contracts. However, the winning defense contractor must be able to obtain the FCL and at the level of the classified work to be performed prior to performing on classified contracts. However, they cannot process their own clearances and must be sponsored by a Prime Contractor or Government entity.

A PCL is linked to the FCL and awarded to employees after an investigation and adjudication process. This award is the administrative determination that an employee is eligible from a national security basis for access to classified information. The security clearance process as discussed here is abbreviated. It is provided in more detail in the book *Insider's Guide to Security Clearances*.

HOW DEFENSE CONTRACTORS GET FACILITY SECURITY CLEARANCES

There are many books written about how to get government contracts and how to become a defense contractor. This book continues that conversation by exploring the cleared defense contractor space. Not every defense contractor is a CDC; only those granted an FCL are. This book begins where other books end after they describe how to become a contractor and continues where *Insider's Guide to Security Clearances* leaves off with how to perform on classified contracts. However, if you have not read these other books, I will give a brief synopsis of the process.

A defense contractor is a business entity that has registered with the US Government and Central Contractor Registration. A CDC is the designation of a U.S. Government contractor facility that has been granted an FCL, authorizing them to perform on classified contracts.

How Uncleared Facilities can Win Classified Contracts

An uncleared defense contractor may bid on a classified contract without possessing an FCL. However, they must be cleared before working on the classified contract.

Many defense contractors may find it difficult to compete for classified contracts. But this should not be a deterrent as uncleared defense contractors may partner with or team with an existing CDC for sponsorship. For example, suppose a major defense contractor is performing on a classified contract for engineering support. Their core competencies provide much needed results but they are in need of a cleared widget maker to make a peripheral piece of hardware. The prime defense contractor is familiar with the excellent work performed by a small uncleared defense contractor. The company does not have a clearance but the cleared prime contractor can award a subcontract and sponsor the winning company for a security clearance.

The Government Contractor Relationship

The relationship includes the The Government Contracting Activity (GCA) who provides classified work to CDCs. The GCA is where the program office, contracts managers, logistics, and contract awarders are located.

The Contracting Officer's Representative / Contracting Officer's

Technical Representative ensures the contract requirements and technical work are delivered as defined in the contract and interact with the contractor. The CSA/CSO oversees protection of the GCA's classified information.

The Facility Security Clearance Process

The FCL is strictly contract based and demonstrates an enterprise's trustworthiness; but the award is not a right nor a guarantee. In this section the reader will learn the FCL process and how defense contractors qualify. The reader will also learn how to maintain the qualification, security clearance, and associated documents for future audits.

The FCL is a result of a thorough investigation and the subsequent determination that a company is eligible to have access to classified information. Additionally, if the company is to possess or store classified material, the contract will determine the need and DCSA will approve the storage level for that company.

The organization desiring to work on classified contracts should work with the GCA, CSA, and CSO. As addressed earlier, remember that the DCSA is the CSO for the Department of Defense (DoD) and this book will refer the CSO and DCSA interchangeably. The DCSA helps the contractor with the security clearance process.

According to the DCSA website, forms and requirements are available at:

https://www.dcsa.mil/Mission-Centers/Critical-Technology-Protection/Facility-Clearance/Checklist-for-a-New-Facility-Clearance/

The facility clearance is required to be in place prior to the contractor performing on classified work. Once the contract is awarded the GCA or prime contractor submits the sponsorship letter to the DCSA, the company can begin the process of applying for the clearance. A contractor has to meet six requirements on the journey to an FCL.

1. Register as a defense contractor for Contractor and Government Entity Code (CAGE)
2. Be Sponsored
3. Sign Department of Defense Security Agreement
4. Complete a Certificate Pertaining To Foreign Interests
5. Provide Organization Credentials
6. Identify Key management personnel

The Six Steps in Depth

Register as a defense Contractor-A business entity should register with the System For Award Management (SAM): *https://www.sam.gov/SAM/*

SAM assists the government contracting activities with information on defense contractors and registration is required in order to be awarded contracts by the federal government.

Once registered, the company will be assigned a Commercial and Government Entity (CAGE) Code. The CAGE code is a form of identification the government assigns to defense contractors. Government agencies use CAGE codes in the course of business with defense contractors. Cleared contractors use the CAGE code to search for classified mailing addresses and conduct business with other cleared contractor companies.

However, registration in no way guarantees that a contract or assistance award will be awarded. Like any business, success is up to the quality of work, reputation, and initiative of the defense contractor.

The following should be obtained prior to registering:

- Data Universal Numbering System (DUNS) Number provided by Dun and Bradstreet (D&B) by Requesting a DUNS number with the D&B web form:
http://fedgov.dnb.com/webform.
- A Tax Identification Number (TIN) and Taxpayer Name used in Federal tax matters. The TIN is either a Social Security Number or an Employer Identification Number assigned by the Internal Revenue Service.

- You can request an EIN from the IRS:
http://www.irs.gov/

Sponsorship-This reflects a need to access classified information. A company cannot apply for a security clearance for business development purposes or to be more competitive. The security clearance process begins with a need which is supported by a legitimate U.S. Government or foreign government requirement and the classified contract will be offered to meet that need. This is in the form of sponsorship.

Department of Defense Security Agreement (DD Form 441)- A security agreement is signed between the US Government and defense contractor. This agreement is legally binding and designates responsibilities of each party to follow procedures established by the OCA and NISPOM.

Certificate Pertaining to Foreign Interests (SF 328)-Defense contractors are evaluated to determine whether or not they fall under Foreign Ownership Control or Influence (FOCI) and to what degree. This is simply a determination of whether or not a foreign entity can make decisions regarding classified contracts or classified material. Defense contractors should not fall under the influence, control or ownership of a foreign entity to the extent that it causes classified information to be in jeopardy of unauthorized disclosure. Contractors that fall under FOCI can still compete for classified work; however, there are measures to be taken to ensure that only U.S. persons control the scope of classified work. DCSA and the GCA will be involved in the process.

Organization-the enterprise must be in good business standings and have a history of demonstrating a good reputation and ethical business practices. The company should prove that they are structured and a legal entity under the laws of the United States, the District of Columbia or Puerto Rico and have a physical location in the United States or territories.

Key Management Personnel (KMP)-These are management or senior leaders who influence decisions regarding classified contracts. KMPs can be members of the board of directors, vice-presidents, directors or other upper level managers. Also, neither the company nor key managers can be barred from participating in U.S. Government contracts. A simple review of Federal Acquisition Regulations (FAR) demonstrates the ethics and legal requirements of companies who wish to participate in these contracts.

The Investigation Process

Once a company is sponsored for classified work and meets the requirements as identified above, DCSA can begin the process of investigating the business for the FCL. The company should posses a CAGE code. In the event of a parent-subsidiary relationship within a corporation, both entities are processed for an FCL separately. Usually, the parent company is granted an FCL at the same or higher level as that of the subsidiary. DCSA should determine whether or not the parent will be cleared or excluded based on mission requirements and the contract. If both need clearances, they will be processed separately and as a result, have different CAGE codes.

Oversight

The company being sponsored will fall under the NISP and NISPOM is the guide for DoD cleared contractors. The sooner the company obtains their copy of the NISPOM, the quicker they will begin to understand their expected role in protecting the nation's secrets. After the contract award, more guidance will be provided by the GCA in the classified contract information is found in the contract related SCG and Contract Security Classification Specification or DD Form 254.

A critical piece of the sponsorship program revolves around DCSA having a good understanding of the subject company and their mission. To do this, DCSA will review organizational structure and governance documentation to determine which leadership positions can commit the company and make decisions. This information includes: articles of incorporation, stock records, corporate by-laws and minutes.

The senior company officer, FSO and other KMPs will be processed for a security clearance. This requirement can include board members and committee personnel. Proof of citizenship and other documentation is needed to determine eligibility for a clearance. The other officers and board members may be excluded from the security clearance process if they will not have influence over cleared contractor decisions [2].

Required Government Forms

Aside from corporate entity documentation; DCSA will collect and process additional forms during the FCL process. These forms include, but are not limited to the Department of Defense Security Agreement (DD Form 441) and the Certificate Pertaining to Foreign Interests (Standard Form 328). DCSA will advise the contractor on how to fill out the forms and answer any questions the contractor may have.

Department of Defense Security Agreement, DD Form 441

The DD Form 441 is a security agreement between the contractor and the government. It lists the responsibilities of both the cleared contractor and the government. For example, the contractor agrees to implement and enforce the security controls necessary to prevent unauthorized disclosure of classified material in accordance with the NISPOM. The contractor also agrees to verify that the subcontractor, customer, individual and any other person has the need to know and possesses a security clearance prior to accessing classified information.

The U.S. Government agrees to notify the contractor of the security classification level assigned to classified information. The agreement states that the government will not over classify material and that they will notify the cleared contractor of any changes in the classification level.

The Government will also instruct the contractor on the handling, storage and disposition of classified material. The Government also agrees to provide security clearances to eligible contractor employees. Classified contract information is found in the contract related SCG and DD Form 254. The Government will also assess the contractor's ability to protect classified material. For DoD, this is done through a review performed by a designated DCSA special agents.

DCSA will make an initial determination of a contractor's ability to protect classified information. They will also assess and review at reasonable intervals the security process; procedures and methods the cleared facilities use and determine whether or not they are in compliance with the NISPOM. Typically, DCSA inspects based on a checklist and the FSO's security plan. These events are scheduled every 12 months for possessing facilities and 18 months for non-possessing facilities. If the cleared contractor is found not in compliance with NISPOM, DCSA will notify the GCA or prime contractor in a written report. On the other hand, if the cleared contractor earns two superior ratings in a row, they are eligible for DCSA's Cogswell Award.

Appendage to Department of Defense Security Agreement, DD Form 441-1

The DD Form 441-1 is an additional document used with multiple facility and parent subsidiary companies. The DD Form 441-1 is an additional form providing the government information about the cleared branches or divisions of an organization. These divisions and branches are also included on the DD Form 441 and the SF 328.

Certificate Pertaining to Foreign Interests, Standard Form (SF) 328

The SF 328 is used by the contractor and the CSA to determine whether or not and to what extent the cleared contractor falls under FOCI. The primary concern is always protecting classified information from unauthorized disclosure. As with determining the amount of control a company officer or board member has over classified contracts, the same holds true of foreign entities with which a company may become involved.

In today's changing world it is not unusual for a cleared company to be involved with international business or be owned by a foreign entity. If classified contracts are under the control of a foreign entity, the classified information could be in jeopardy of unauthorized disclosure. If a contractor falls under FOCI, the CSA will work with the GCA to evaluate the contractor's ability to mitigate the extent of foreign influence concerning classified information and approve, deny or revoke the FCL.

Granting FCLs

A facility clearance follows the life cycle of the classified contract. Close coordination and consultation with DCSA can help with the speedy processing of the FCL. If DCSA determines the company is eligible for access to classified information, they will award the appropriate security level. At that point the company can begin the process of PCL requests and putting procedures in place required to perform on classified work.

The FCL is a determination that a legal entity is trustworthy and able to safeguard classified information. This FCL relates to an organization and not a physical location or building. For example, a cleared contractor organization can move locations, keep the FCL and the clearance remains in place until either party terminates it. If for some reason the contractor no longer requires access, can no longer protect classified information, is no longer eligible for access to classified material or either party terminates the FCL, the contractor must return or destroy any classified material and provide proof to the GCA [3.]

Personnel Security Clearances

According to Executive Order 12968—Access to Classified Information, employees should not be granted access to classified information unless they possess a security clearance, have a need to know the classified information involved, received an initial security briefing and have signed a nondisclosure agreement.

The contractor and DCSA have joint responsibilities with the PCL process as they do with the FCL process. Applicants complete a

Questionnaire for National Security Positions, also known as Standard Form 86 or SF 86. They submit the application to the FSO who then reviews and forwards to the CSA. An investigation is conducted and the Central Adjudication Facility (CAF) makes a security clearance determination. The determination is then entered into the CSAs information system for maintenance. Once the information is updated, the FSO can access the information system and perform PCL processing functions such as determine the security clearance awarded and grant access based on need to know and the clearance level [4.]

In some instances a clearance can be denied, revoked or suspended. The employee's background is investigated thoroughly for the initial clearance and again every five to fifteen years while maintaining a clearance and depending on the required security clearance level. In the event that a security clearance is denied, suspended or revoked, DCSA will also notify the FSO. The FSO will then deny access to classified material to that employee and update the system.

Investigation

Prior to granting a security clearance, DCSA will ensure the security clearance background investigation is conducted. Two primary types of investigation included the Single Scope Background Investigation (SSBI) and the National Agency Check with Local Agency Check and Credit Check (NACLC) [5.]

The FSO's role is to initiate the security clearance request and liaison between the CSA and the employee. Whether a new employee needs a clearance or a cleared employee is going through re-investigation, the FSO performs a similar function to notify the employee and get the investigation started. The FSO notifies the employee to begin the application by completing Electronic Questionnaires for Investigations Processing (e-QIP) SF 86.

The FSO should work with the applicant and review the SF 86 for accuracy and completeness. The FSO may be tempted to but should not perform adjudication functions or inform the employee that they are either eligible or ineligible for a clearance, this is the adjudicators role.

The federal investigator verifies the information by interviewing references, employers or others who have known the subject socially or professionally. To facilitate an efficient investigation, applicants should complete the SF 86 accurately and completely.

The SSBI is the most detailed investigation and is used to process TOP SECRET (TS), and Sensitive Compartmented Information (SCI) clearances. The SSBI will also cover periods of employment and education institutions attended. The applicant should be truthful about the attendance and degrees, certificates or diplomas credited and provide contacts or references as completely as possible. Other areas subject to investigation include places of residence, criminal records and involvement with law enforcement and financial records. The investigators may contact those with social and professional knowledge of the applicant, and divorced spouses.

The NACLC investigation is required for SECRET (S) and CONFIDENTIAL (C) levels of security clearances. Investigations are conducted to determine security and suitability for a clearance, fingerprint classification and a background check using a search of the Federal Bureau of Investigation's (FBI) database. Investigators also conduct a credit check based on residence, employment and education locations. The investigation will also cover law enforcement issues at all locations listed on the SF 86.

Once assigned a case, investigators will use the submitted request to research factors about the employee's life to help determine suitability. The security clearance is not a right, but a privilege based on an employee's ability to protect classified material and not be subject to compromise. The suitability is assessed by a trained adjudicator based on an approved background investigation.

The FSO also forwards supporting documentation for clearance requests. Signature forms authorizing the investigation and fingerprint cards are necessary to begin the investigation process. The FSO collects this information from the applicant and submits it to DCSA through the information management system (IMS), facsimile and mail channels. The signature pages are sent through facsimile or IMS and the fingerprint cards are sent electronically or mailed depending on the technology available to the contractor. Once the investigation is complete and the access is granted or denied the hardcopy SF 86 has served its purpose. The FSO should then destroy or return it to the applicant. The SF 86 soft copy is saved in a protected online national database. The cleared employee can access the SF 86 during the scheduled Periodic Review (PR).

The granted security clearance investigation is reciprocal and honored across agencies and no additional investigations should be conducted to access classified information at the same level or lower of the PCL. If an employee has a security clearance granted by any agency with an investigation meeting the same or higher requirements, access to classified information can usually be granted without further investigation.

Once a cleared contractor determines the employee's need to access classified material, they should verify that the subject is a U.S. Citizen. There are several methods of proving citizenship. The preferred method is a birth certificate containing a raised seal if the state provides a seal. Uncertified birth certificates are unacceptable as well as birth certificates issued more than a year after the actual birth. Supporting documentations such as hospital birth records or circumcision certificates can be used to substantiate unofficial birth certificates. Supplemental information can also be submitted showing baptism records, entry in a bible, and other traditional methods subject to approval. A passport or a record of military service (DD Form 1966) is also acceptable as proof of citizenship. If a person becomes a citizen by naturalization, then the subject can present a certificate of naturalization [7].

The FSO should submit the clearance request using the current CSA provided IMS and e-QIP. There, the applicant completes the online application and submits it to the FSO for review. The FSO and supporting staff are required to protect the applicant's privacy and personal information from public access. The FSO should notify the employee in writing that they will review the SF 86 only for adequacy and completeness. The notification also includes a statement that the information will not be used for any other reason nor shared with anyone in the company [5].

Cleared contractors usually benefit from hiring employees

who already have clearances. This is accomplished by transferring jurisdiction of the new employee's security clearance information in the IMS from the losing CDC to the gaining CDC. Newly cleared contractors may request clearances investigations for existing employees or well qualified potential employees. In both cases, defense contractors should invest in efforts to hire ethical employees up front. Human resources should be involved with the hiring process by initiating employee background checks prior to hiring an employee. Using fair and standard practices to hire ethical and qualified people is a good way to increase the possibility of hiring employees eligible for a clearance. The cleared contractor may have the luxury of hiring a worthy employee and assigning them to other tasks until the needed clearance is granted.

However, if the employee is not granted a clearance, the wait can prove to be costly. This is a hard lesson if the employee was not granted a clearance for something the contractor could have discovered using reasonable methods.

Employee background checks should be conducted before any hiring action. They are vital to good company morale, future employee relations, and life safety issues. They can help employers hire qualified employees, but they are not used to determine security clearance eligibility.

The 13 Adjudicative Criteria

Security clearance investigations are more in-depth than typical employee background checks. Investigators report the results of their investigations and the government determines suitability. The results of the investigation are used to determine whether or not the subject is stable, trustworthy, reliable, of excellent character, judgment, and discretion; and of unquestioned loyalty to the United States. The determination is based on 13 investigation criteria [6]:

Allegiance to the United States-The applicant should demonstrate an unquestionable loyalty to the United States. If the investigation reveals that the subject belongs to or has belonged to organizations or individually supporting the overthrow of the U.S. government there is a good chance that a clearance will be denied.

Foreign influence-Ties with foreign nationals are usually not a problem unless the relationship creates a security risk. The employee's relationship with family, friends, and other situations could cause them to compromise classified information. Questionable business partners, banking, investments and other business or financial involvement could cause the employee to be under obligation or duress that could present a national security risk. For example, an employee may be under foreign influence while married to a foreign national spouse with close family ties in an oppressive country. In that situation, the employee could be coerced into providing secrets to spare foreign family members.

Foreign preference-An employee might lean toward being sympathetic to or have idealistic attitudes toward another country greater than that of the U.S. This could present a security risk. Recently a defense contractor cleared employee gave classified information to Israel. Ben-Ami Kadish was recruited by a foreign agent who exploited his sympathy toward Israel. He received no payment, but contributed based on his sentiments [8.]

Sexual behavior-Sexual practices or desires of a criminal intent could indicate emotional or personality disorders. Such a person could be under duress, easily influenced, asked to return favors or be under obligation to protect their practices or keep them from being discovered. Examples of risky behavior include: trading sex for drugs or money, becoming obliged to someone to keep practices quiet or a history of arrests for a sex related crime.

Personal conduct-The subject should demonstrate good judgment, trustworthiness, honesty, candor and a willingness to comply with rules. Any behavior otherwise may indicate irresponsibility and unsuitability to safeguard classified material. An example of this is stalking, excess speeding tickets, arrests or terminated from a job for unethical or illegal behavior.

Financial considerations-Investigators will look at financial records, levels of debt or other indicators of ability to meet financial obligations. Unexplained affluence or conducting criminal activities may be indicators of someone who could be tempted to divulge national secrets.

Alcohol consumption-Symptoms of alcoholism, driving under the influence, being drunk on the job or drinking in excess may indicate irresponsibility which could lead to questionable judgment.

Drug involvement-Aside from making poor choices, abuse of prescription drugs is illegal. Inappropriate drug use leads to legal problems, personal problems and judgment issues that may make it difficult for the person to safeguard classified material.

Psychological conditions-Persons suffering under mental, personality and emotional challenges could be unable to perform in normal social or work environments. This could also affect their judgment and suitability for a clearance. Emotional, mental and personality disorders can cause a person to make bad decisions concerning classified information or make them incapable of protecting classified information.

Criminal conduct-Committing crimes or having a criminal record indicates instability, poor judgment and lack of ability to follow rules and regulations. Persons displaying criminal behavior indicate a security risk and may not be suitable to protect classified material.

Handling protected information-Person's who cannot protect privacy, physical inventory or other privileged information may have problems protecting classified material. Employees who have demonstrated willingness to violate security policy could prove a risk to national security.

Outside activities-Sometimes work or activities conflict with the ability to maintain a security clearance. This involvement with outside activities also includes volunteer or non-profit work.

Use of Information Technology Systems-Breaking company policy concerning the use of technology and computer systems can indicate lack of obedience to rules and regulations. Inappropriate use of the internet, computers, fax machines, alarms and networks could indicate that an employee cannot adequately protect classified systems.

Subjects who fall under any of the above criteria will not automatically be denied a security clearance. There are situations where people have committed crimes or used drugs, but have had clearances awarded because of corrective behavior or other mitigating circumstances. They may have sought professional counseling or other types of treatment. Employees who had abused alcohol may have attended rehabilitation. Some may have demonstrated disqualifying behavior because at the time they suffered emotional problems from incidents us as a death or divorce, or the indicated incidences had transpired way back in their personal histories. When considering a person for a clearance, the adjudicator will assess each case based on the whole person concept. For more information on the 13 Adjudicative Criteria, see the book, *Insider's Guide to Security Clearances.*

It is important for the applicant to fill out the security clearance request information accurately and completely. The adjudicator will only be able to rely on the information provided in the investigation and the applicant's SF 86. Willful or voluntary disclosure of adverse information can prove helpful during the adjudicative process.

Periodic Reinvestigations

The granted security clearance is part of a continuing evaluation process. Once a security clearance is granted the cleared employee will be periodically reevaluated and reinvestigated if the clearance is to remain in effect. When cleared employees require access to classified material beyond the scope of the initial investigation, the security office will submit a request for a PR. The adjudicator makes decisions concerning whether or not the subject's allegiance is still to the United States, they can still be trusted to protect classified information and they will still be able to carry out their duties at all times.

The PR for the TOP SECRET clearance is the same level of investigation as was initially conducted. The SSBI-PR is conducted every 5 years as needed. For SECRET, the NACLC is conducted every 10 years and for CONFIDENTIAL the NACLC is conducted every 15 years [5.] Part of the security education process covered in later chapters describes the importance of continuous evaluation of the cleared employee. This evaluation is a requirement for cleared employees to report any information on themselves and other cleared employees that may demonstrate an inability to protect classified information.

The Continuous Evaluation Process

Cleared personnel should also continue their demonstration of suitability after the security clearance is determined. Cleared employees are responsible for notifying their security offices anytime they or another cleared employee violate any of the criteria. This is referred to as reporting adverse information. Failure to report adverse information could result in risk to national security. On a more personal matter, failure to report adverse information could manifest during the PR. For example, adverse information discovered on a subject during the PR that should have been self-reported, may raise questions of trustworthiness. Self reporting of adverse information demonstrates trustworthiness and helps mitigate the event's impact. Cleared employees with such concerns should seek qualified legal counsel.

The Adjudicative Process

Whether considering an initial investigation or a PR, the adjudicative process requires an authority to consider all evidence and make a decision of whether or not a person is suitable to have a security clearance. The adjudicator weighs decisions based on information the subject provided in the SF 86 as well as the results of the investigation. The adjudicator will use the information to determine whether or not the person is stable, reliable or subject to coercion based on the whole person concept. The whole person concept allows an assessment of many factors that may help mitigate negative findings. In evaluating the relevance of an individual's conduct, the adjudicator will consider the following factors:

The nature, extent, and seriousness of the conduct-There are varying degrees of impact and circumstances of individual conduct. Looking at each incident case by case will provide better details useful in determining whether or not a person is given security clearance.

The circumstances surrounding the conduct-There are situations that may cause someone to take adverse action. People under stress or duress react in different ways. For example, a person is arrested for murder but released after proving self-defense.

The frequency of the conduct and when it occurred-Conduct may be habitual or a onetime incident. Adjudicators can use the information discovered to make a better determination. For example, a subject has a record of drug counseling from twenty years earlier. The incident occurred in the past and was a onetime occurrence.

The individual's age and maturity at the time of the conduct-Minors are not held accountable for their actions the same way as adults. For example, a subject had several moving violations during the first year after obtaining a driver's license. Incidents may have resulted from immaturity and not a reflection of who the person is now.

The willingness to participate-People can be coerced into doing things they do not want to do. Some people volunteer freely to commit crimes or engage in risky behavior. Both situations are taken into account during the adjudication process. For example, a subject joins a group hostile to the U.S. Government after an invitation is extended; they volunteered freely. Coercion involves a person forced to engage in adverse behavior to avoid certain consequences.

The presence or absence of rehabilitation and other pertinent behavioral changes-Adjudicators may consider whether or not the subject sought counseling or other psychological help with addiction, grief, anger and other behavior issues that can affect the ability to obtain a security clearance. For example, a subject receives counseling to manage their anger.

The motivation for the conduct-The adjudicator may consider the reasons a person behaved adversely. Justice, revenge, anger, self-defense or duress are examples of different types of motivation that can change behavior. For example, a subject attacks and injures a bystander only after friend plies them with alcohol.

The potential for pressure, coercion, exploitation, or duress-There are some situations that can make people vulnerable; peer pressure, alcohol or drug tolerance, coercion and exploitation are a few. These are also taken into consideration to determine whether or not a security clearance and an applicants' situation would create vulnerability. In an earlier example, a subject married to a foreign national from an oppressive country may be coerced to help an adversary obtain privileged information.

The likelihood of continuation or recurrence-Information on a subject is used to determine whether or not the behavior will happen again. For example, a person had been in counseling for an alcohol related event. Both the counseling and the alcohol related event occurred 15 years prior. Since then there have been no further indicators of alcohol abuse. The adjudicator may determine that the likelihood of recurrence is low. Each case will be judged on its own merits, and any doubt concerning personnel being considered for access to classified information will be resolved in favor of national security.

Summary

A defense contractor is required to have an FCL to perform work on a classified contract. The FCL is not a requirement of eligibility to bid on classified contracts, but the process of the FCL is initiated upon award of the contract. A company cannot process their own clearance for the sake of looking competitively attractive, but is a result of sponsorship by the Government or a prime contractor. The FCL is strictly contract based and demonstrates an enterprise' trustworthiness to work on classified contracts.

A PCL is the administrative determination that an employee is eligible from a national security basis for a security clearance. The PCL is based on a contract and the FCL. The FSO provides justification for an employee clearance and submits a clearance request to DCSA who then assigns an investigation based on the clearance level. The investigations are thorough and based on 13 criteria to determine eligibility. Once the investigation is complete, the clearance request will go through an adjudication process.

Problems

1. Aside from corporate documentation, what three government forms will a CDC compile for DCSA to begin the process of granting a facility clearance?
2. What characteristics must a company display to qualify for a

facility clearance?
3. What determines the security clearance level to which an FSO be cleared?
4. Name three criteria that are considered during the adjudication process.

REFERENCES

1. Defense Counterintelligence and Security Agency, *Checklist for New Facility Security Clearances*, https://www.dcsa.mil/mc/ctp/fc/
2. Department of Defense, DoD 5220.22-M, *National Industrial Security Operating Manual*, section 2-106, February 2016
3. Department of Defense, DoD 5220.22-M, *National Industrial Security Operating Manual*, section 2-110, February 2016
4. Department of Defense, DoD 5220.22-M, *National Industrial Security Operating Manual*, section 2-202, February 2016
5. Department of Defense, DoD 5220.22-M, *National Industrial Security Operating Manual*, section 2-201, February 2016
6. Bennett, J W (2020), *Insider's Guide to Security Clearances*, Huntsville, AL: Red Bike Publishing
7. Department of Defense, DoD 5220.22-M, *National Industrial Security Operating Manual*, section 2-208, February 2016
8. *FBI Claims a Confession in Israel Spy Case*, NY Sun, Joseph Goldstein, April 2008 http://www.nysun.com/national/fbi-claims-a-confession-in-israel-spy-case/75129/

HELPFUL WEBSITES:

e-Qip website
http://www.opm.gov/e-qip
Security Clearances
http://www.DCSA.mil/isp/fac_clear/fac_clear_check.html
Security Forms
http://www.archives.gov/isoo/security-forms/

CHAPTER 4 CONTRACTING PROCEDURES

Introduction

It is important for the CDC to understand the contractual requirements and how to specifically perform the classified work. The Government Contracting Activity (GCA) or prime contractor should provide the guidelines and information about the classified work to be performed. Along with the Security Classification Guide (SCG), the DD Form 254 or Contract Security Classification Specification is issued to describe the classification level, location of classified work performance and type of classified work to be performed. This chapter will explain security requirements identified in the NISPOM and the DD Form 254 and how to interpret and prepare.

Identifying Customer Requirements

Whenever the GCA or prime contractor awards classified work to a cleared contractor or subcontractor, they should describe the classified work to be performed, the level of classification, and guidance. This security guidance is provided during all phases of the contract negotiations including the Invitation for Bid (IFB), Request for Proposal (RFP), Request for Quotation (RFQ) or other means of business solicitation [1]. The DD Form 254 (Figures 1-3) is issued by the GCA or prime contractor and is used to identify the type of classified work the cleared contractor is expected to perform, the classification level of the work to be performed and how to protect the classified information under the cleared contractor's control.

The FSO's role is to work with contracts, engineers, program managers or other involved departments to ensure that the company understands how to protect classified information. The NISPOM requires the contractor to provide input to the DD Form 254 and how it is applied in the company [1]. The FSO should at least review the DD Form 254 with cleared employees to ensure it is accurate, clear and that everyone performing on the contract understands the security requirements.

Additionally, the FSO should ensure they receive the SCG from the GCA or prime contractor customer. The performing cleared contractor should abide by requirements in the DD Form 254, SCG and NISPOM. It is the CDC's responsibility to ensure that the cleared employees understand and apply the security requirements. DCSA will inspect the contractor to determine how well they understand and apply the NISPOM and requirements identified in the DD Form 254 [2].

FSO responsibilities include providing a good assessment of any security product and service costs necessary to meet requirements. For example, the defense contractor agrees to abide by the NISPOM. Therefore, the contractor pays for all of the costs required to implement the NISPOM at their location.

Interpreting Requirements in the DD Form 254 and NISPOM

A cleared contractor can help reduce costs by preparing ahead of time. This is where an FSO can anticipate expenses, perform risk assessments while implementing NISPOM and advise on ways to reduce costs while being compliant. The earlier into the process the assessment is conducted the better the company performs. Conducting a cost impact analysis or coordinating with DCSA only after committing to the contract may place the contractor in the tough position building closed areas, ordering more GSA approved containers (safes) and meeting tough governmental compliance with short notice. Lack of planning could prove costly.

The FSO should form a team consisting of key players such as: program managers, engineers, security staff, contract representatives and others responsible for developing business with the prime contractor or GCA. This team should be able to make decisions to bring to the company leadership before they commit to perform as the contract specifies. The FSO contributes by providing information and guidance on protecting classified information in the process and such planning could translate into significant cost reduction.

Understanding how to advise and assist in the development of the DD Form 254 provides the ground work for ensuring the customer security requirements are clear, applicable and understood. Since the government provides the protection requirements, getting in on the ground level development can only benefit the contractor.

The DD Form 254 requirements can be a baseline to help the FSO assess the current state of security to determine whether or not the company has enough classified storage space, the right type of storage space, whether or not alarms are needed and other physical security needs to support the contract. Other performance requirements may indicate the need for classified computer processing, upgrading facility and personnel clearances, and increasing storage level and capability.

The DD Form 254 could be used to identify training needs concerning how to perform on the classified work. Training should be contract specific to protect the classified information while meeting the customer's needs. Training topics include familiarization with the SCG, details specific to the DD Form 254, insider threat, derivative classifier, and a refresher of the initial security training topics as they could be impacted with the new work. Depending on the requirements, DCSA may have to provide additional briefings to the FSO such as NATO, COMSEC, intelligence and others. In turn, the FSO will be expected to brief designated cleared employees.

Interpreting the DD Form 254

Non-possessing Facilities

In most situations, non-possessing facilities are not authorized to store classified information on site. The non-possessing CDC will manage security clearances for employees who provide classified products and services at other locations as indicated in the DD Form 254. The DD Form 254 describes the classified performance even though that performance may not be at the same location as the CDC.

The DD Form 254 will specify the contract requirements for possessing and non-possessing facilities. Beginning at the top of the DD Form 254 the reader can see the important information concerning the CDC's identity, clearance level and oversight agency. Included is the description of the facility clearance level of the CDC and level of classified storage, both of which are in lines 1a and 1b of figure 4.1. The expected clearance level should be typed in the appropriate boxes indicating CONFIDENTIAL, SECRET or TOP SECRET [3]. Part 1b indicates the highest level of classified storage required for performance on the contract. For non-possessing facilities, this should be "Not Applicable". Though the FCL may be at the TOP SECRET level, no classified information will be authorized for storage on site. In other words, the CDC will require valid facility clearance at the level indicated to perform on the contract, but classified work will not be conducted at the FCL address.

In Item 2a, the issuing activity will enter the contract number. This contract number provides authorization for the facility and personnel security clearance request, upgrade, or maintenance and the current level. If a prime contractor is issuing a subcontract, the issuing authority will fill out Item 2b. In that case, they provide the original prime contract in Item 2a. Item 2c is filled out for Requests for Proposal, Requests for Quote, Invitations for Bid or other requests for business.

Figure 4-1

Item 3 offers several choices of status; original, revised, or final. It allows for only one check mark for options a, b, or c. Original is checked to indicate the type of contract. The original document is retained on file and all additional future changes or revisions will refer to this original document.

The "Revised" choice is selected when there is a change to the DD Form 254 (Items 4-5). In the case of a revision, the revision number and the date of the revised DD Form 254 are entered. Since the original DD Form 254 is always the source, the date of the original DD Form 254 is entered in Item 3a. Both DD Forms 254 are filed and accounted for in a manner facilitating quick reference and access.

Item 6 is required when the Government issues a contract to a prime contractor. The contracting activity enters the contract company name, Commercial and Government Entity Code (CAGE), and the DCSA address in Items 6a through 6c. Item 7 requires the same information when it is a subcontract.

Item 8 notifies the contractor the location where actual classified work will be performed. If work is performed in multiple locations, that information is added in Item 13 to include company name, CAGE code and the serving CSO. A copy of the DD Form 254 is submitted to the FSOs of the other companies. When work is performed on a government facility, the information is listed in Item 13.

The GCA or prime civilian contracting officer provides a clear, unclassified description of the work to be performed in items 9 and 10. Descriptions and titles should be unclassified when at all possible to provide a means of cataloging, filing and retrieving and for ease of access. If a classified description is entered, then the DD Form 254 itself would be classified. A possible security violation could arise if the actual DD Form 254 were not stored in an approved location.

Item 10 (Figure 4-2)provides all the information that the contractor needs to know and the access they are required to maintain on the contract. The access blocks are marked with an "X" indicating "Yes" or "No" for access requirement. Again, this work will not be performed in the non-possessing facility. In that case the FSO or appointed representative may need to provide security briefings for the different types of required access levels. Otherwise, the security manager at the location where the classified work is performed may conduct the training. Coordination should be made between program managers and security offices to ensure understanding and compliance.

Figure 4-2

Item 10 addresses sensitive information determined to require additional protection. The NISPOM primarily addresses CONFIDENTIAL, SECRET and TOP SECRET. However, item 10 covers areas that may require additional security countermeasures. This book will not address security requirements for Item 10, but an affected contractor can get more in depth guidance from the government customer or prime contractor and DCSA. In this example of a cleared contractor of a non-possessing facility, all checks in item 10 will indicate "No" or no special types of access required.

Moving on to Item 11 we discover how to perform on the contract. Item 11 identifies where and how classified information should be accessed. For example, all the access listed earlier is not necessarily required to occur on company campus. In some cases, a DD Form 254 will identify that a company will have a facility clearance and no storage requirement. In the example our non-possessing facility has no special access and will perform all work at a US Government location.

Item 11a indicates whether or not access to classified information ONLY occurs at another facility. The word "ONLY" indicates that the work will be performed elsewhere and not be conducted on the company campus. In the example, the answer is yes and Items 11b through 11f are marked "No". Since 11a is yes, then Item 13 may indicate the location of classified access.

When the contractor is afforded the use of the Defense Technical Information Center (DTIC), then "Yes" will be indicated in Item 13g.

When the opportunity comes for a contractor to gain access to DTIC services, the government agency's GCA or the prime contractor will sponsor the company for access. The DTIC access is tied to a contract. The GCA will submit the Registration for Scientific and Technical Information Services, DD Form 1540, to the DTIC [9]. The prime contractor submits the request form through the GCA for verification of need to know. Once registered with DTIC, the contractor can apply for access to unclassified, military critical data from Department of Defense. The request is sent using Military Critical Technical Data Agreement, DD Form 2345, to the Defense Logistics Service Center.

Items 11g through 11k indicate COMSEC, TEMPEST, OPSEC, Defense Courier Services requirements or access by the contractor. Item 11l. is a recent requirement that identifies controlled unclassified information. This is not classified, but the contractor or subcontractor must be made aware of their responsibility to participate in a program to protect qualifying information.

For Item 12, the cleared contractor should seek approval from the GCA prior to releasing information to the public. The NISPOM also requires contractors to seek approval before releasing certain unclassified information relating to a classified contract [3]. Because of the nature of classified contracts, even the release of some unclassified information related to the contract could compromise a program. All release of any information concerning a classified contract should be discussed with and approved by the GCA or prime contractor.

The GCA or prime contractor provides specific classified performance guidance and how to implement security measures in Item 13. The contractor or subcontractor has an equal responsibility to understand the security requirements identified on the DD Form 254. The information in Item 13 should include clarification on the existing SCG, identification of source and what makes the information or product classified, and any other information to let the contractor know just what to protect and how to protect it while performing classified work off-site.

Item 14 (Figure 4-3) is identified as early as possible. Additional security requirements could increase costs. The earlier costs are identified the better. The contractor or subcontractor is responsible for ensuring that they are able to provide the specified additional requirements. These additional requirements are reflective of precautions necessary for intelligence and special access. Good coordination between the GCA, contractor and DCSA conducted early

Figure 4-3

will ensure the contractor is prepared to implement the required level of security without providing undue burden.

The final pieces consist of certification, signature and distribution. The signature and certification represent that the DD Form 254 has been staffed and is complete and accurate.

When done correctly, this last part is more of a formality after a great coordination effort and understanding of all parties involved. The contractor should not be reviewing the completed DD Form 254 for the first time at this point, but should have been involved with the coordination throughout the creation. Additionally, they should not be left to filling out their own requirements for the GCA or prime contractor to approve.

Possessing Facilities

For possessing facilities, most of the form is completed as with the non-possessing facilities. However, we should go back and visit Items 1b and Item 3. Item 1b indicates level of classified information to be stored at the possessing facility. This is a great time for the FSO and the CDC to determine resources necessary to protect classified information. They should understand how much information, what format it is in so that they can acquire space and protection resources.

In some cases classified material is authorized for retention for a period of longer than the two years if authorized after the associated contract closes. When retention is necessary, the contractor should request an extension from the GCA or prime contractor. Upon approval, the issuing authority submits a final DD Form 254 to reflect the change. In that case, Final (Item 3c) will be selected and the new DD Form 254 date is annotated. The date of the original DD Form 254 will be completed in Item 3a (Figure 4-1).

Item 8 notifies the contractor the location where actual classified work will be performed. If work is performed in the contractor company or the subcontractor company, "Same as Item 6a or 7a" is annotated. If work is performed in multiple locations, that information is added in Item 13 to include company name, CAGE code and the serving CSO organization is completed. A copy of the DD Form 254 is submitted to the FSOs of the other companies. When work is performed on a government facility, the information is listed in Item 13.

Item 10 provides all the information that the contractor needs to know and the access they are required to maintain on the contract. The access blocks will be marked with an "X" all that apply for access requirement. The FSO or appointed representative may need to provide security briefings for the different types of required access levels. Coordination is made between program managers and security offices to ensure understanding and compliance with the requirements of the government or primary contract holder.

If COMSEC requirements are annotated in 10a, accounts are created for COMSEC items with National Security Agency's Central Office of Records (NSA COR) oversight [4]. The GCA will have to approve a subcontractor's access prior to a prime contractor awarding the affected contract. The NSACOR requires notification prior to bargaining for the contract requiring access to COMSEC. This coordination is necessary for sponsorship to enable the approved companies to apply for and receive the COMSEC accounts. Keep in mind that some COMSEC material may not require the contractor to have a COMSEC account.

When COMSEC accounts are required by the DD Form 254, the FSO appoints a cleared employee as a COMSEC Custodian. The

COMSEC Custodian does not have to be the FSO or other senior leader. Any appropriately cleared employee capable of performing the job is eligible. The appointed employee attends training and develops a compliant accountability program depending on the type of COMSEC and the classification level assigned. The custodian is responsible for conducting periodic inventory, conducting employee COMSEC briefings and other administrative actions. DCSA conducts briefings for the FSO, COMSEC and Alternate COMSEC Custodians. The FSO or COMSEC Custodian in turn briefs the company employees [5].

Items 10b, c and d are designated for access to additional security measures, information and items affected by the Department of Energy and Nuclear Regulatory Commission. RESTRICTED DATA (RD) Critical Nuclear Weapon Design Information (CNWDI) and FORMERLY RESTRICTED DATA (FRD) require structured briefings prior to accessing the information.

Recall that, CONFIDENTIAL and SECRET clearances require NACLC clearances and TOP SECRET requires an SSBI. However, RD has different background investigation requirements. SECRET RD requires a favorable SSBI where plain SECRET requires only a NACLC [6]. The FSO should ensure the proper security clearance is requested based on the identified DD Form 254 need.

The FSO should use the DD Form 254 requirements to prepare for the receipt and storage of new material. This is where they provide return on investment to their employers. Knowing the requirements of the DD Form 254 will help them prepare for budgetary requirements that come from company overhead, not customer provided. Heightened preparation includes anticipating supplies on hand in anticipation of properly marking classified information. In addition to the classification markings, the FSO should prepare for other marking capability to indicate special handling instructions.

Item 10e falls under the jurisdiction of the Director of National Intelligence (DNI). However, the GCA ensures security requirements identified by DNI are implemented in the contractor security procedures. As with earlier items, releasing agency approval is necessary prior to a contractor providing a subcontractor access to the intelligence information [7].

If access to SCI is required, then special security requirements are necessary to protect intelligence information. The contractor or subcontractor will need to know what physical security, access control, alarms, briefings and other measures are necessary to protect the classified product. DCSA typically has the responsibility of inspecting the contractor's ability to protect classified information. However, DCSA will not have oversight of this particular area without an agreement in place with DNI. When an agreement has not been made, the DNI has oversight and DCSA is "carved out".

Access to intelligence information is identified as requiring either SCI or Non-SCI. If access to a Sensitive Compartmented Information Facility (SCIF) to protect intelligence sources and methods is required, then the FSO should be prepared to protect classified information by investing time, money and personnel to prepare and properly mark such intelligence products. The FSO should use the DD Form 254 to identify security requirements and resources such as stamps and ink pads and other equipment to mark generated classified material.

Item 1of notifies the contractor whether or not access to Special Access Programs (SAP) is necessary. The GCA's Program Security Office approves all contractors for access to program material. Any additional security requirements should be identified in item 13. Whether or not the CSA is "carved out" or deemed not responsible for inspecting the program will be noted in Item 15.

If SAP access is required. The contractor and subcontractor gets guidance in Item 13 (Figure 4-2) as well as special security requirements as identified in Item 14 (Figure 4-3). Where SAP inspections are not conducted by the DCSA, Item 15 will be marked to indicate "Yes" for inspection to indicate that DCSA will not be providing the inspections.

Though not addressed in NISPOM, the DD Form 254 preparation guide instructs that NATO and Foreign Government Information (FGI) both require GCA approval prior to a contractor granting access to a subcontractor. The FSO will also give briefings prior to granting access to contractor employees. Item 10i no longer applies and will therefore always have "No" selected. FOR OFFICIAL USE ONLY (FOUO) requires GCA to provide security guidance as it is not classified and is not covered in the NISPOM. The GCA provides the guidance in Item 13. Item 10k is filled out if there are other access requirements not identified in the DD Form 254. If there are any, the "Yes" box is selected and the specifics are provided in Item 13.

Consider the case where a CDC has access to COMSEC, RESTRICTED and FRD, CNWDI, SCI and non-SCI Intelligence information, NATO, FGI and FOUO material. Each access will require separate briefings. Recall that DNI has oversight over intelligence information and DoE and NRC has oversight over RD and CNWDI. Each access will also have different agency oversight and inspection requirements unless an agreement between agencies is in place.

Moving on to Item 11 we discover how to perform on the contract. Item 11 identifies where and how classified information is to be accessed. For example, all the access listed earlier is not necessarily required to occur on company campus. In some cases, a DD Form 254 will identify that a company will have a facility clearance and no storage requirement. If that is the situation, then work will be identified to take place at other locations and Item 10 describes the access levels. There will not be security instructions for work performed outside of the facility. Additionally, companies that perform work on site have in depth security instructions to best safeguard classified information.

For Item 11b, the contract issuer will indicate whether or not the company will ONLY receive classified information. This is opposite of Item 11a, meaning that the access identified in Item 10 is to occur on the company campus and that the company will ONLY receive the information and not generate classified material. In some cases the scope of work may require the company to generate classified material. Since it is difficult to predict the possibility, the contract issuer can add flexibility by annotating Item 13. "Situations may require the generation of classified material. Always mark classified material to the level of the source material."3

If a contractor will be authorized to receive and generate classified material, the GCA or prime contractor selects "Yes". If the contractor is to receive and generate classified material as outlined in Item 10, additional security classification guidance is necessary. The guidance is added to Item 13 and provided in the associated SCG.

The contractor may be required to fabricate, modify or store classified hardware. If so, "Yes" is selected in Item 11d. Detailed information is vital to the proper security of the hardware. Item 13 is used to include information such as how much hardware, use of Closed or Restricted areas and any other information to indicate what type of storage is necessary.

Item 11e identifies whether or not the access to classified information is for services only. If "Yes" is checked, then the type of services should be identified in Item 13. For example, the type of service examples may indicate some of the following situations:

Editing only-_Services to perform include editing classified documents for accuracy of content, technical information, and grammar. Classification markings are already provided.

Janitorial – Services to perform involve cleaning rest rooms, hallways and closed areas. Cleaning employees are cleared at the SECRET level.

Quality - Consult on how to improve first time yield of manufactured parts. These parts are classified at the CONFIDENTIAL level.

When situations arise where the cleared contractor will have access to classified information outside the U.S., Puerto Rico, U.S. Possessions and Trust Territories, the "Yes" block will be checked. Item 13 could have the location of the work to be performed to include the city, state and country of the performance. The contractor company will provide a DD Form 254 to DCSA.

When the contractor is afforded the use of DTIC, then "Yes" will be indicated in Item 13g.

Item 11g is marked indicating whether or not a COMSEC account is necessary. A COMSEC account is required when a company is engaged in using accountable Communication Security equipment or devices. The GCA informs the contractor of the need to have a COMSEC account and the contractor will inform DCSA of the names of primary and alternate COMSEC Custodian and the FSO to the NSA Central Office of Record and the GCA.

The GCA may require the contractor to provide Operations Security (OPSEC). The OPSEC plan is designed to help a contractor identify areas of weakness that could be exploited by an adversary. The

OPSEC plan is designed to deny an adversary unclassified information. The OPSEC information is usually unclassified, but would cause some damage to a company or individual. For example, a contractor may forbid customers or vendors from taking notes or bringing cell phones into meetings in efforts to protect proprietary information. The government may specify that a company must have a plan in place to shred all unclassified material associated with a certain contract.

If a contractor is required to use the Defense Courier Service, the GCA will approve it. The prime contractor will seek this approval prior to requiring it from the subcontractor [10]. Item 11k is for additional information not covered in earlier items. Specifics are usually included in Item 13.

The contractor should seek approval from the GCA prior to releasing information to the public. The NISPOM also requires contractors to seek approval before releasing certain unclassified information relating to a classified contract [3]. Because of the nature of classified contracts, even the release of some unclassified information related to the contract could compromise a program. All release of any information concerning a classified contract should be discussed with and approved by the GCA and DCSA.

The GCA or prime contractor provides significant guidance on how the contractor or subcontractor is to protect the classified information and work provided by the contract. The DD Form 254 is the venue for providing such guidance and how to annotate security measures in Item 13. The contractor or subcontractor has an equal responsibility to understand the security requirements identified on the DD Form 254. The contractor should review each item and ensure they have an understanding of how to safeguard the classified items and what exactly is classified. The contents of Item 13 should be quite clear to the user. The information in Item 13 should include clarification on the existing SCG, identification of source documents whether or not classified hardware will be produced or provided, what makes the information or product classified, and any other information to let the contractor know just what to protect and how to protect it.

Item 14 is identified as early as possible as additional security requirements could increase costs. The earlier costs are identified the better. The contractor or subcontractor is responsible for ensuring that they are able to provide the specified additional requirement reflective of precautions necessary for intelligence and special access. The final pieces consist of certification, signature and distribution.

Summary

The DD Form 254 is a powerful contracting tool to ensure that classified information is protected. Beyond oversight, the CDC can use it as a method to develop and implement their security program. The 254 is used to both relay requirements from the prime contractor or GCA and ensure the subcontractor understands the level of effort. The DD Form 254 is the result of cooperation between the issuer and receiver on how to perform on the classified contract.

Problems

1. Your company has just won a major contract supporting the Department of Defense. A program manager is sure that your company will not need to access classified material on campus, but needs verification. Where will you find that information?
2. What type of information should be included in Item 13 of the DD Form 254?
3. Explain why the DD Form 254 is important to a company's ability to protect classified material.
4. Who provides the security briefings to the FSO and COMSEC Custodian?
5. An FSO should be prepared to point out to senior executives any additional security requirements and the impact. What are some things an FSO should consider when preparing for storage of SCI information. In other words, what are some expenses to consider that go above and beyond non-SCI security?

REFERENCES

1. Department of Defense, DoD 5220.22-M, *National Industrial Security Operating Manual*, section 4-103, February 2016

2. Department of Defense, DoD 5220.22-M, *National Industrial Security Operating Manual*, section 1-207, February 2016

3. Defense Security Service Academy, *A Guide for the Preparation of a DD Form 254*, Defense Counterintelligence and Security Agency Academy, MD, https://www.cdse.edu/documents/student-guides/IS128-guide.pdf, downloaded May 2020

4. Department of Defense, DoD 5220.22-M, *National Industrial Security Operating Manual*, section 9-403, February 2016

5. Department of Defense, DoD 5220.22-M, *National Industrial Security Operating Manual*, section 9-404, February 2016

6. Department of Defense, DoD 5220.22-M, *National Industrial Security Operating Manual*, section 2-201, February 2016

7. Department of Defense, DoD 5220.22-M, *National Industrial Security Operating Manual*, section 9-108, February 2016

8. Department of Defense, DoD 5220.22-M, *National Industrial Security Operating Manual*, section 9-303, February 2016

9. Department of Defense, DoD 5220.22-M, *National Industrial Security Operating Manual*, section 11-202a, February 2016

10. Department of Defense, DoD 5220.22-M, National Industrial Security Operating Manual, section 5-402a, February 2016

CHAPTER 5 RECEIVING CLASSIFIED MATERIAL

INTRODUCTION

What happens when you win the classified contract and all of the work begins to arrive? This chapter explains how the CDC should prepare to receive customer provided classified information and perform the work according to the DD Form 254. Protecting classified information begins with the introduction of classified information into a cleared facility and ends with the successful removal through return to customer, destruction or further dissemination of classified information. Also included is a recommended organizational structure to ensure only cleared personnel have access to classified material.

THE INFORMATION MANAGEMENT SYSTEM (IMS)

The cleared contractor is required to protect all classified material and be able to retrieve it within a reasonable amount of time [1]. Though the NISPOM only requires the cleared contractor to keep accountability of TOP SECRET information, cleared contractors should keep a document trail for all classified information. The NISPOM requires receipting action whenever SECRET and TOP SECRET information is transferred to or from a cleared contractor. However, it is a good practice to track deliveries and send receipts for outgoing CONFIDENTIAL information as well; we'll discuss how to do this in more detail later. Confirmation of receipt and visibility of the internal transfer of classified information will also help an FSO retrieve stored classified information or identify its location. A defense contractor can possess anywhere from a few to thousands of classified documents. An IMS should help track and find classified material at any time no matter how much classified information is involved .

Classified information can arrive at a cleared contractor in many different ways. Delivery through cleared contractor employees, government employees, contractually related customers, Defense Courier Service, secure fax, secure e-mail, US Postal Service, overnight delivery services and other approved means of transmission, delivery or other methods of dissemination. Regardless of how classified material arrives, the FSO should plan for the reception of classified material by authorized cleared employees. The receiver of classified material plays a role in both safeguarding classified material after it arrives as well as identifying discrepancies and security violations that may have occurred in transit.

CENTRALIZED CLASSIFIED INFORMATION PROCESSING

FSOs should control the introduction and dissemination of classified product with a centralized document control system. The process directs the arrival of visitors, couriers, mail carriers, overnight delivery companies, and others. Through a process of document control, FSOs receive, inspect, sign receipts, document arrival, safeguard or make available for authorized employees.

Without such controls, classified information could be vulnerable to unauthorized disclosure, loss, or compromise. Possible scenarios include having it on site in an unauthorized manner such as: not contract related, improperly marked, improperly stored, provided to unauthorized employees, or even removed from the premises without authorization. To prevent the unauthorized delivery, classified deliveries should be made to ONLY the authorized mailing address. This address should be synonymous with the centralized classified information processing location.

Remember that a defense contractor registers for and obtains a CAGE code. They also provide a classified mailing address as part of the clearance processing. These addresses are listed with DCSA. Multiple receiving locations in a facility can cause confusion during deliveries. However, providing guidance to cleared employees on where to deliver classified information will help resolve any confusion.

Controlling Introduction Reduces Security Violations

The uncontrolled introduction of classified information can cause serious accountability problems, potential security violations and compromise of classified material. The FSO conducts investigations into security violations to determine whether classified information is lost, compromised or suspected to be compromised. Many security incidents are investigated internally and resolved at the lowest level. However, if the investigation reveals that classified material is lost, compromised or suspected to be compromised, the information should be reported to DCSA.

Train Cleared Employees How to Introduce Classified Information

The FSO should create company policy demonstrating how classified material is introduced and removed from the company and train cleared employees on the procedures. The intent is to establish an enterprise where everyone has a clear understanding of policy and minimize any customer generated security violations. For example, the FSO can ensure that the government customer understands that classified deliveries are to be made through the cleared contractor's security department and not directly to the cleared engineer. Assuming that cleared employees will know what to do without verifying that knowledge can lead to the security program's failure.

One trigger point to plan the reception of classified information is upon notification of a classified visit request. When cleared employees visit another cleared facility, their organization submits the visit request. At that point, the receiving FSO can coordinate directly with the sending security manager for delivery of classified material. Furthermore, if a classified visit or meeting is taking place the FSO or representative can provide a security briefing covering accountability of all classified notes or other items necessary for the meeting.

Restrict Flow of Visitor Traffic

A follow on method of controlling the introduction of classified information is to restrict or direct the flow of visitor traffic into the cleared facility. Cleared facilities may have multiple entry points and visitors should have access to only designated entry points. To help with maintaining control of the classified environment, FSO's can employ information technology or human controls to direct pedestrian traffic into their facility. Access controls with biometric, pin card or data card access provide an excellent opportunity to flow all traffic through an authorized area. When budget does not permit the purchase or subscription to expensive information technology, high security hardware such as door locks and crash bars are adequate to prevent entry into unauthorized doors.

When controls are in place, pedestrian traffic is filed through a reception area where visitors are received warmly and reminded to check in with the security or reception desk for all classified deliveries. Additionally, the NISPOM requires the prominent display of signs notifying employees and visitors to a cleared facility that their personal effects are subject to inspection [2]. Human resources and legal corporate entities should be consulted and actions coordinated to ensure that privacy is respected and laws are followed. The technology and physical security measures are designed for the FSO to control who enters the facility, the reason for entry, and the further control of introduced classified material.

Inspecting Classified Information Deliveries

The FSO should ensure all classified deliveries are inspected and received into accountability. This due diligence is necessary to ensure that a classified delivery has not been compromised, is related to a contract, and is properly marked. Regardless of transmission methods of physical items (mail, courier, overnight, hand carry and etc) classified material should be double wrapped. Each layer serves to protect the classified material from inadvertent and unauthorized disclosure and should be addressed.

The classified package should be wrapped and sealed in opaque material or envelopes. A good practice is to cover seams with rip-proof opaque tape or other material that prevents and detects tampering. All seams of the outer layer should be sealed with opaque tape in an effort to create a solid layer of covering. The item should be wrapped and sealed with the first layer containing the classification level and to and from address lines. Two copies of receipts should either be attached to the first layer or inside the first layer. The outer layer should not contain classification markings and be addressed to a cleared contractor and not a person's name [3].

The sender may contact the receiver to notify that classified material is being sent to their facility and alerts the receiver to expect the delivery. Many times program managers, engineers or other technical employees are anticipating the delivery, but may not have all the details of delivery times and dates. However, an FSO to FSO coordination can provide all the information of the transaction in advance.

Detailed Inspection Requirements

Regardless of transmission methods, the recipient should examine the outer wrapping for evidence of tampering or to otherwise inspect that there has been no compromise of classified material. Classified packages should be double wrapped with two independent layers of protection. Each layer consists of opaque material such as: an envelope, paper, box or other strong wrapping material. The first part of the inspection should be conducted to look for evidence of tearing, ripping, re-wrapping or some other means of unauthorized access to the product.

Next, the shipping label should be reviewed for full approved classified mailing address and return address. There should be no classification markings on the outer layer of the item; the outer layer should not draw attention to the classified material inside. Classification markings on the outside of a package are a security violation.

The inner layer should be inspected the same way as the outer layer for evidence of tampering or unauthorized disclosure (Figure 5-1). However, the inside wrapping should contain the full address of the recipient as well as classification markings on the top, bottom, front and back (Figure 5-2). TOP SECRET and SECRET material should have a packing list or receipt of contents either on the outside or inside of the container. Receipts are not necessary with the shipment of CONFIDENTIAL material. If a receipt is included, the receiver should sign it and return it to the sender.

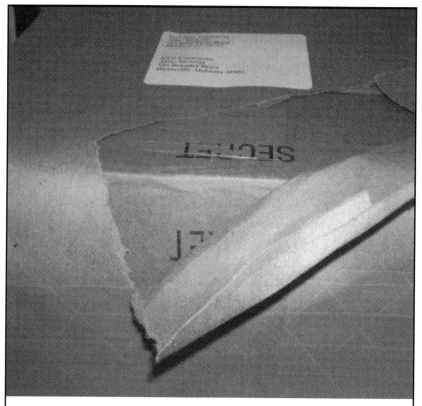

Figure 5-1 This package is ripped. The receiver would notify the sender that the shipment packaging was damaged. It may be necessary to investigate and determine whether or not classified information was compromised.

The receiver should then check the receipt against the contents to ensure the item has been identified correctly and all items are accounted for. The receipt should list the sender, the addressee and correctly identify the contents by an unclassified title and appropriate quantity. Since the receipt may be filed for administrative and compliance purposes, the inspector should ensure information on the receipts are unclassified. If the receipt contains a classified title, the sender may be able to coordinate for an unclassified title for internal use. Listing classified titles in an unclassified IMS data base is a security violation. Also, since the receipt contains a classified title, it must be protected as classified. The receiver should prepare to store the receipt long term in a GSA approved container because of the classification level.

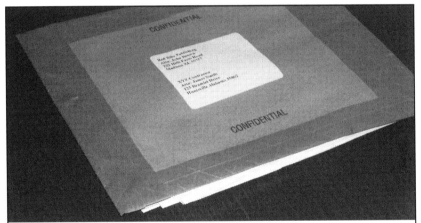

Figure 5-2 This inner layer is addressed and stamped correctly. It is typical of the inner wrapper of a package a cleared facility might receive via mail, delivery or courier. Notice the anti-rip tape on all major seams.

If a signed receipt is to be returned to the sender, the FSO should ensure it is prepared for delivery. The receiver should compare the classification identified in the receipt with that annotated on the inner wrapper. These markings ensure the package is handled correctly once the outer wrapping has been opened or removed. The receiver should compare the classification marking on the contents with the wrapper and the receipt to once again verify the classification level and prevent unauthorized disclosure. Once all the checks and verifications are complete, the receiver can then sign a copy of the receipt and return to the sender, thus closing the loop on the sender's accounting responsibilities (Figure 5-3).

Items to inspect when receiving classified deliveries:

1. Outside layer:
   - Evidence of tamper
   - Seams sealed with anti-rip tape
   - Label is addressed to organization (not individual)

2. Inside layer:
   - Evidence of tamper
   - Seams sealed with anti-rip tape
   - Inside label addressed to recipient
   - Inside wrapper is marked with appropriate classification
   - Receipts / packing list included for SECRET and above
   - Compare receipt/packing list against contents
   - Ensure items are classified properly
   - Sign receipts and return to sender

Figure 5-3 The FSO should ensure that all classified deliveries are inspected prior to bringing them into accountability. Such checks are necessary to ensure items were sent properly, were not tampered with in transit, contain correct items and are authorized for storage in the classified holdings.

Top Secret Control Official

Cleared contractors that are granted a TOP SECRET FCL and are authorized to maintain a TOP SECRET inventory are required to appoint a TOP SECRET Control Official (TSCO). All transactions involving TOP SECRET information require documentation through access and accountability records. This requirement is for the life cycle of the information and includes reception, transmission, destruction and storage. Additionally, the contractor is required to perform an annual accountability inventory unless a waiver for the requirement is on file.

For example, all TOP SECRET information and material is documented by numbering them in a series. This allows the contractor and owner of the classified information to know exactly how many there are and what to look for during inventory. Any incoming material, copies generated or faxes transmitted are documented with the number and accounted for by the TSCO using the numbering and a continuous receipt system.

Reporting Requirements

It is the sender's responsibility to ensure deliveries arrive at the intended destination. The sender should be aware of the shipment and follow through until they receive a receipt or verify arrival. The receiver should report discrepancies to the sender, notifying them of a possible problem with their shipping policy. The sender can then take the opportunity to investigate the root problem. Once the root of the security infraction is discovered they can conduct training, review policy and otherwise put measures into place to improve their security program. If the notification responsibility or the report itself is ignored, then more severe problems could develop.

Security violations resulting in loss, compromise or suspected compromise of classified material, should be reported to DCSA. There is value added with sharing discrepancy information with the right agencies and parties. Reasons for reporting include risk reduction and to provide feedback from which all parties concerned can benefit to better implement and direct security policies.

Safeguarding the Classified Information

The FSO should design a policy to maintain strict control. The NISPOM requires strict control at the TOP SECRET level [4]. However, all material entering the facility, produced, or reproduced in any fashion should be brought into possession for control, audit and inventory purposes using an IMS [4]. This provides visibility over the classified material and allows for preventative measures against unauthorized disclosure or identification of security violations.

The FSO should employ a security training and discipline program to compel cleared employees to act as force multipliers increasing security effectiveness. In that role, cleared employees will know to deliver all newly introduced classified material to the FSO for accountability purposes and into the IMS. When security personnel practice good customer service and enforce procedures, good relationships develop making procedures easy to follow as well as rewarding for all employees.

Once the material is received and the delivery inspected against the receipt, the FSO or security specialist can input the information into a retrievable database or IMS. This database can be something as simple as logging the information into a notebook or through technology such as software sold on the market. As a reminder, caution should be taken to ensure only unclassified titles and descriptive information is entered in to an unclassified database.

An example of a classified information accountability record can be seen in Figure 5-4. An accountability record is an excellent tool for controlling classified information introduced into the defense contractor facility. With the accountability record, documents are managed with additional receipting action. Some accountability records track document status from introduction to dissemination on the same record. Contractors are not limited to a certain method of document control other than the ability to track the status of classified information the cleared facility possesses.

Because of the positive identification and control involved, inventories should be conducted for all classified deliveries. If during the course of inventory, a document cannot be easily located, a more thorough search takes place. Input into the IMS record as documents are used or moved throughout the organization provides information for a growing data warehouse that may prove beneficial in finding the misplaced product.

Date of Receipt	How Received	Contract No.	Document No.	Title	Classification	Copy No.	Location
2/11/2011	Express Mail	ABC1230-00-7-A-0000	08-012	Gravy SCG (U)	SECRET	1	Safe 12875

Figure 5-4 Sample Information Management System record.

Commercially available IMS use information technology to create a detailed database that helps FSOs track classified material through many dispositions from receipt, inventory requirements and final disposition. Some produce receipts, tie to a barcode scanner, report statistical data that can help determine use and much more. For example, if an inventory reveals missing classified information, the database can provide valuable information to help reconstruct the history.

Databases can be tied to scanner software. Barcodes can be printed and applied to classified items for scanning. If an item is destroyed, shipped, filed, loaned or returned, it can be scanned and the status updated. These databases provide reports identifying when and where the barcode on the classified document was scanned and the last disposition. The FSO can use the technology to research dates, methods of receipt, contract number, assigned document number, assigned barcode, title, classification, copy number, location, and name of the receiver as follows:

Date of Receipt or Generation-This information is recorded to indicate the day the document arrived. It can be used as the countdown date for an inventory requirement or as a time line or search method in case an employee needs to retrieve it. If a document cannot be easily traced, those conducting the inventory can use the date in reference to narrowing down search locations or options.

How Received-Did the classified item arrive through USPS mail, overnight delivery, courier, hand carry, electronic means, derived from other research, printed or duplicated? This information is important to the FSO for use during DCSA's annual review of the contractor's ability to protect classified material. This column can be linked to the receipting action bringing the classified document to the company from external locations or perhaps from an internal customer request.

Contract Number-Contract numbers are important in situations where a contractor may have hundreds of classified contracts including directions that the material classified at certain levels must be stored separately. This added column can assist with determining need to know, quick retrieval of receipts, records or the classified item itself. Additionally, the FSO can pull documents by contract number to return to customer during contract closeout.

Document Number-Cleared contractors operating an IMS can generate an internal document number for classified product entering the company. This system generates a unique number that allows for quick filing and retrieval by that designation. Each contractor may assign a unique internal document number.

Barcode-The barcode is an excellent tool for document filing, retrieval, inventory and internal tracking for cleared contractors with large inventories. Classified information is received, assigned a barcode number and a physical code is placed in an easy to scan location. The barcode reader is used to scan the item during inventory and any other transactions. An FSO can assign any value to the document record necessary to know the status of any classified material at any time. Major retail stores use the same technology in their inventory and logistics process.

Unclassified Title-Because the title information could be stored in an unclassified computer, file cabinet, desk top or drawer, unclassified titles should be used. If a receipt arrives with a classified title, the receipt will have to be protected as classified. However, the receiver can make arrangements to assign a new unclassified title with little confusion. If an unclassified title is not possible or desired, arrangements will have to be made to protect all records and receipts. The classified title cannot be put on an unclassified database.

Classification Level-Data with the classification identified at the TOP SECRET, SECRET, or CONFIDENTIAL level helps during the retrieval process. Classified information with the additional designations or caveats of: FGI, NOFORN, INTEL, NATO and others should be filed separately according to regulations and contract requirements.

Copy Number-Copy numbers are used for multiple copies of existing classified material. For example, five copies of the same type of classified document could arrive or be duplicated on site. Each duplication should be safeguarded at the same level as the original document. For example, XYZ Contractor numbers their documents sequentially. Document number 35601-02 is the 35,601st document entered into the system. Additionally, the -02 identifies it as the second copy of that document.

Location or Disposition-The exact location of classified material helps with the easy retrieval. To log a document into accountability with no location is fine for companies possessing a limited amount of documents. Those contractors or agencies with multiple documents and possible locations will want to identify the assignment for quick retrieval. An additional data field can be used to input shelf, GSA container, room or building number. The more details the better. Additional comments and supporting documentation is necessary when the classified material leaves the accountability system through any means.

FSOs may also want to track the use of classified information checked out of a central location. This is similar to what a library does. Tracking the check out dates can help reconstruct where and when a document is used to find lost documents, help enforce need to know and provide better document control.

Summary

A good security program begins with the reception of classified information. These packages should be delivered to an approved mailing address. Prior to delivery, the sender should contact the receiver and notify them of the intended delivery. The receiver should then prepare for the delivery and ensure that only the employee cleared to the appropriate level receives it. The receiver should inspect the delivery for wrapping, address, and delivery method. After inspection, they should sign a receipt and return it to the sender. The inspector should then enter the classified items into an IMS. Once filed, they can make the information available for use to those with clearance and need to know.

PROBLEMS

1. After receiving classified material, the receiver inventories the contents and inspects the package. Name three items for possible inspection?
2. You have just received a classified package. Upon comparing the contents of the package with the receipt, you notice a misspelled title. What should you do?
3. Who should the FSO or senior security specialist notify in the event of a potential or suspected compromise of classified material?

REFERENCES

1. Department of Defense, DoD 5220.22-M, National Industrial Security Operating Manual, section 1-303, February 2016
2. Department of Defense, DoD 5220.22-M, National Industrial Security Operating Manual, section 5-103, February 2016
3. Department of Defense, DoD 5220.22-M, National Industrial Security Operating Manual, section 5-406, February 2016
4. Department of Defense, DoD 5220.22-M, National Industrial Security Operating Manual, section 5-201, February 2016

HELPFUL WEBSITES:

For additional training and resources on introducing classified information into a possessing facility, visit:
https://www.bennettinstitute.com

CHAPTER 6 MARKING CLASSIFIED MATERIAL

INTRODUCTION

Performing on classified contracts begins with recognizing and applying classification markings. Classification markings are provided as a method of warning and informing of classification level, the exact information to be protected, downgrading and declassification instructions, reasons for classification and sources of classification, and special access, control or safeguarding requirements (Figure 6-1). The classification level is applied to the front and back covers, top and bottom of pages, paragraphs, figures, tables and charts of classified documents. They are placed in conspicuous locations on objects, computers and other types of media. This chapter demonstrates how to inspect classified items for proper markings and how to properly mark classified items originally created or derived.

GUIDANCE FOR MARKING CLASSIFIED MATERIAL

Executive Order 13526 delivers guidelines for assigning classification levels to objects and information. The Government classifies information to provide safeguarding and prevent unauthorized disclosure, loss or compromise of classified information [1]. The amount generated should be kept to the minimum needed to build any system or accomplish any mission.

When receiving classified information, the FSO should check it against a receipt, inspect it for proper identification and markings and bring it into an IMS. If there are marking discrepancies, the receiver should rectify the situation by either sending it back or fixing the mistake themselves according to directions in the appropriate SCG.

Reasons for Applying Classification Markings

Classification markings can be found on the top and bottom, front and back of classified items. Markings are also found in internal pages, paragraphs and other locations inside documents, books, manuals and other paper based products.

- Warn and inform a user that an item is indeed classified or sensitive
- Conveys what exactly needs protection
- Identifies levels of classification or sensitivity
- Provides vital information and instruction on when to downgrade or declassify the material
- Gives sources and reason for classifying the item
- Warns of special access, control, dissemination or safeguarding requirements

Figure 6-1 Reasons for Classification

Security violations could occur if classified material is not marked. Suppose an engineer of XYZ Contractor goes to the company's centralized document storage area and signs out a document classified as SECRET. According to company information management policy the user is to return the item to document control prior to the end of the work day, or when they leave the office. The engineer takes the document back to his office and works with it. After a while his eyes get tired and he grabs his day planner to check his schedule.

He is reminded of an upcoming meeting with the social committee and begins to reflect on the near term company picnic. He gets up and walks to the window to look at proposed picnic location. While gathering his thoughts, he hears a knock at the door and walks over to open it. As he passes his desk his eyes glance at the document's markings of SECRET on the top and bottom of the opened pages. He then closes the classified book and picks it up. With the book closed and firmly secure in his hands and the outside protected by a cover sheet he opens the door and sees his buddy from across the hall. They both have clearances, but are working on two different contracts. His buddy has no need to know of the contents of the book.

In the example, the markings served to remind the engineer of the classified information in his possession and ensured that he maintained proper control and accountability. The marking also reminded the cleared employee of the responsibility of verifying clearance and "need to know" before disclosing it.

Classified markings also convey what exactly needs protection. For example, a cleared employee reviews a classified document and is able to determine from the portion markings which information is TOP SECRET, SECRET or CONFIDENTIAL. This information is important as a cleared employee would need to correctly transfer the classification of any information derived from the document to incorporate into a new document (derivative classification). Additionally, if any UNCLASSIFIED information needs to be removed for a sanitized product, the information will be properly identified in the portion markings.

Downgrade and Declassification

Classification markings also convey information and instruction for when to downgrade or declassify the material. These instructions are identified with "Declassify on:" and "Downgrade on:" followed by an event or a date. The downgrade and declassification instructions assist cleared employees in keeping classified material to the minimum necessary [2].

Executive Order 13526, directs that the OCAs assign a date or event for the declassification based on the sensitivity. Once the date or event transpires, the information should be declassified. This date or event should occur within the following 10 years and be annotated on the "Declassify on:" line. If declassification within the next ten years will still be sensitive enough to cause a measure of damage to national security, the OCA can extend "10-year rule" to a total of 25 years [3].

SECRET

For training purposes only

(U) Classified Material Marking Guide

Classified by: Jon Dow RBP/1022 DDMA

Reason: 1.4(e)

Declassify on: 31 July 2031

SECRET

For training purposes only

Figure 6-2a Front Cover

SECRET

For training purposes only

(U) Classified Material Marking Guide

SECRET

For training purposes only

Figure 6-2b Cover Page

SECRET

For training purposes only

(U) Classified Material Marking Guide

(U) First Page Markings

(U) Since this is the first page of the main part of the document, classification markings will be applied to the top and bottom that reflect the highest level of overall classification.

(C) For training purposes, this porting is classified CONFIDENTIAL but the page will be marked with SECRET on the top and bottom. The classification level of the portion markings on the first page have no bearing on the classification marking of the page.

SECRET

For training purposes only

Figure 6-2c First Page

SECRET

For training purposes only

SECRET

For training purposes only

Figure 6-2d Back Cover

Marking a Sample Classified Document

Figure 6-2 shows the overall marking requirements for a classified document. Here, the document is designated with a classification level of SECRET. In classified documents, the overall classification level is applied to the front and back covers, the title page and the first page of the document. The front cover page has an unclassified title as indicated by the portion marking (U) applied just before the title text. The "By:" line is on the cover page. Jon Dow of the fictional RBP Agency office designation 1022 DDMA provided the classification based on guidance from section 1.4 of Presidential E.O. 13526. The OCA listed Reason as 1.4 (e) (Figure 6-3) because the document contained information that would reveal "… scientific, technological, or economic matters relating to the national security, which includes defense against transnational terrorism" [4]. In this example, assume that the current date is 31 July 2021. He also assigned a declassification date for a duration of within the next ten years hence "Declassify on: 31 July 2021".

In another example of a classification "By:" line, information could be classified if unauthorized revelation could compromise military plans, weapon systems, or operations. In such cases a document or item assigned a classification because of this reason could have the statement "Reason: 1-4a". The 1-4a refers to section 1-4 of the E.O. 13526 (Figure 6-3). The reason line could also read, "Reason: Military plans, weapon systems or operations". The "Declassify on:" line could carry a date as indicated in the above paragraph, or an event such as "Declassify on: When the Ambassador Smith returns from her posting."

The top right page of Figure 6-2 is an example of the title page also with the "SECRET" markings on the top and bottom of the page. The page classification level is indicated by the "(U)" for UNCLASSIFIED as shown in the title. However, this is one of the mandatory four pages reserved for the markings of the highest level of classification, therefore the overall classification marking is SECRET.

The page on the bottom left is also to be marked with the overall classification even though the OCA has indicated that the highest level of the page is a paragraph marked with the "(C)" for CONFIDENTIAL.

The back cover is the final page requiring overall markings. This page will also indicate the highest level even if the highest level markings are the only classification markings on the page.

Sec. 1.4. Classification Categories

Information shall not be considered for classification unless it concerns:

(a) military plans, weapons systems, or operations;

(b) foreign government information;

(c) intelligence activities (including special activities), intelligence sources or methods, or cryptology;

(d) foreign relations or foreign activities of the United States, including confidential sources;

(e) scientific, technological, or economic matters relating to the national security, which includes defense against transnational terrorism;

(f) United States Government programs for safeguarding nuclear materials or facilities;

(g) vulnerabilities or capabilities of systems, installations, infrastructures, projects, plans, or protection services relating to the national security, which includes defense against transnational terrorism; or

(h) weapons of mass destruction..

Figure 6-3 Reasons for original classification authority to assign a classification.

SPECIAL HANDLING

Special access, control, dissemination or safeguarding requirements and warnings are also identified in the classification markings. These alert the holder of special handling instructions in addition to protection provided by the classification level. These handling instructions are more precisely "need to know" oriented. Some other warnings may require additional briefings beyond the induction required for standard TOP SECRET, SECRET and CONFIDENTIAL clearances.

MARKING CLASSIFIED INFORMATION

Cleared contractors are not OCAs and do not perform original classification tasks. However, they may perform derivative classification based on contractual requirements found in the DD Form 254. The cleared employees perform derivative classification where they apply appropriate markings to items generated, reproduced or compiled. Failure to apply timely markings could lead to inadvertent security violations such as forgetting to lock classified items in a GSA approved container, vault or other approved storage; improper processing to include mailing or delivering in an unauthorized manner and unauthorized disclosure to those without clearance and need to know. The lack of proper notification could lead to compromise, suspected compromise, loss and theft of classified material.

Classification markings are required on all classified material regardless of the type of information or media [5]. Documents such as reports, books, white papers and notebooks are physically easier to apply classification marking to. But because of the multiple pages and portions, they may require a greater volume of markings. Objects such as computers, machinery, weapons and other large end items require fewer markings, usually on the top and bottom of each side. Computer software and media such as floppy discs, flash drives and CDs require small labels. Smaller items are very difficult to apply classification markings and exceptions exist. However, every effort should be made to ensure that classification level is clearly identified. DCSA can assist and advise in the proper procedures for non conventional marking issues.

Caution

Working on classified projects may seem intimidating at first. Overtime, the work may quickly become routine and perhaps mundane. The cleared employee can quickly go from being impressed with their responsibilities and alert in their actions to having a more relaxed attitude as they become accustomed to the work. Soon the classified items and the markings can become invisible and ineffective. Many modern examples of security violations include cleared employees leaving classified information unattended at their desks, lunch rooms and other areas. Such actions have led to possible compromise as security containers have even been left open and unattended or accidentally removed from a cleared facility with contents still inside.

REMINDERS

Markings should not be the "stand alone" security measure. FSOs might be tempted to add additional markings to already cluttered media hoping to prevent a user lapse in judgment. Once again the effectiveness begins to wear off and man hours are wasted on efforts that may not increase awareness. To counter the effects, the holder of the classified material must remain vigilant and aware of their surroundings and situation at all times. This is a proactive posture and requires a bit of imagination. Such security is accomplished with solid training and reminders of responsibilities while possessing it.

Simple Solutions

Simple acts such as maintaining a clean desk policy has helped reduce security violations. In this situation, an employee removes everything from the tops of their working surfaces or desks except for the classified material. That simple practice could make a busy employee more aware that any articles on the desk requires extra diligence and must never be left unattended. When no longer needed, classified information should be locked up in a security container or closed area. If a desk is empty, the cleared employee can also assume that there are no classified items out. This discipline creates an environment that reduces the chances of the employee leaving a classified item vulnerable to compromise if they forget to secure it prior to taking a break or leaving for the day. Also useful is the posting of a desk tent and door hanger with an important reminder that classified items are left out. As the employee leaves their work area, they will encounter the warnings on their desk or door handle.

Types of Classification Markings

Classification markings are broken down into categories to assist with proper protection and control. These categories of markings help reduce the risk of security violations, loss, compromise or suspected compromise. The categories are as follows:

- Identification Marking
- Overall Marking
- Page Marking
- Component Marking
- Portion Marking
- Subject and Title Marking
- Derivative Marking

Identification Marking

Identification markings provide the contact information of those responsible for preparation of the classified material and the date of classification. This is usually completed by the original classification authority (OCA) or the person assigning derivative classification markings.

Overall Marking

Overall markings display the highest level of classification contained in the document. The overall markings are conspicuously placed to allow for easy identification and protection of the highest level. Classification markings should be more prominent than any other letters, characters or otherwise stand out for easy identification. Markings can be applied with a stamp, hand written, branded, printed on labels or any other method of permanently identifying the classification level.

The overall classification is placed on the top and bottom of the outside front cover, the title page, first page and the outside back cover (Figure 6-2). The overall classification provides the highest level contained in the document. For example, if a document contains CONFIDENTIAL, SECRET and TOP SECRET information, the overall classification of the document is marked TOP SECRET, the highest level. Computers, discs, drives and other objects, are also marked on the top, bottom, front and back. If this is not possible, markings should be placed in such a manner that there no doubt of the classification level.

Page Marking

Page markings are for classified documents with single and multiple pages such as books, notebooks or other multi-page manuals. Except for those pages reserved for overall markings, the remaining document's pages are marked on the top and bottom with the highest classification level contained on that particular page. For example, if a page in the TOP SECRET document contains only CONFIDENTIAL information, the page will be marked "CONFIDENTIAL". If the page contains SECRET and CONFIDENTIAL information, then the page marking will be "SECRET" even though the overall document classification will be TOP SECRET (Figure 6-4) [6]. However, this is offered as a choice and not a hard set rule. Some organizations mark all pages at the highest level of the document.

Component Marking

Component markings refer to documents with stand alone sections such as annexes, appendixes or other components. These could be parts of plans, programs or projects with attachments. In the case of a major section containing UNCLASSIFIED material, only the top and bottom of the first page should be marked "UNCLASSIFIED". A statement is included with wording such as "All portions of this component (identify the component as an appendix, section, letter, annex, etc.) are UNCLASSIFIED [6].

Portion Marking

Subject and title markings should be unclassified. When the unclassified title or subject is marked in a classified document the

CONFIDENTIAL

For training purposes only

(U) Pages are marked top and bottom according to the highest classification on the page. Mark with material that will stand out from the rest of the document.

(C) The marking on the top and bottom of the interior page reflects the level of the paragraph or portion with the highest classification.

CONFIDENTIAL

For training purposes only

Figure 6-4a Portion Markings

UNCLASSIFIED

(U) Even though the overall classification may be SECRET, this page is marked UNCLASSIFIED.

(U) Each portion is UNCLASSIFIED, therefore the entire page will be marked as such.

UNCLASSIFIED

Figure 6-4b Overall Markings

SECRET

For training purposes only

(U) Portion markings reflect the classification of each part, paragraph or portion of an item.

(C) Depending on agency, portion markings can be put to the front or behind the actual portion.

(S) Abbreviate (TS) for TOP SECRET, (S) for SECRET and (C) for CONFIDENTIAL when marking portions.

SECRET

For training purposes only

Figure 6-4c Portion Markings

SECRET

For training purposes only

(U) The term "portion" also includes charts, graphs, pictures, etc. The following table has a full portion marking inside the table and an abbreviated marking in the caption.

Vehicle	Speed	Ceiling
Helicopter	100 KPH	12,000 Ft
Airplane	150 KPH	15,000 Ft
Jet	450 KPH	30,000 Ft
Rocket	17,000 KPH	22 Mi
SECRET		

SECRET

For training purposes only

Figure 6-4a Graphics

(U) will be inserted at the beginning or end depending on the OCA's requirements. This unclassified title allows for documenting, filing and adding to other unclassified databases. If a classified title is used, the database or files would have to be protected as classified.

Figure 6-4a demonstrates how page and portion markings should be applied. The markings on the page on the upper left corner carry the highest classification of the material found in the paragraphs and portions. Here, the second paragraph is classified at the CONFIDENTIAL level, marked with a (C) [7], and the classification is transferred to the top and bottom as the overall page marking. Primarily, pages are marked at the highest level of classification found on that page.

Figure 6-4b provides an example of a page within a classified document containing unclassified information. All portion markings are marked with "(U)" indicating that the highest level of classification on the page is indeed UNCLASSIFIED. The overall marking of the page is therefore UNCLASSIFIED.

Figure 6-4c is classified at the SECRET level and marked as such on top and bottom. This marking is directly linked to the portion marked with "(S)". Portion markings containing text use abbreviations of the classification and are placed either before or after the portion depending on agency requirements. TOP SECRET is abbreviated with "(TS)", SECRET is abbreviated with "(S)" and CONFIDENTIAL with "(C)" [7].

Finally, Figure 6-4d is classified SECRET because of the table's classification. Portion markings on tables, charts, figures, diagrams, illustrations, etc, should not be abbreviated but spelled out and placed conspicuously as to indicate the classification level [7]. The text identifying the feature uses abbreviations as seen in "(U) Aircraft capabilities".

Though these examples have demonstrated overall markings on certain required pages and page markings throughout the document, some GCAs may require that all pages are marked with the overall classification regardless of the highest classification on that page. For example, if the overall classification of a document is Secret, then the each page will be marked SECRET even when the highest level of classified information on the page is CONFIDENTIAL.

SECRET

For training purposes only

The Testing Agency

Washington, DC

June 21, 2011

MEMORANDUM FOR CHIEF

From: Deputy of Development

Subject: Test Results

(U) This is the original classified document. If a cleared employee conducts research based on this and/or other documents, then they will transfer the classified information.

(S) The classification level of the information used will determine the classification level of the new document

Classified by: Jon Dow RBP/1022 DDMA

Reason: 1.4(e)

Declassify on: 31 July 2021

SECRET

For training purposes only

Figure 6-5a Page markings on original document

Derivative Marking

According to the NISPOM, "Contractor personnel make derivative classification decisions when they incorporate, paraphrase, restate, or generate in new form, information that is already classified".

Original classification occurs when information meets classification criteria as described in Executive Order 13526, *Classified National Security Information*. Classification determination is usually considered as events, programs or missions develop.

Remember, the product of original classification is a security classification guide, classification markings and the DD Form 254.

SECRET

For training purposes only

Local Research Park

Decatur, IL

October 2, 2011

MEMORANDUM FOR DIVISION

From: Jon Smith, Senior Engineer

Subject: Fireworks

(U) This paragraph contains original information from independent research. The information is unclassified.

(S) The classification level of the information used will determine the classification level of the new document. This information was extracted from the document Subject: Test Results.

Classified By: John Jones, Engineer

Derived From: Memorandum dated June 21 2009

Subj: Test Results

The Testing Agency

Declassify on: 31 July 2021

SECRET

For training purposes only

Figure 6-5b Page markings on derivative document

Derivative classification occurs when information is used that has already been determined to be classified and is provided in a new product such as report, item, or event. Information is already known to be classified. In this case a security classification guide or previously classified information is used to identify the existing classification level. The product of derivative classification is labeled based on guidance in the DD Form 254, Security Classification Guide and/or previously marked source documents.

Where the OCA makes classification determinations, contractors carry over classification markings on existing material. Copying or duplicating is not considered derivative classification; it's just copying. A new product or application using existing classification better fits the derivative classification description.

The following is an example of derivative classification. While writing a report to enhance the "Zenith System", XYZ Contractor engineers pull three classified documents from the classified holding area. They conduct background research based on the documents and begin to understand not only how the system works, but how they can improve the system to work better in rain storms. The engineers are working with a document classified SECRET and two documents classified at the CONFIDENTIAL level. By the time they completed the report, they had used portions of all three documents thus the finished product is classified SECRET.

Derivative classification products are marked the same as any other classified product. The top, bottom, front and back of objects and the front and back covers, title and first pages of documents are marked with the highest overall level. The difference between original documents and derived documents exists in the area reserved for information about the classification. Derived documents also have a "Classified by:" line and a "Derived from:" line (Figure 6-5b). The "Derived from:" line provides a connection between the original source document or security classification guide and the new document. In some cases there are multiple security classification guides or source documents, thus the contractor should simply state "multiple sources". When using the "multiple sources" designation, the derivative classifier documents the sources to preserve a continuous record of the derived document and the basis for classifying the product.

Since the definition of derivative classification covers all production, assembly, paraphrasing, word for word transition, and many other tasks, this training is significant; no training, no work performance. Employees performing derivative classification must also be cleared at the appropriate level, have need to know and have access to classification guides or other references to provide sources of markings.

The CDC should provide derivative classifiers with training every two years[1] and derivative classifier training is available through:

http://www.dcsa.mil
https://www.bennettinstittue.com
https://www.redbikepublishing.com

Previous Classification Guidance

There are still many documents, machines, objects, computers and other products that have been classified by an OCA using previous Presidential Executive Orders. The markings on such classified material are sufficient if they are legible and provide safeguarding and identification notification. There is no guidance to re-mark such material and the task may prove to be a tremendous burden on contractor and government personnel [8]. In such cases where this classified information is still available, it can be stored and worked with no changes. If there is a need to re-mark the documents the responsibility falls on the OCA. These previously classified documents can be used as source documents.

Where the documents have no portion markings or page markings, the derived document will carry over the markings of the overall source document classification. If classification guidance or markings need clarification, the holder should inquire with the Agency responsible for the original classification [9]. Every effort should be made to clarify any confusion to prevent unauthorized disclosure or compromise. The "Declassify on:" line uses dates and other information contained in the DD Form 254 and the SCG or from the original source documents [10].

When to apply classification markings

Part of good IMS is a formal request process for copying, creating, transmitting and destroying classified material. The NISPOM requires hand receipt action for the transfer of material classified at SECRET or above and also require accountability measures for items classified at the TOP SECRET level [11].

An FSO can control use applying many techniques. One way is to create and implement forms for each classified transaction executed by the cleared employees. For example, when cleared employees compile classified research projects into a new document they can submit a request to the classified document custodians for those originating classified documents. On the request they would specify the name of the new document, the sources of compilation by in-house document number, type of media the document will be create on (disk, CD, data stick, book, etc). The FSO can then prepare the derived classified document as they assign a new document number and either add the required classification markings to the new media, or review the new document to ensure correct markings have been applied. The FSO can also create a process and implement request forms for destruction, transmission, duplication and other transactions.

Alternative Marking Methods

There are exceptions to marking guidance as not every product follows a typical form or structure. Items can be too small, large, odd shaped or bulky, thus preventing the application of classified markings in the directed method. In all cases, the NISPOM requires a clear identification of the protection level regardless of the shape or form.

The NISPOM does provide information on how to mark various forms of classified material. Classified files, folders, envelopes, binders, and etc are to be marked in an obvious method with the classification. Markings must be placed directly on the object and a cover sheet should be provided when removed from a closed area or security container [11]. Classified e-mail should also be properly marked within the message. The first words on the first line should contain the classification level. Also included in the e-mail should be the "Derived from" line. Certain agencies may also require a "classified by:"and "Reason for classification:" lines. More contract specific classification information is available in the program SCG. If the e-mail is printed, then the classification marking should stand out above the other print in the document [12].

Objects that are too small to be read with the human eye should be marked such that the markings can be seen when read with magnification equipment. For example, microfiche items should be marked in such a way to be immediately recognized, and the storage container should be marked to protect it from unauthorized disclosure. Since the print is small on the original document, other markings large enough to be read with the unaided eye should be placed on the container. The original classified document should be marked in such a way as to be recognized when magnified.

Transmittal Papers

Transmittal papers accompany a document while it is transferred from one location to the other. It provides administrative data about the classified product being transmitted. The transmittal document should be marked at the highest classification level of the information in the entire document packet. A statement of the classification level when classified attachments are removed from the compiled document should be included. For example, if there are unclassified attachments included with the classified document, the statement would read: "Unclassified when separated from classified enclosures." In another example, attachments could include those classified with higher classification documents included. This would include the statement, "CONFIDENTIAL or SECRET when separated from enclosures." (Figure 6-6) [13].

Compilation

In the event unclassified items are grouped with other unclassified items, the SCG may identify the compilation to be classified. When events warrant such classification, the compilation will carry markings of the highest level and a statement of the reason for classification will be affixed to the item in a visible location. Unlike other documents, portion markings on compiled information are not necessary [14].

Unclassified information can be developed while performing on classified contracts. In this case, the material should be protected at the overall classification level. For example, suppose a company is making a classified item. Some of the by-products, or rejected products may not be usable and will be destroyed. Until then, they should be treated as classified material [15].

CONFIDENTIAL

For training purposes

(U) Understanding Marking Requirements-Unclassified Transmittal Documents

When an unclassified transmittal document is attached to a classified document, mark the

transmittal document with the highest classification level transmitted to include all attachments.

Some agencies do not require portion markings on the unclassified transmittal document.

(U) Include the statement: "This document is UNCLASSIFIED when removed from the package."

Enclosures

This document is UNCLASSIFIED when removed from the package

CONFIDENTIAL

For training purpose

Figure 6-6 Transmittal Documents

Training Aids

Training is vital to an organization's improvement. They are great resources as students are able to observe and participate in exercises to help improve their skills and performance on the job. Where employees practice protecting classified material they may need to use training aids labeled with classified markings. Unclassified training material is marked to indicate that it is UNCLASSIFIED but is assigned a classification for training purposes only. For example, an unclassified document is marked to portray a secret memorandum. Here, the preparer or trainer may mark the document to indicate it is unclassified, but deemed classified for training purposes with the following or similar markings: "UNCLASSIFIED SAMPLE", "SECRET FOR TRAINING OTHERWISE UNCLASSIFIED", "CONFIDENTIAL for exercise only", etc [16].

~~SECRET~~

UNCLASSIFIED

For training purposes

(U) Classified Material Marking Guide

Classified by: Jon Dow

RBP/1022DDMA

Reason: 1.4(e)

Declassify on: 31 July 2008

~~SECRET~~

UNCLASSIFIED

For training purposes

Figure 6-7 Example of a document that has been marked as UNCLASSIFIED after the "Declassify on:" date has passed. Original classification has been crossed out and the new UNCLASSIFIED marking has been added.

DECLASSIFYING INFORMATION

When the classification duration has expired according to the markings on the classified material, the holder of the information should begin the process of declassifying. Contractors should coordinate with the GCA before beginning the declassification or downgrading process [17]. Regardless of the approval method, when the holder of the classified material is authorized to begin declassifying or downgrading, they should re-mark appropriate areas. For documents, the holder cancels the old classification markings and re-applies the new downgraded markings (Figures 6-7 and 6-8). This action also depends on how the involvement impacts operation. If the impact is too great, the GCA's can provide guidance for alternative markings or notices. A classified document with multiple pages may look as depicted in Figure 6-9.

~~SECRET~~

CONFIDENTIAL

For training purposes

(U) Classified Material Marking Guide

Classified by: Jon Dow

RBP/1022DDMA

Reason: 1.4(e)

Downgrade to Confidential on: 31 July 2008

Declassify on: 31 December 2020

~~SECRET~~

CONFIDENTIAL

For training purposes

Figure 6-8 Example of a document that has been marked as CONFIDENTIAL after the "Downgrade to:" date has passed. Original classification has been crossed out and the new CONFIDENTIAL marking has been added.

UPGRADING INFORMATION

Some activity, discovery or action could indicate that the classification assigned does not offer the correct level of protection necessary for safeguarding the classified material. In these cases the GCA may require that the document be upgraded and re-marked from CONFIDENTIAL to SECRET or TOP SECRET or from SECRET to TOP SECRET [18]. The person responsible for the re-marking should cross out the old classification and re-mark with the upgraded classification in all the appropriate locations. They then enter the information of the authority responsible for the upgrade and the reason for the upgrade and notify all users of the information.

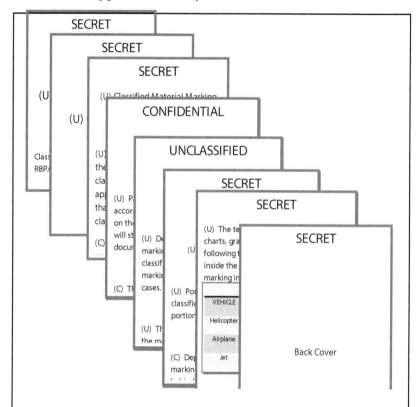

Figure 6-9 Putting it all together. This is an example of a multiple page document (composed of figures from this chapter). The front, back, title and first pages are marked with the overall classification. The internal pages are marked with the highest level on each page. (Each page is classified for training purposes).

CHALLENGING CLASSIFICATION

Users of classified information have an obligation to report any confusing classifications or wrongly marked classified material [19]. This is challenging the classification. Measures are in place to prevent employees from suffering any form of punishment or retribution for raising the issues. This reporting assists with proper markings, preventing over classification and ensuring that classification is based on legitimate reasons.

Those who discover classification discrepancies should challenge the classification. The SCG provides information on challenging classification with the GCA.

Summary

Cleared employees who perform on classified contracts should be able to recognize what is classified and know how to protect the classified material based on the markings provided. Classified objects and products are marked on the top, bottom, sides, front and back. If the item is bulky, odd shaped or otherwise a size and configuration that makes mandatory marking difficult, the markings should be placed as clearly as possible to convey the proper classification level. Multiple page classified documents have many places reserved for classification markings.

Additionally, the source of classification, reason for classification, and duration are applied to classified items. Derived classifications will have a statement indicating the source. While working with classified items, cleared employees are responsible for challenging any classified information that has been incorrectly or unnecessarily classified, should be downgraded or upgraded to another classification level or that security classification guidance is incorrect or not sufficient.

Problems

1. As a document custodian, your responsibilities involve receiving and inspecting documents for proper classification markings. You receive a properly wrapped classified document from a Government agency with the following characteristics:
    - Contains UNCLASSIFIED, CONFIDENTIAL and SECRET information
    - Created on June 21, 2017

- Reason for Classification is 1.4 (a)
- Contains 400 pages
- Classified by: Jon Wain, RBP, 1022 DDMA
- Classification guidance is found in the Zenith Security Classification Guide

1a. Based on the above description, what are the major areas you would expect to see classification markings?

1b. Write out the "By:" line describing who classified the material, reason for classification and the declassify on date.

1c. Which classification marking would you expect to find on the overall marking?

2. Your security team is conducting an annual inventory of your company's classified holdings. In the course of the inventory, they come across a 30 page document entitled *Weather Capabilities (U)*. The document is slightly worn but otherwise in good condition. Your team notifies you that a page is loose and that the document needs to be repaired. They also ask your opinion on some findings concerning internal illustrations; none of the graphs, pictures or containers contains classification markings. Additional information for the document follows:

- Created in 1986
- Contains the following marking on the first page:
- Classified by: RBP, 1022 DMDA
- Reason for classification: Military capabilities
- Declassify on: OADR
- Contains overall classification of CONFIDENTIAL.

2a. What would you direct your team to do concerning the portion markings?

3. An engineer is about to print a report based on classified information. This report is a summary of information found in two different documents. As you prepare to help her correctly mark the derivative document you take into consideration the two source documents that she has provided. The source documents are the same as example questions 1 and 2.

3a. The derived document contains information classified

SECRET, how would the "Classified by:" line be filled out?

   3b. What should be put on the "Reason for classification:" line?

   3c. What would be the duration of classification?

4.   You are making the rounds of your security team's area and overhear a heated discussion between your team members and a technical writer. In order to diffuse the situation, you politely interrupt the conversation and ask the technical writer if you can be of any help. He informs you that "your" security specialist has rejected acceptance of the document based on classification marking errors. He states that it is a good product and no one would notice the mistake anyway. What would you say to him?

5.   A program manager knocks on your door and asks if you have a moment for something important. He asks you to take a walk with him to a secure area where he shows you a piece of hardware. The object is small enough to fit in your hand. You notice a commercial CONFIDENTIAL label; the kind that a manufacturer might install at the factory. The manager lets you know that he has been informed that the object is not classified at all, but that the manufacturer installed the labels as classified material would be added at a later date. The program manager would like to bring the item to an unclassified meeting seeing that "it's not classified anyway." You notice that the object is well worn and does not look new at all.

   5a. Where can you go to discover whether or not the item is classified?

   5b. Are there any other sources?

   5c. After speaking with the right people and consulting the authoritative documents, you are now more confused than ever. You decide to challenge the classification to seek the clarification you need to properly protect the item. Describe the process you would employ.

REFERENCES

1. Department of Defense, DoD 5220.22-M, National Industrial Security Operating Manual, section 4-200, February 2016

2. Department of Defense, DoD 5220.22-M, National Industrial Security Operating Manual, section 4-107, February 2016

3. The President, Executive Order 13526, Classified National Security Information—National Industrial Security Program, section 1.5, (Federal Register, Dec 2009)

4. The President, Executive Order 13526, Classified National Security Information—National Industrial Security Program, section 1.4e, (Federal Register, Dec 2009)

5. Department of Defense, DoD 5220.22-M, National Industrial Security Operating Manual, section 4-201, February 2016

6. Department of Defense, DoD 5220.22-M, National Industrial Security Operating Manual, section 4-204, February 2016

7. Department of Defense, DoD 5220.22-M, National Industrial Security Operating Manual, section 4-206 February 2016

8. Department of Defense, DoD 5220.22-M, National Industrial Security Operating Manual, section 4-209, February 2016

9. The President, Executive Order 13526, Classified National Security Information—National Industrial Security Program, section 1.8, (Federal Register, Dec 2009)

10. Department of Defense, DoD 5220.22-M, National Industrial Security Operating Manual, section 4-208, February 2016

11. Department of Defense, DoD 5220.22-M, National Industrial Security Operating Manual, section 5-202, February 2016

12. Department of Defense, DoD 5220.22-M, National Industrial Security Operating Manual, section 4-210, February 2016

13. Department of Defense, DoD 5220.22-M, National Industrial Security Operating Manual, section 4-211, February 2016

14. Department of Defense, DoD 5220.22-M, National Industrial Security Operating Manual, section 4-213, February 2016

15. Department of Defense, DoD 5220.22-M, National Industrial Security Operating Manual, section 4-215, February 2016

16. Department of Defense, DoD 5220.22-M, National Industrial Security Operating Manual, section 4-216, February 2016

17. Department of Defense, DoD 5220.22-M, National Industrial Security Operating Manual, section 4-217, February 2016
18. Department of Defense, DoD 5220.22-M, National Industrial Security Operating Manual, section 4-218, February 2016
19. Department of Defense, DoD 5220.22-M, National Industrial Security Operating Manual, section 4-104, February 2016

CHAPTER 7 PERFORMING ON CLASSIFIED CONTRACTS

INTRODUCTION

Performing on classified contracts should incorporate excellent products and services and the provision of sound security practices. A good security program protects classified information from unauthorized disclosure. Otherwise national security could face varying degrees of damage depending on what information is disclosed and how it was used. We have seen how classified information is identified with markings so that the user will understand the classification level and how it should be protected from unauthorized disclosure. An Information Management System (IMS) is a good tool the FSO can use to record the disposition of classified information while security containers and closed areas protect classified information when not in use.

PROTECT ORAL TRANSMISSION

CDCS should protect classified information as communicated verbally in conversation, meetings or presentations. This applies to both possessing and non-possessing cleared facilities. A classified conversation may occur during a visit or meeting and should be conducted only as necessary and in controlled environments. For example, classified conversations are authorized in areas where access and need to know have been verified. These classified communications should never take place in hallways, around the water cooler, in public places or car pools. Just as the holder of classified documents verifies a receiver's need to know and security clearance before transferring it, the same is true for releasing classified information verbally.

MEETINGS AND VISITS

As an example, suppose a GCA desires to sponsor a classified meeting at XYZ Contractor as part of contractual requirements. The government holds and controls the release of classified information while XYZ Contractor provides the facilities and controls the access. The government organizes the meeting and provides the need to know. They also verify that access controls are in place. Their responsibilities include setting up the meeting and authorizing the release of classified information. The attendees then use the approved method of filing a visit authorization through government's data base.

On the day of the meeting, an XYZ Contractor cleared employee verifies the identification and clearance levels of all authorized attendees based on the information provided by the points of contact. Once verified, the visitor is given a pass and escorted to the conference room which has been previously approved for conducting classified discussions.

Prior to the start of the meeting the FSO ensures that someone provides a security briefing notifying attendees of the classification level of information to be discussed, whether or not taking notes is permitted and if so, how classified notes will be controlled. When classified notes are permitted, they will have to be properly marked and prepared for dissemination (hand carry with the attendee, faxed or mailed at a later date).

In situations where classified conversations are required over telephone, radio, or other means, each party must be in a location authorized for classified conversation. Additionally, the discourse must occur while using devices authorized for classified discussions such as the National Security Agency (NSA) approved Secure Telephone Unit (STU) or Secure Telephone Equipment (STE).

END OF DAY SECURITY CHECKS

Non-possessing Facilities

End of day checks apply to facilities where classified work is conducted and or classified meetings have taken place. The primary purpose is to protect classified information by double checking that it has been returned to classified storage. Non-possessing facilities should implement this practice in situations where classified conversations and note taking have occurred or any instance where classified information has been carried into the facility. It is also a good idea to implement such checks to protect other sensitive or critical information or for life safety issues.

Possessing Facilities

The following is an example of a typical workday involving classified documents signed out from the company's central classified document repository. At the end of the day, the FSO reviews an IMS database to identify any classified material not returned. Satisfied of the accountability, she closed her safe and left for the evening. A few hours later, the contracted guard service informs the on call security specialist of a possible security violation. The FSO has left a classified document unattended on top of a security container.

To prevent the above violation, end of day checks serve as a precaution against leaving classified material unattended. The designated responsible employee should complete a check list prior to leaving an area where classified material is used, stored, transmitted or is otherwise accessed. The checklist should address secure containers, tabletops, walking surfaces, printers, copiers, and computers to ensure that no residual classified material is left unattended. The end of day checks are not required when an area is manned 24 hours per day, seven days per week [1].

Though not required by NISPOM, government forms are available as methods of strengthening of security programs. Companies are free to use these forms or create their own. One such form available is the Activity Security Check List, Standard Form 701. The FSO can adapt it by removing inapplicable information or even adding to the checklist. For example, the government form includes a block for checking whether or not coffee pots are turned off. This may or may not be important to the FSO. Regardless of the system used, the security checks are effective measures and have proven successful. Unsecured classified information would have otherwise been susceptible to compromise.

Magnets and Reminders

When conducting end of day checks, the designated, last to leave or other responsible person determines whether or not the security containers are locked. This involves spinning the dial and attempting to open the security container. They should inspect the security container check sheet, Standard Form 702 to ensure it has been properly annotated with initials, date and time of persons locking the container and sign the SF 702 as the checker.

The inspection continues with searching tables, desks, printers, trash cans and other areas where classified material may be left unattended. Removable hard drives, classified papers left in printers and copiers, and other classified material should be properly stored before departing. Then they should check doors and windows to ensure they will lock properly. Finally, they should set locks and alarms, ensure magnets display the CLOSED side, and annotate the end of day check sheet. These SF Forms 702 are not required, but do have useful fields for annotating the date and time opened, initials for person opening the lock, date and time closed with initials of person securing the lock and the date and time verified that the lock is indeed closed with the verifier's initials. The final fields are for guards to annotate their checks if necessary.

Other Inspection

The following does not pertain to non-possessing facilities. Perimeter controls are required for certain areas containing classified information in possessing facilities. Such controls set the tone for the successful security program. Perimeter controls provide an additional physical security layer between unauthorized persons and classified material. Controls begin with an assessment of the risk facing the classified information in the holder's possession. Depending on the assessment results and contractual or NISPOM guidance, controls may manifest in the installation of cameras, alarms, reaction force and physical reinforcements to deter and detect forced entry.

The NISPOM requires physically inspecting employees in possessing facilities [2]. Inspections enhance classified document accountability and the myriad compromise opportunities while working with classified information. Establishing a system to deter, detect and deny the unauthorized introduction or removal of classified material is critical. Such a system notifies employees, visitors, contractors and vendors entering and exiting a cleared facility that they are subject to inspection. Posting signs and performing random inspection gives the organization an active measure to set the stage for compliance. Laptops, electronic items and other materials where classified information is stored should be searched. Searching electronic data such as laptops, disks, or other storage devices with a keyword list can also help detect and prevent the unauthorized removal of classified information. Sample keywords might include "secret, program, proprietary, export," or other words that could tip off security that unauthorized information resides in the information system or storage device.

Such measures encourage and remind others not to remove or introduce classified material without going through proper channels. These measures make economic and intelligence espionage more difficult. However, FSOs consult with legal council before conducting inspections of persons or their belongings.

DEVELOP EMERGENCY PROCEDURES TO PROTECT CLASSIFIED INFORMATION

During 9/11, a jet slammed into the Pentagon. Fuel, fire and concussion waves smashed into the most secured of areas. Sensitive and classified military information and material, communications equipment and secure containers became vulnerable to loss or compromise. In 2005, Hurricane Katrina flooded much of the Alabama, Mississippi and Louisiana low areas. Residents and businesses evacuated the area leaving classified information locked in security containers. Flood waters caused tremendous damages that could have left unprepared businesses with unsecured classified material.

Regardless of the type of disaster, man-made or natural, those in possession of classified material should have a procedure for protecting it based on the risk analysis. Life safety is the top priority. However, when possible, classified information must be protected. Creating emergency procedures and rehearsing them regularly can save lives and protect classified information. Such procedures should support the overall security program and be in harmony with the risk assessment and practical enough to execute. The contingency plan includes written policy and rehearsals to ensure everyone understands their role in protecting classified material.

For example, an FSO may use the risk analysis to discover that fire and severe weather are the biggest and most disastrous of threats. Any emergency causing the evacuation of the facilities makes classified information vulnerable. Risk analysis helps the FSO develop a plan to account for any classified material that could be in use and otherwise vulnerable when disaster strikes. Such an effort requires the implementation of a team of all affected business units to map out a written policy and scheduled rehearsals.

What happens when a disaster occurs while classified information is in use and not properly stored in a secure container? The resulting emergency requires that when possible, cleared personnel will evacuate their work areas with classified material. Time permitting, identified cleared employees should lock security containers and grab emergency kit bags (Figure 7-1) and classified document sign out sheets. All employees should report to their designated assembly areas where security representatives relieve them of their classified material and provide adequate protection from unauthorized disclosure.

Emergency Kit Bags

- Marking supplies (Pen, stamp, preprinted labels, etc)
- Opaque bag or wrapping paper
- Opaque security tape
- Cleared personnel roster
- TOP SECRET, SECRET and CONFIDENTIAL cover sheets

Figure 7-1 Suggested contents of emergency kit bags. These bags should be kept up to date and readily available during emergency evacuations.

CLASSIFIED INFORMATION ACCOUNTABILITY PROCESS

The NISPOM requires cleared contractors to maintain access and control of TOP SECRET information. Since the unauthorized disclosure or compromise of TOP SECRET information has the potential to cause exceptionally grave damage to national security, the cleared contractor must designate a Top Secret Control Official (TSCO) [3].

This official maintains records and accountability of TOP SECRET information entering and leaving the facilities. They also conduct an annual inventory and maintain a chain of custody on actions pertaining to the TOP SECRET holdings. Receipts, records and accountability of all items are continuous from reception to destruction. Additionally, destruction and reproduction receipts should be maintained for two years [4].

The TSCO tracks the movement of the TOP SECRET information. They know at all times where an item is stored or located at any given time. Each TOP SECRET item is cataloged and numbered in a series. This includes items photocopied, derived, couriered, electronically, or otherwise properly received. As the item is stored, moved, disseminated and or destroyed, the paper trail and catalog numbers are annotated accordingly. This tracking system allows for constant status surveillance.

TOP SECRET Control Officials are authorized to:
- Receive
- Transmit
- Maintain access and accountability
- Conduct annual inventory

Information Management Systems (IMS)

Though NISPOM directs the duties and appointment of a TSCO, it is a good practice to control all classified information. Receipting actions, reproduction, destruction, and other activities concerning classified information should be documented. This can aid in the control, protection and investigations concerning discovering the disposition of classified information. Also, NISPOM identifies the use of an IMS, but does not provide implementation details [5].

Basically, the IMS should allow for documenting receipting actions, transmission, receptions, storage location and other transitions involving all classified information. IMS can be a spreadsheet for small inventories or for complicated inventories, software is available from vendors and may be worthwhile for contractors with large classified holdings inventory.

Working Papers

The accounting process for TOP SECRET includes any unfinished products such as notes, files and workbooks used for more than 30 days or transmitted outside of a facility. The creator should mark working papers with the date created, the classification level and annotate "Working Papers". These TOP SECRET working papers become finalized after 30 days and a control number and documentation by the TSCO should begin. Working papers at the SECRET and CONFIDENTIAL classification levels are finalized at 180 days and again when sent outside of the facility [6]. The working papers should become a final product at the end of the time period. If not needed they should be destroyed.

Classified information not a finished product? No problem
- *Mark date created*
- *Mark classification level*
- *Annotate "Working Papers"*
- *Working papers are to be marked as finished document when:*
  - *Over 30 days old for TOP SECRET*
  - *Over 180 days for SECRET and CONFIDENTIAL*
  - *Sent outside of facility*

Classified Material Storage

TOP SECRET material is normally required to be stored in a GSA approved security container. If items are too large or bulky, they can be stored in approved vaults or closed areas with supplemental controls. SECRET material can also be stored in the same manner as TOP SECRET except that it can be stored in a security container, but without supplemental controls (Figure 7-2)[7]. Supplemental controls are intrusion detection systems or an approved guard force and are required for SECRET stored in closed areas and all TOP SECRET information. However, NISPOM does not require supplemental controls for SECRET as long as it is in GSA approved containers.

Figure 7-2 Classified information should be stored in GSA approved security container unless open bin storage is approved.

Classified Reproduction

Classified information should only be reproduced in response to a contractual requirement such as in the performance of a deliverable. Reproduction should not be made as a matter of convenience as it puts classified information at unnecessary risk and it requires dedicated resources. The FSO can enforce resource discipline with procedures to ensure classified information is reproduced only as necessary and using only approved equipment. They can also ensure only trained and authorized personnel are able to reproduce classified information. This control should include procedures to govern the use and type of designated reproduction equipment.

Copy machines, scanners and other reproduction equipment should be identified and designated for classified information reproduction. All other enterprise equipment should be off limits to classified reproduction. This can be accomplished through signs identifying authorized equipment as "Approved for Classified Production at the _____ level". Other equipment would be identified as "Not authorized for the reproduction of classified information".

TOP SECRET information is authorized for reproduction to meet contractual requirements such as when directed. Any other use should be approved by the GCA. SECRET and CONFIDENTIAL information should also be reproduced only as part of a subcontract, in furtherance of a contract, or as part of a business proposal or in the preparation of a patent.

The FSO should consider the type of equipment the company purchases, leases or rents. When service contracts expire, repairs are needed, equipment is to be replaced or other transactions replacing or removing the equipment occur, the hard drive or memory should be destroyed or wiped in an approved manner to remove all stored classified information. DCSA can help determine this approved method and guidance is available.

Cleared employees should understand that only trained and authorized persons are authorized to make classified copies. The FSO can make the determination of how many and who to authorize. This can be based on contractual needs, workload or other valid reason.

However, procedures should be established that identify authorized persons and train them how and when to copy classified information and how to protect it. Procedures should include detecting and deterring unauthorized reproduction, documenting, marking, storing and disseminating copies.

In large enterprises the FSO might limit access, creating an environment where classified information is stored in a central area and issued to those who need access by document custodians. On a smaller scale, classified information might be stored in a security container where a few cleared employees possess the combination. Additionally, access can be limited to a designated copier where it controlled and a code is provided before copies can be made. In this situation, the FSO can control who can make copies as well as audit authorized access.

But the real threat may exist when an employee copies classified information in uncontrolled environments. Limiting reproduction to authorized equipment and personnel only protects it as reproduced by honest employees. It does not protect against acts of espionage where employees access classified information and copy it at uncontrolled copiers, load them to unauthorized disks, and fax them using unauthorized machines all in an effort to remove it from the company undetected. This can also be controlled by requiring a login code on reproduction equipment, putting all reproduction equipment in access controlled areas, or controlling all copying functions. However, the ultimate protection resides with controlling who accesses it, when they access it and what they do with it.

Remember, managing a security program takes valuable resources. When copies are made they should be afforded the same protection as the original and may require re-marking, additional storage space or dedication of security focused man hours. Also, FSOs should assign document numbers to track the amount of copies made. For example, if a copy of a document assigned an internal document number 401 is copied, the new number might be 401 copy 1 or 401-01.

Restricted Areas

Restricted areas provide temporary solutions for performing classified work and may apply in both possessing and non-possessing facilities. These are designated areas, but not dedicated areas. In other words, they are temporary and can be created from existing locations. These locations can then be returned to their original function almost immediately. A cleared employee may find it necessary to use a restricted area in the performance of a contract. This may arise from many reasons to include emergencies, because the product or process is large, bulky or of other unique size and such that work cannot be performed in the normal work area. When the need for working in a temporarily classified location arises, the cleared employees and FSO can create and occupy a restricted area.

Restricted areas should be clearly identified and access controlled to prevent unauthorized entry or compromise of classified material [8]. Physical barriers such as walls, doors, or barricades are not necessary, but access control should be present to prevent unauthorized personnel from entering and to keep control of classified material prior to introduction and removal. The restricted area can be as simple as stringing yellow caution tape around an accident site, or as complicated as using a hardened area such as a room or cafeteria. Cleared employees should challenge all who enter and verify clearance and need to know. Since restricted areas are temporary, all classified material should be returned to secure storage when no longer needed.

The creation of temporary restricted areas can solve problems of growing companies. In situations where closed areas are non-existent, work can be performed in a designated restricted area. Additionally, restricted areas can be created in non-possessing companies when the need arises to have a classified meeting or conversation. Restricted areas can be created for the introduction of classified information when needed and returning it to proper storage when no longer required or at some point before the work day ends.

Reminders should be posted in the restricted area to remind cleared employees to control access and to ensure classified material is returned to secure storage. Depending on the company's mission, warning signs could be posted outside of the restricted area to notify employees that only those with the appropriate clearance and need to know will be granted access.

Closed Areas

Closed areas are a more permanent solution for possessing facilities and when classified items are difficult to store in a GSA approved container. When unique sizes and shapes do not fit into conventional GSA container storage capability, the FSO should seek approval from DCSA for open shelf or bin storage.

Closed areas are necessary for storing bulk information. However, TOP SECRET material should be stored in a GSA approved container with supplemental protection such as a guard force and or intrusion detection systems are required for TOP SECRET in all cases [9]. SECRET material also requires supplemental protection in a closed area when not stored in a GSA approved security container. As with restricted areas, closed areas require access control either with an ever present, cleared employee checking a roster or through a supplanting access control system such as biometrics, access card, pin number, and retina scan readers. Supplemental protection is not necessary at the time when the work area is occupied.

Physical security measures employed in a closed area prevents unauthorized access at any time. Reinforced doors, windows and other access points should be installed to prevent anyone from easily breaking in or going around current security precautions. DCSA approves new construction, modifications, and repairs of closed areas. When building closed areas, the FSO should ensure pictures of progress are taken as evidence of compliance with construction requirements.

The construction standards require that all hardware is of heavy-gauge material and the hinges and jams are pinned, brazed or spot welded to prevent removal. Walls, windows, doors and ceilings are made of materials that can detect and resist unauthorized entry. Barriers should be constructed to prevent removal and access to classified material [10].

Closed areas are used to store classified material that won't fit into

a GSA approved container with the following stipulations:
- Access is controlled
- Supplemental protection for SECRET and TOP SECRET
- Qualify structural integrity at required intervals
- CSA approves open shelf/bin storage of SECRET and CONFIDENTIAL
- No open shelf or bin storage of TOP SECRET

Vaults

When constructing vaults, the FSO should also ensure pictures of progress are taken as evidence that the contractor is in compliance with construction requirements. Vaults have additional construction requirements outlined in the NISPOM to offer a protection level necessary for the classified material stored. The doors and frames are GSA approved furnishings.

Openings to the vault are constructed the same as with openings of closed areas and designed to prevent and reveal evidence of tamper. Wire mesh, screens and other efforts installed to provide barriers that prevent people or objects from entering. These barriers must not be easily removed and should detect and prevent forced entry. Pipes and conduits should be installed during construction to maintain better integrity. Construction gaps remaining between the pipes and conduit should be filled with waterproof and tamper resistant caulking or material [11].

Security Containers, Locks and Combinations

The GSA approved security containers provide the appropriate amount of protection as identified on the classification levels. The containers are rated to withstand break-ins and detect attempts of break-ins. Security containers come in many forms and sizes ranging from single drawer to five drawers. Containers can have one locking drawer to secure the entire container or each drawer can have a separate lock.

Security containers are available in many makes and models,

but unauthorized modification can degrade the security level of the container. For example, painting the container to match the office décor or removing the large GSA label will cause the container to lose its certification.

Security containers should be used only for storing classified material. Though not addressed in the NISPOM, alcohol, tobacco, firearms, personal items and valuables should never be kept in a GSA approved security container. Also, the classification level of the contents must never be displayed on the outside of the security container [12]. The tops and the surface of security containers should be free of debris, books, plants and anything else other than the SF 702 and the OPEN/CLOSED or combination reminder magnets. The proper use of classified information and the protection using GSA approved storage containers help to prevent security infractions.

The containers are certified and so must the maintenance and upkeep of the security container. All maintenance should be performed by approved repair persons using approved parts or approved cannibalized parts and approved methods. Repairs are either performed using authorized cleared employees or by escorting authorized technicians [13]. Once the repairs are made, the authorized repair technician issues a certificate of repair and the certificate is kept in local files. Unless the repair person is a cleared employee with a need to know, they should never be allowed to change or set the combination. Combinations are classified at the same level as the contents of the security container. Providing combinations to unauthorized personnel is a security violation.

Key and Combination Control

The number of authorized employees having knowledge of combinations or access to keys should be kept to the minimum necessary. FSOs should maintain a roster of those who have access to the combination and remind those who sign for the combinations to protect the combinations based on the highest classification level of the contents.

The FSO should either perform as or assign someone as a

combination control person to maintain administrative records and combination control to protect classified information [12]. The FSO should also maintain a log of those with knowledge of combinations. A good practice is using the Security Container Information Form, Standard Form 700. The SF 700 can be filled out every time the combination is changed. When used, a copy is stored inside the locking drawer of the security container. The SF 700 tear sheet is stored in a separate security container approved for storage at the same level of the container contents. The SF 700 is a great tool for controlling security container access and keeping records up to date.

When in possession of multiple security containers, vaults and closed areas, FSOs could make a combination access binder. This binder can be used to keep up with who has access to the combinations, serial numbers of the containers and when the locks were last changed. Where facilities have multiple security containers, this binder can serve as a reminder of combinations. Instead of remembering every combination, the list of combinations can be stored in a security container with equal or greater security classification storage capacity.

Combinations are meant to be memorized and not written down or stored in computers, phones or Personal Data Assistant devices. The combination should be protected at that same level of the contents in the security container. For example, if the contents of the security container are CONFIDENTIAL, then so is the combination. To ease with memorization, combinations can be created with six letter words or the first six letters of longer words. Instead of memorizing a long six digit number, they create a word and use a rotary phone image for the corresponding numbers.

Magnetic combinations reminders similar to telephone touch pads are also available. For example, the number 2 corresponds with ABC, three with DEF, etc. When cleared employees have access to multiple safes, word reminders help prevent security violations that occur when cleared employees write the combinations down for personal use. Using combination word clues and providing an administrative security container helps reduce the risk of such violations. You can get these telephone touch pad magnets from internet sites such as:

http://www.redbikepublishing.com/magnet.

According to NISPOM, combinations should be changed upon initial use, change in status of authorized users, compromise or suspected compromise of container or combination, when safe is left open or when required by FSO or DCSA [14].

When a security container is brand new or has been pulled out of service for repair or resale, it should be set to an industry standard combination of 50-25-50. This universal combination allows the resale, reuse or temporary disposition until needed later. Upon initial use and after ensuring the certification of the container, the new owners of the security container should reprogram a new combination. The new combination is issued to authorized personnel and those having knowledge of the previous combination will no longer provide a security vulnerability.

Employees having knowledge of combinations and who can no longer protect the classified material or otherwise no longer have clearances and need to know provide a significant security risk. When an employee having access to a combination has had their clearance revoked or suspended, is transferred away or loses employment or otherwise has a change in status affecting their eligibility to provide the proper security of the classified information, the FSO should change the combination.

Security violations occur when combinations are revealed to unauthorized or non-cleared persons. Combinations spoken out loud, written down, or otherwise broadcast in an unauthorized manner put classified material at risk of compromise. Likewise security containers that no longer work properly or have suffered damage significant enough to affect the required security capability may make compromise a possibility. When the combination or security container has been compromised or is suspected of being compromised, then the combination must be changed and an investigation conducted.

Keyed Locks

The procedures, recommendations and security effectiveness of padlocks and keys are similar to managing and accounting for classified combinations. FSOs using padlocks and keys must maintain a registry of those who have possession of keys and locks. A monthly change of custody key and lock inventory ensures that keys remain on the premises and are stored to offer the correct level of protection [15].

The key and lock roster is the administrative accountability and assignment document. The FSO should ensure that only the amount of cleared personnel necessary is assigned access to keys and locks. Their role is to provide classified storage and accountability of classified material inside the security container. The key and lock custodian keeps account of persons and the specific keys and locks for absolute access control. The register is helpful during inventories, investigations, or when someone loses the assigned locks or keys.

Keys and locks protecting classified information should be inventoried regularly. FSOs should conduct this inventory monthly to ensure keys are secured properly and are where they should be [14]. If any keys are missing or are not stored to offer the proper level of protection, an investigation should be initiated to determine whether or not classified information has been compromised. Keys and locks should also be inventoried when reassigned to new or additional cleared employees.

Keys should remain in the secure facilities. Putting keys on personal key rings or bringing them home is equivalent to writing down a security container combination and keeping it in a wallet or other unauthorized location. Such actions are violations and increase the potential for loss or compromise of classified material. To provide better control the locks are changed or rotated annually and replaced when keys become lost or compromised. Master keys must not be duplicated as key control could be lost and thus degrade security and lead to the possible compromise of classified material.

Control keys and locks to classified containers using the following:
- Appoint a custodian
- Maintain register of lock and keys
- Audit keys and locks monthly

- Inventory keys upon change of custody
- Keep keys on premises
- Protect at the level of contents
- Rotate or change locks annually and replace when keys become lost or compromised
- Keep tight control of inventory and never make master keys

ACCESS TO CLASSIFIED INFORMATION

The possessor of classified information is required to protect it from unauthorized access [15]. According to the NISPOM, the term access is the ability and opportunity to gain knowledge of classified information [16]. This results from a determination that a person is trustworthy as proven in a thorough background investigation. Recall that there are varying degrees of background investigations depending on the level of classification the person is required to access. For example, a person with access to information at the SECRET level has had a NACLC conducted. Once a person is determined to be trustworthy, the clearance will be granted and the individual signs a non disclosure agreement, Standard Form 312.

A successful background check conducted and a clearance granted is just part of the process. A cleared person also has to have need to know. Need to know can be determined by using an access roster, information on the DD Form 254, statement of work, the SCG and other documents listing the classified work requirements. Typically, an FSO will have a way to verify the security clearance. Need to know is trickier, but usually resolved with familiarity of who works on a classified program or verification from another cleared employee.

SUMMARY

The FSO creates a security program and trains the employees on the proper procedures to protect all disciplines of classified work. Whether the work is conducted in a closed area, restricted area, vault, or other location of the facility, care is taken to ensure no unauthorized persons have access to the classified information. All cleared employees are responsible for protecting classified information. Restricted areas are used for temporary work and not authorized for permanent classified information storage. Defense contractors should use closed areas and vaults to work with and store classified information designed as a permanent working solution.

PROBLEMS

1. You are an FSO of a growing defense contractor. One of the executives approaches you about the need for more space to conduct classified work. He is agreeable to implementing your recommendation to use a restricted area and would like you to prepare a security briefing for his team. Prior to your briefing, you conduct the necessary research. Describe the reason for a restricted area and when cleared employees would use a restricted area. Keep in mind access control and storage requirements.

2. You have just sat down to eat lunch and receive a phone call from a cleared employee. She tells you that the security container's drawers are closed, but the dial on the combination lock has not been engaged. She explains further that according to the SF 702, the container had been locked and checked 20 minutes earlier. She is sure that was "about the time everyone left for lunch." What would you direct her to do?

3. Your colleagues leave for the day. On their way out, they inform you that you are the last to leave. The facility is authorized to store classified materials. What will you check for prior to leaving?

4. As part of the building project, you are responsible for providing input into the projected classified contracts and the

required work space and storage requirements. As you put together a presentation, you research the requirements of a much needed closed area. Describe how a closed area should be constructed. Who approves the construction requirements?

REFERENCES

1. Department of Defense, DoD 5220.22-M, National Industrial Security Operating Manual, section 5-102, February 2016
2. Department of Defense, DoD 5220.22-M, National Industrial Security Operating Manual, section 5-103, February 2016
3. Department of Defense, DoD 5220.22-M, National Industrial Security Operating Manual, section 5-201, February 2016
4. Department of Defense, DoD 5220.22-M, National Industrial Security Operating Manual, section 5-603, February 2016
5. Department of Defense, DoD 5220.22-M, National Industrial Security Operating Manual, section 5-200, February 2016
6. Department of Defense, DoD 5220.22-M, National Industrial Security Operating Manual, section 5-203, February 2016
7. Department of Defense, DoD 5220.22-M, National Industrial Security Operating Manual, section 5-303, February 2016
8. Department of Defense, DoD 5220.22-M, National Industrial Security Operating Manual, section 5-305, February 2016
9. Department of Defense, DoD 5220.22-M, National Industrial Security Operating Manual, section 5-306, February 2016
10. Department of Defense, DoD 5220.22-M, National Industrial Security Operating Manual, section 5-801 a-h, February 2016
11. Department of Defense, DoD 5220.22-M, National Industrial Security Operating Manual, section 5-802 a-e, February 2016
12. Department of Defense, DoD 5220.22-M, National Industrial Security Operating Manual, section 5-308, February 2016
13. Department of Defense, DoD 5220.22-M, National Industrial Security Operating Manual, section 5-311, February 2016
14. Department of Defense, DoD 5220.22-M, National Industrial Security Operating Manual, section 5-309, February 2016
15. Executive Order 12968—Access to Classified Information,

section 6.2, Federal Register, August 1995
16. Department of Defense, DoD 5220.22-M, National Industrial Security Operating Manual, Appendix C, February 2016

Helpful Websites:

Access to DCSA Training
https://www.DCSA.mil

Area Studies/World Fact Book
http://www.cia.gov

Federal Bureau of Investigation
http://www.fbi.gov

ITAR
http://www.ddtc.gov

ITAR, NISPOM, and NISPOM Security Books
http://www.redbikepublishing.com

NISPOM Require Training to Download and Present
http://www.redbikepublishing.com
http://www.bennettinstitute.com

Training Pamphlets
http://www.archives.gov/isoo/training/

Travel Advisory and Travel Briefing Information
http://www.state.gov

Various Security Forms
http://www.archives.gov/isoo/security-forms/

CHAPTER 8 CLASSIFIED COMPUTER SECURITY

INTRODUCTION

Since much of the work that Cleared Defense Contractors (CDC) perform is on automated systems, it is important to understand how to protect classified information that resides on information systems (IS). The intent of this chapter is to demonstrate that the protective measures for classified IS are very similar to those that are described in other NISPOM chapters. This is our explanation of how classified information should be protected equally, no matter what form it takes. In other words, SECRET hardware should be afforded the same protective measures as SECRET software.

I write this to demonstrate that a Facility Security Officer (FSO) should not be intimidated by any IS security discussions; they are similar to protective measures employed for all forms of classified information. Some security managers may be intimidated by an IS discussion because of perceived lack of technical experience. Ether they do not work with IS or they if they do, it is in a limited capacity. In these cases, they may turn over the entire process to the Information System Security Manager (ISSM) and remain hands off. However, it does not need to be that drastic. A broad overview of this chapter provides enough information for a non-technical security manager to successfully supervise a security program on IS. The trick is to consider the guidance in NISPOM chapter 8 just like the guidance that is applied in NISPOM Chapter 5. Chapter 8 is not much different if you just think about the classified IS as part of your security program to protect classified information and it may appear less intimidating.

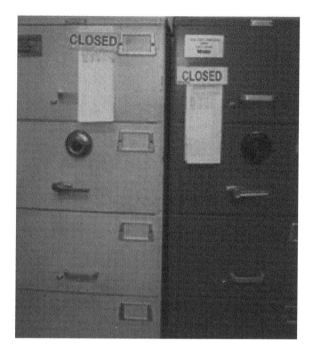

Figure 8-1 Just like other classified information, classified Information Systems and media must be protected in a security container or closed area.

At the end of this chapter, you should have a better grasp of how to employ classified IS protection and measure your program's effectiveness. Additionally, you may be able to use this information to better prepare for security certifications like Industrial Security Professional Certification and Industrial Security Oversight Certification.

INFORMATION SYSTEMS PROTECTIONS

Chapter 8 recommends that a set of controls be implemented to protect classified information residing on IS. As with all other classified information, regardless of format, the government owns the information and the contractor protects it according to NISPOM.

For IS, the contractor requests approval to store and use the classified information on an IS and the government certifies the contractor to do . This is of course an over simplification, but I hope it gives you more confidence in your ability to execute the guidance in a practical and effective way.

Is Oversight

The Cognizant Security Agency (CSA) dictates how all classified information is to be protected in NISPOM Chapter 5 and as discussed earlier in this book. NISPOM Chapter 8 re-purposes the same information and applies it to IS. As usual, the Government Contracting Activity (GCA) has a role because they own the information and then the CDC has a responsibility to protect the classified information and certify that is protected. The CSA provides the guidance and approves the CDC's response through their CSO as well as any other organization who provides the Authorization to Operate.

The assessment authorization defines IS terminology, determines how the contractor is awarded Authorization to Operate, and identifies the government entity to perform audits. This information is grounded on the security controls that determine protective measures to be in place as dictated by the CSA to protect classified information residing on IS.

When CDCs use IS to process classified products and the information systems become part of the security program. Therefore, they fall under the FSO purview. The FSO may appoint an ISSM who may also delegate an Information System Security Officer (ISSO) and together they will implement a protection program that ensures IS are in place and the security controls are in line with the security requirements.

CDCs should determine what the classification level is of the information that will reside on the systems since that IS will then become classified at the level of the information introduced to it. If the facility clearance is only at the SECRET level, the classified information residing on those IS can be no higher than that level. It can support information that is CONFIDENTIAL, but it cannot host TOP SECRET information.

The CDC should also determine any threat to that classified information. Many times, we understand that when information is classified as SECRET, the impact to unauthorized disclosure is potentially serious damage to national security. However, we don't always need to identify the threat; just the impact. Therefore, CDCs will have to do some research to discover what exactly the attack vector is. Is it something through a cyber-attack? Is it through somebody breaking in? Determining the threat within the operational environment is key. Throughout this chapter, we define these controls and we define how to protect this classified information.

COUNTERMEASURES TO BE EMPLOYED BASED ON IMPACT LEVEL

The CSA will determine the guidance for protecting the IS that are at the cleared defense contractor location. The CSA gives the guidance and provides tools and other capabilities for the contractor to use in the conduct of continuous monitoring of IS. This monitoring includes information covered earlier with alarms, guards, tools and capabilities that are on the IS themselves. We can use these to determine how the IS protects and performs such as when unauthorized persons attempt to gain access. Security managers can pull up logs to discover activity on classified IS. For example, the observation of cleared employees conducting suspicious activity on IS.

Why Robust Protection

The classified IS that conduct classified processing are often commercial computers that are available worldwide. The CDCs and government employees procure them from the global supply chain. These IS are produced with the purpose of performance over security. These consumers are likely college students, gamers, and many value the computers for various reasons. The security settings may be set very weakly and performance capabilities strong. This is not a good solution when procured to process sensitive information. At that point the IS requires enhanced security measures to protect classified information and monitor use such as downloading, copying, and transmitting capabilities that occur on that information system.

The Set of Protective Controls

The CDC is responsible for maintaining an IS security program that is consistent with the CSA guidelines. The contractor will then respond to these guidelines and ensure that they are applying them and describe how they are doing so. These guidelines should be ground in a risk-based set of controls that include management, operational and technical controls.

Management controls are broken down into other definable terms as well. Information security risk levels, information system, life cycle and where the IS reside are some of the things that you will need to be familiar with. Therefore, an FSO or ISSM should determine how the IS will be used to process classified information. They will then implement information system user training which will include insider threat training.

The CDC will implement information system policies, procedures and practices that fit best with the CSA guidance. They will have to crosswalk and balance the safeguards with the results of applying the safeguards. It is best to know what the requirements are then build policies around them. This is a mixture of NISPOM compliance and the CDC policies in place. The CDC implements continuous monitoring and describes the process and how the security program will be monitored

The risk to the assets residing on the system should be considered. What classification level are they and what is the threat to these systems? In other words, how are they vulnerable? These are the type of questions the CDC both asks and answers. If the risk is unacceptable, countermeasures or remedial actions should be applied to reduce that risk and those measures should be tested. The desire is to reduce and document the reduction. This documentation will be used later for the Authorization to Operate. The CDC's IS should be able to detect, report, and respond to incidents as well as conduct a self-inspection to make sure all of these measures are in place.

THE SYSTEM SECURITY PLAN (SSP)

The SSP describes how the CDC will protect information that resides on classified IS. The plan describes the assets to be protected, potential risks to exposing the information to unauthorized disclosure, and the plan to mitigate risk in detail. As with most security policies, the plan can refer to existing risk reduction, security, or other applicable documents.

For example, consider the Program Protection Plan (PPP) specific to some weapon systems. Similarly, assets and risks are identified and risk reduction plans described. This PPP also references other programmatic documents such as the security classification guide, the cyber security plan, the physical security plan, etc. Instead of writing additional pages, the PPP makes reference to already existing and accessible documents.

This SSP should be constructed in a similar method. The security manager provides a risk assessment in the document as well as reference programmatic, corporate, and other applicable processes, procedures and practices. The SSP might reference the Authorization to Operate, contingency plans, etc. These can appear as references, appendices or annexes; no need to rewrite.

The SSP should be written in response to CSA guidance. The CSA instructs the CDC to protect the assets at a specific classification level and then conduct a risk assessment. Once the CDC completes the risk assessment, they should address the risk in detail and document the results in the SSP. Then the CDC certifies to the CSA that they have implemented a risk-based plan to reflect these controls.

Information System Security Manager (ISSM)

CDCs that perform classified work on IS may appoint an ISSM to assist with tasks. The option for the CDC is appointing or hiring an employee who understands networks, computing, and implementing the CSA provided guidance. The ISSM will oversee the SSP implementation and evaluate the insider threat. Much of their job will be in consult with the FSO and the Insider Threat Plan Senior Official (ITPSO)

The ITPSO is responsible for recognizing and mitigating the insider threat. A great place for an insider threat to best impact the organization is in networks, computer systems and designing software. IS are extremely vulnerable and the ITPSO, FSO and ISSM can work together to prevent unauthorized access to or unauthorized action on a classified information system. Examples of insider threats to an information system can be found with the cases of Reality Winner, Eric Snowden and Chelsea Manning. Each one of these examples were of cleared users who gained authorized access to acquire and release classified information in an unauthorized manner (to the uncleared general public). For this reason, this ITPSO, FSO and ISSM team is extremely important.

Cleared employees should practice risk mitigation as described in the SSP, regardless of job title. Any cleared employee should be able to report risks to the FSO, ITPSO, or ISSM. Each of these important appointed positions should take issues seriously and use the information appropriately to either report security violations, strengthen the security plan or conduct a new risk assessment. The FSO and ISSM should be focused on the three controls: Management, Operation and Technical.

The ISSM has many tasks including:
- Writing out the IS security plan and describe eloquently to those who need to read this
- Determine where the classified information resides
- Describe how the classified IS performs
- Describe how the classified information residing on the IS is protected.

SELF-INSPECTIONS

The ISSM conducts or oversees the self-inspection and the corrective actions. A good place to start with the self-inspection is the Self-Inspection Handbook for NISP Contractors, available at the

Defense Counterintelligence and Security Agency website:
http://www.dcsa.mil

 A printed version is at:
https:*//www.redbikepublishing.com*

 This handbook covers the entire NISPOM self-inspection topic. The ISSM will be responsible for doing the checks that are listed in there for chapter eight and for the insider threat portion of chapter eight.

 Where the self-inspection identifies vulnerabilities, the FSO and ISSM should address those vulnerabilities and provide corrective actions. The ISSM should understand how to identify significant vulnerabilities in the system, provide mitigations and countermeasures and implement the countermeasures, meeting CSA guidance.

Information System Security Officer

 The ISSM, depending on the scope of work, may appoint or hire in an assistant. The Information System Security Officer (ISSO) assists the ISSM and the ISSM can delegate tasks such as verifying the SSP, the self-inspection task and more.

The Information System User

 The cleared employee system users are those who perform on the contract and do the day-to-day work such as the engineers, software designers, testers, statisticians, etc. They are authorized to enter the workspace and gain access to the systems. They should have a good grasp of the SSP requirements as it is up to them to protect the system and contents of the system.

 Users should not share any of their authentication mechanisms such as what they use for authentication or for gaining access to computers. To gain access to the computer system, the user should enter information describing what they are and who the are. For example, they would verify that they are an authorized person. This can be achieved with a user name and a CSA approved password, a computer access card, a token, etc. No matter how convenient to do so, users should not share that information or let anybody use their account for performing classified work.

Just as classified security container combinations are classified to the level of the information in the container, so is the authentication mechanism at the highest classification level that is accesses. If the information inside the computer is SECRET, then it should be protected at the SECRET level. Users should also understand and acknowledge that their access and interaction is monitored. This should be evident and of no surprise as most activity in and around classified information is monitored. For example, security container access is protected as the removal and introduction of classified information within and out of cleared facilities and classified reproduction is monitored. Additionally, the continuous monitoring program for cleared persons provides another example of insider threat mitigations.

AUTHORIZATION TO OPERATE

The CSA has a role in the CDC's use of classified processing as the CDC requires Authorization to Operate. In this case, the CSA designates an authorizing official and their job is to assess and authorize the CDC's IS. The CDC assures the CSA that the security capabilities are implemented. The ISSM is responsible for writing the CDC's response and demonstrates compliance by answering the following:
- How the CDC implement requirements
- How the CDC tests ISs to identify vulnerabilities and threats
- How the CDC validates IS functions according to CSA guidance
- How the CDC mitigates risk

The ISSM works with the government to make sure that the CDC plan is approved by the CSA, and then further approved by the designated Authorizing Official. The CDC will certify and attest to the CSA that their information system is working according to

CSA requirements and according to the CDC plan in place. The CDC conducts the assessment and documents results and the CSA approves it. The government authorizing official provides the CDC the Authorization to Operate based on the CDC's implementation. The CSA will continuously monitor, including during opportunities while conducting the annual security review. Finally, the CDC should not process any classified information on the IS prior to the authorization.

Interim Authorization to Operate

Interim Authorization to Operate functions similarly in concept as does the interim security clearance process. There are cases where the operating system may not be fully authorized because there might be further information needed but the CDC may have presented a case where, "Hey, I think we're up and running. I think we're good to go." At that point the Authorization Official (AO) might respond, "Well, I've got to do some more research on this. It looks good thus fare and I'm going to give you a temporary authorization, an interim Authorization to Operate and it's good for 180 days. It can be expanded for another 180 days."

After the trial period, the government will evaluate and make a decision of whether or not to authorize full operations or rescind the temporary. On the other hand, the interim authorization may not ever be implemented as that Authorization to Operate may be provided without the need of the interim period. Just like the interim security clearance; it is available, but may not be necessary. The point of the comparison is that just because one part of NISPOM is carved out for a dedicated purpose such as a separate chapter for IS, guidance should crosswalk within NISPOM.

The CDC should crosswalk all the NISPOM requirements and implement them based on the classified work performed within the CDC. Security requirements are all the same as with other classified material regardless of form. For classified information in hardcopy, the CDC protects it in a GSA approved container, for soft copy, the CDC applies security procedures to where the classified information resides on computing devices, printers, faxes, servers networks, etc.

Changes in Security

There are occasions when security relevant changes occur, such as the modifications to the system or a breakdown in the system somewhere. The CDC should notify the CSA immediately where the IS security measures do not protect the classified information as described in the Authorization to Operate. This is also similar to requirements found in NISPOM Chapter 2; reporting requirements where CDC or cleared employees are no longer capable of protecting classified information.

The CDC should notify the CSA as soon as possible of any facility or IS security changes according to the requirements of the system security plan or the requirements flowed down from the CSA. Once changes in security are reported, the CSA will make a risk based decision based on the report. The decision is whether or not to revoke the authorization or reauthorize after further assessment.

The security relevant changes include occurrences of information system or network malfunctions, repairs, or replacements. It could be a hardware or software replacement that impacts the security of the system. Such changes may generate a new request for an Authorization to Operate. Some other examples include, modification to the networks, the nodes, system ports, protocols, or a new computer. That's significant enough especially since the component's function should be evaluated as well as when software or cryptologic devices are replaced, upgraded, or repaired. Additionally, if DoD updates NISPOM, the CSA issues policy changes, national security policy is updated, directives or regulations that require additional requirements or even the threat changes; this should trigger an evaluation if current security measures are affected. The CSA should review the Authority to Operate and forward their evaluation decision-making authority. The authority then makes the decision to either renew or revoke the authorization.

Reevaluation of the authorization

The CSA will reevaluate every three years. However, keep in mind that the CSA will be conducting other vulnerability assessments during the annual reviews. In the interim, other reviews such as self-assessments, software updates, CSA audits and other events will help determine security issues between the three year window.

The CSA will determine how the CDC applies guidance and evaluates risk to the system. If risks are higher than what is acceptable, the CSA could withdraw that Authorization to Operate. Additionally, the CDC should report when detrimental changes to security of the system occur. They should continuously evaluate security relevant changes without waiting for the three-year event. The continual relationship between the CSA and CDC should allow for good communication and constant evaluation of the IS.

Security Controls Defined

Security controls describe as a minimum the controls that protect the IS and are expected to be implemented.

Management Controls.

The management controls are further described with subcomponents such as: system acquisition, planning, security control assessments, program assessments and risk assessments.

a.   System and services acquisition - how security requirements are implemented. Concerns include:
- Resources in place to acquire new components
- How software updates are acquired and integrated
- How hardware updates are acquired and integrated

b.   Planning - the CDC should describe the security controls in place or that are planned to be in place. The CDC should describe how the cleared employee user will access and interface with these systems, how they will be trained and what their user role and privileges will be.
- How is the system deployed?
- What does it look like once deployed?

c.   Security controls
- How well is the system protected?

- What additional protections are necessary?
- What are the residual risks?

d. Program Management

e. Risk Assessment

Management controls include a risk assessment after reviewing the security controls. Do they work? Do they always work? Are they recording their function? This is a continuous evaluation. The CDCs evaluate the risk assessment cycle of identifying assets, identifying threats, vulnerabilities, determining risk and assigning countermeasures. Risk assessment does not end once the CDC assigns countermeasures. Instead, the CDC reevaluates them to determine residual risk and whether or not additional countermeasures need to be in place. Risks evolve as quickly as new technology, thus the repetitive risk cycle.

The CDCs respond to the classification requirement to determine which IS are going to be used to process classified information based on the information's classification levels. The risk calculation includes the impact of unauthorized access to the classified information based on the classification level: CONFIDENTIAL, SECRET and TOP SECRET. This impact is already determined when the original classification authority provides the classification level. CONFIDENTIAL information has lower risk, SECRET is moderate, and TOP SECRET is high impact to national security.

Under risk assessment, the requirement still exists for the confidentiality levels of low, medium, and high risk or low, medium, high impact based on the classification level. There are some cases where the contract requires additional considerations. The NISPOM describes the requirement to protect classified information on IS and protect it based on the confidentiality level. This requires the IS to be established with the capability of protecting classified information at the appropriate level. The confidentiality level is the only NISPOM requirement, but contract language may require additional evaluations such as the integrity and the availability of the system.

Integrity simply means that a system can perform as it is intended to, without being degraded.

Availability means accessing information when necessary and that a failure will not occur or a repair will not need to be made.

Users should be able to access information to do their jobs. Again, NISPOM requires only confidentiality. If you have a contract in place, they may want you to do the integrity and availability.

CDCs should monitor their systems for impact changes. If an incident occurs to the IS that impacts its ability to protect the information at the appropriate classification level, the CDC should notify the AO that classified information is at risk.

Operational Controls

The operational controls involve almost everything that the CDC information system is required to perform. This ranges from personnel security to employee awareness and training. The operation control measures include many sub-topics.

Personnel security.

Security clearances, need to know and accessing the classified information is part of personnel security controls. Classified information on the IS requires limiting access as provided by human interaction. The CDC should monitor this interaction and make sure that the humans are acting appropriately on these classified machines. The CDC should be tracking people's security clearances and ensuring authorized users are able to access the classified information based on their clearance level and their need to know.

Physical and environmental protection

This describes where the IS actually operates and how the CDC controls access to the IS, physical security measures for the building housing the IS or the physical location of the IS. It also includes contingency planning for natural and man-made disasters that may impact protection levels.

Configuration management

This is the establishing and maintaining of an IS baseline configuration. The configuration should be tightly controlled so that only authorized persons can implement changes for authorized purposes. As with the unclassified network, the classified IS should prevent unauthorized changes such as software downloads or updates or connect unauthorized hardware into the system. Only authorized users should be able to change the configuration of the information system and controls should be in place to prevent contradicting opportunities.

Maintenance

The CDC should assess the information systems to make sure that software updates are implemented correctly. They should also ensure that existing control tools perform as required

Information integrity

CDCs should protect the IS from insertion or creation of malicious code and determine how software patches are uploaded or software is updated for the mitigation software. Security should be capable of preventing an insider or even authorized persons from unintentionally uploading a threat into the system through the introduction of thumb drives, DVDs or CDs into a classified system that also may introduce malware. The malware could affect or impact the controls that are in place, so it is necessary to protect the media that's in the systems.

In the performance of classified processing, users may need to insert a removable hard drive or download classified information on to some type of media. If so, the media should be marked with the correct classification levels and visible to the naked eye so that it is not removed or disclosed of in an unauthorized manner. The information within the removable media should be marked as well as the removable media itself. That way classified media can be afforded the appropriate protections with physical security access controls to prevent unauthorized employees from gaining permission.

Additionally, some classified IS should be destroyed and not recycled when no longer needed. For example, in the case of a classified reproduction machine, any hard drives or anything that captures data should be completely sanitized or destroyed prior to removing it from protective custody.

Trusted downloading

Trusted downloading is the authorized removal of unclassified information from a classified document. The cleared person performing the task determines that no classified information exists on the downloaded document. For example, if a user downloads FOR OFFICIAL USE ONLY (FOUO) information, a set of controls are in place that allows some to download it and certify or authorize that the download is indeed FOUO. We want that trusted downloading capability, but we need to review it, test it and certify that it is indeed bringing down unclassified information and that classified information is not inadvertently spilled. Those performing trusted downloading should be knowledgeable through required derivative classifier training.

Incident response

The cleared contractor confirms with the CSA that the incident response ability works as required. If there is anything wrong with the security system, the cleared defense contractor will be able to mitigate whatever risks there are through an emergency response plan.

Awareness and Training

Another component of the operation control is the requirement for IS protection awareness and training. Training should include annual security awareness training, initial security awareness training, derivative classifier training, and insider threat program training. This required training is available at the CDSE website:

http://www.cdse.mil
https://www.redbikepublishing.com
https://www.bennettinstitute.com

Technical controls

Technical controls are security controls as executed by the information system. They do not involve human interaction; they're actually designed in the system to protect the classified information. They are the security in place to prevent unauthorized access and do so by detecting violations. For example, a contractor ISSM sets a control that prevents documents from being printed and an employee attempts to bypass those controls to print documents, the action will be reported. Another option is to prevent the overnight downloading of 5,000 copies onto a floppy disk, which would be detected and reported.

Identification and authentication

Cleared defense contractors should apply, identification and authentication. These answer the user questions: Who am I and why do I need to access this system? The CSA usually provides direction on the length and the content of passwords, but the CDC will be authorized to generate those passwords. You might have a card with a PIN number instead of a password or you might have a user name and a password that is really difficult to remember. Cleared employees should not be permitted to write down, record or otherwise keep this classified password on their person or in an uncleared location; the passwords are classified to the level of information on the IS.

Access controls

Contractors will limit IS access to authorized users, processes acting on behalf of authorized users, or authorized devices (including other ISs). Access must be limited to the types of transactions and functions that authorized users are permitted to exercise.

Audit and accountability

The audit and accountability just means reviewing and approving log-on actions. The CDC should enable authorized access to detect unauthorized access or intrusions as well as protecting how the IS communicates. Do we e-mail from the system? Are we able to fax? Are we able to make copies? What communicates and are those communication ports open or closed depending on how they are used or needed?

System and Communications Protection

Cleared contractors should maintain an information system audit to discover or prevent inappropriate use as well as appropriate use of the system. This monitor and control capability should include the protection of the communication devices that are on that information system. Part of documentation includes the IS architectural design and software development techniques to ensure that the system is working and cannot be bypassed by a bad actor.

Special Categories

Additionally, special categories of these security controls exist. These special categories include tactical systems, embedded security information systems or special-purpose systems. The tactical embedded or data acquisition or legacy systems and special-purpose systems are just categories that are not normally covered by a CDC. These are situations where these units might be really old and can't protect themselves such as in a legacy system. Mobile systems exist such as shelters or weapon systems that maneuver to various locations or mobile office space that has to move around and as it sets up in a new location. While mobile they should be capable enough to protect that classified information residing on it.

Compensating security systems

These are additional and above the normal security systems available as described earlier. They may include guards, extra alarm systems, components, and firewalls to protect the information system from unauthorized access. The AO assesses all these risks that exist in these special categories.

Where the AO determines a risk is too high, they may require the contractor and the GCA to acknowledge that they understand the risk. The GCA, which will be the owner of the classified information, will say, "Yes, I understand the risk. I will accept that risk". But if the GCA determines it's too high, they may need an alternate plan or they may need additional compensating controls in place.

SUMMARY

With classified IS, the CDC possesses classified information that's owned by the GCA, the program executive office. The GCA provides the classified information to the CDC through a classified contract. The CDC performs on the classified contract as authorized by the CSA. The CSA inspects the security plans and makes sure that the CDC is applying the required security measures.

The protective measures found in NISPOM Chapter 5 are similar to those for classified IS. The CSA provides the protection requirements for operating an IS. The contractor applies the guidance and then writes out a plan on how the IS will be protected. The CSA evaluates the plan and sends it to an AO who grants either an Authorization to Operate or an interim Authorization to Operate that lasts 180 days and can be extended for another 180 days.

To assist with the IS protection tasks, the FSO can assign an ISSM that will be responsible for making sure the IS can protect the classified information as described in the SSP while using the technical controls, operational controls and management controls.

CHAPTER 9 REMOVING CLASSIFIED MATERIAL

INTRODUCTION

CDCs should be prepared to display the disposition of all classified information under their care. This includes the status of the material from inception to disposition. So, what's the best way to do so?

The NISPOM requires accountability of TOP SECRET items, but the same type of accountability is not required for classified information at SECRET and below [1]. Additionally, CONFIDENTIAL information does not require receipting action when transferred between cleared facilities as does SECRET and TOP SECRET [2]. Where accountability and receipting is not specifically required, the NISPOM states that cleared facilities should be able to retrieve classified information during a reasonable amount of time using an IMS [3].

This chapter also provides recommendations on how to use an IMS to meet requirements. Other topics include structuring the organization to ensure only cleared personnel perform the dissemination functions. This removal of classified information from a cleared facility is authorized in the following situations:

- Mail-Send properly wrapped and documented classified media via the United States Postal Service (USPS)
- Hand Delivery – Authorize cleared employees to personally deliver classified material via air, land and sea transportation
- Courier –Deliver classified information via approved escort services
- Electronic Transmission – Use computers, email, internet and other approved means to send classified information
- Destruction –obliterate classified material no longer needed by

the GCA
* Retention of Classified Material – Request to maintain classified material beyond the contract expiration date

ACCOUNTABILITY

According to the 32 CFR Parts 2001 and 2004, Classified National Security Information (Directive No. 1); Final Rule, classified information should be transmitted and received with the appropriate level of accountability [3]. Classified material should be transmitted in such a way as to prevent accidental opening, detect tampering and ensure expedient delivery. Persons sending classified material should ensure that the recipients have the clearance and need to know [4].

These protective measures not only address classified material within a cleared facility but extends to classified transmission from the cleared facility and beyond. The organization disseminating classified material by any of the approved methods has the responsibility of doing so in such a manner that prevents and detects attempts by unauthorized persons from gaining access at anytime. Preventive measures include wrapping, getting approval for and selecting the transmission methods, coordinating and arranging pickup and delivery, and surveillance of the classified material while in transit.

Classified Information Dissemination Process

Prior to removing classified material from a cleared facility, FSOs should verify that the action is absolutely necessary. Because of inherent risks with air, land, rail and sea movement, removing classified material should be a last resort. The shipper or receiver cannot control the environment but must rely on services provided. The person disseminating classified information should perform due diligence and understand the risks and available countermeasures. These measures include removing the items from the cleared facility's IMS, preparation of the item for delivery and documenting the authorized receiver's acknowledgment of receipt.

When a contractor needs to transfer classified information,

the FSO should verify that the recipient is authorized to receive it. Verification is performed through the DCSA's database. This database lists facility contact information, address, phone number, CAGE code, facility clearance and classified storage capability if applicable.

Once verified, the FSO should update the classified information's status in the IMS. This action serves as a reminder during document inventories and annual inspections that the classified items are no longer in the facility. After removing the classified item from accountability and generating a receipt, the FSO should wrap the item for shipment. Nothing on the final preparation (container, box, envelope, etc) should indicate that the item is classified. Additionally, any attempts to gain access to the classified information should be detectable at some point during transit or identified upon receipt at the destination. Other than the tracking process or physical controls, the package should look like every other package.

Recall that CONFIDENTIAL classified information does not require a receipt. However, a good practice is to always generate a receipt and request signature. This provides a close out or evidence that the items arrived and were received. Once transferred, the receipts should be signed by the receiver and returned to the sender. The IMS process begins with the receipt of the classified document. The sending industrial security office receives the signed receipts and closes out their responsibility and tracking process for that classified material.

Classified Material Preparation for Shipment

The classification level should be the first consideration when determining how to remove classified information from an approved location. According to the NISPOM, regardless of how information is removed, it should be wrapped with opaque durable material such as cardboard, envelopes, or boxes. It should be transmitted in a way to prevent accidental and unauthorized disclosure and detect tamper.

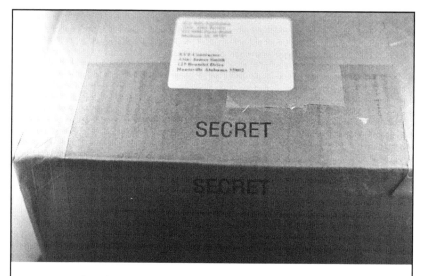

Figure 9-1 Classified information is prepared in two layers. Notice that the inner layer is wrapped with rip proof tape and is marked with the classification level on the top, bottom and all sides.

Inner Layer

Classified information can be sent using almost any material as the packaging. A good practice is to cover seams with rip-proof opaque tape or other similar material. Next, the FSO should mark the package on the top and bottom of all sides with the classification level (Figure 9-1). They should then add the "to" and "from" with two copies of receipts either attached to the first layer or inside the first layer [5]. Internal contents that come in contact with the wrapper could be imaged or observed in certain situations. To prevent this, the preparer can place wrapping paper, patterned paper, receipts or fold the documents in such a way that they cannot be read through the wrapping.

Outer Layer

The outer wrapper is the second line of defense for the classified information. Once it leaves the cleared facility, the level of protection is severely reduced. The wrapping requirements are similar to those of the inner wrapper and should be the same size to prevent looseness or movement that could fray or damage the inner wrapping's seams. The outside label should not identify the recipient by name. Office numbers or symbols should be used to prevent associating a classified package with a particular person. When addressing shipment labels to contractors, the outer label should be addressed to "FSO" or "Security". When addressing shipment labels to military agencies, the outer package labels should be "Commander". Additionally, addressing deliveries to an authorized department ensures the package is received by authorized persons. Providing a person's name on the outside label could cause problems if they are not around to receive it and could result in returned packages.

The inner layer identifies that contents are classified. The intent is to provide warning against further unauthorized opening. For example, suppose a carrier truck overturns and the contents of the carrier are strewn over a large area. Clean up efforts ensue and all packages and containers are recovered. If a classified package is recovered with no damage, it can continue to its destination. If the outer wrapper is torn or destroyed, the package can be controlled to ensure it does not fall into unauthorized hands.

A good practice is to use strong, durable wrapping material readily available at postal or office supply stores. A good rip proof tape is heavy lined with string and is somewhat difficult to rip, remove or cut without leaving evidence. The protection level can be strengthened with the addition of tamper resistant and detecting seals. The seals are numbered and can be logged in a record. If tamper occurs the seal will stretch out of shape or break thus preventing re-application. When the classified shipment arrives, the receiver can compare the seal with a shipping document or receipt. If a new seal has been applied or the existing seal indicates tamper, the receiver can report the suspected compromise. Together the wrapping material and seals can prevent and detect unauthorized persons from accessing the classified material without leaving traces of the attempts.

The following scenario provides an example of how classified material can be prepared for shipment. A cleared employee approaches the FSO with a request to mail a package to their government customer. He identifies the item, recipient, date needed, and preferred method of delivery. The FSO pulls the document and consults the security classification guide and the DD Form 254 to determine whether or not classified items can be mailed and the approved delivery methods. The FSO then accesses the DCSA database for the mailing address.

She enters the document transaction in the IMS to indicate removal of the classified information. She prints two receipts identifying the document title, where it is going and method of delivery. Then she puts the receipt copies in the package and marks the calendar to remind her that a signed receipt is due back within 30 days.

CLASSIFIED PACKAGE WRAPPING CHECKLIST

INNER WRAPPING:
1. Mark opaque envelope with highest classification
2. Label with recipient company name and address, ATTN: Recipient's name, section, mail stop, etc.
3. Seal all seams with opaque tamper-proof tape

OUTER WRAPPING:
1. Label opaque envelope with company name, address, ATTN: Facility Security Officer
2. Seal with opaque tamper-proof tape covering all seams.
3. Include two copies of receipt inside or attached to inner opaque envelope

Classification or other restrictive markings are not annotated on outer wrapper*

Figure 9-2 A classified package wrapping checklist serves as a reminder of how to prepare classified information for delivery. Improperly packaged classified material could lead to loss or compromise of classified information.

To help with wrapping procedures, the FSO consults an internally produced classified package wrapping guide (Figure 9-2). The FSO places the classified document and the two receipts on the wrapping table. She wraps the items and marks the package as SECRET, according to the classification of the document and affixes the address label. Next, she applies the outer wrapping and label, but does not apply the classification level (Figure 9-3). The package is now ready to be delivered through the mail, hand carry, overnight, courier, or whatever approved means desired by the customer.

Figure 9-3 The classified document outer wrapper does not have classification markings, but does have the rip proof tape.

Alternate wrappings

Large sizes, bulk, weight, mission requirements or other structural make up could prevent transmission of items by traditional means. These could be machines, vehicles, aircraft, missiles, or other cumbersome, odd shaped, heavy or odd sized items. Brief cases, canvas courier bags, hard cases, shipping crates, large tarps and other types of containers can serve as wrapping provided they are approved by DCSA [5]. The containers are a part of the process to provide multiple layers of protection, deny accidental access, detect tampering and ensure expedited transport.

Transmitting material by classification level within the U.S. and Territories-Overview

TOP SECRET

Contractors can only transfer outside of a cleared facility with the approval of the Government Contracting Activity (GCA). Only Federal agencies authorize the transfer of TOP SECRET material within their agency control. The approved methods for dissemination of TOP SECRET within the US and territories follow [6] (Note that USPS shipments are not authorized for TOP SECRET):

- CSA approved or designed cryptographic means
- Defense Courier Service when authorized
- Appropriately cleared and approved DoD courier or escort (courier orders (Figure 9-4)) on approved commercial air or ground transportation

SECRET [7]

- Any means as authorized for TOP SECRET
- United States Postal Service Registered and Express Mail
- Cleared commercial carriers
- CSA approved overnight delivery services
- Cleared local messenger service
- Other methods as approved by the GCA

CONFIDENTIAL [8]

- Any means as authorized for SECRET and TOP SECRET
- Commercial carriers do not have to be "cleared"
- USPS Certified Mail

TRANSMITTING MATERIAL WITHIN THE U.S. AND TERRITORIES IN DETAIL

TOP SECRET

National Security Agency approved or designed cryptographic means

One of the largest threats facing the United States is economic espionage. Billions of dollars worth of damage occurs monthly as companies lose their valuable technological edge. Though other nations and enterprises seek to steal technology, much of it is released because employees do not understand how to protect their company and privacy information. Unencrypted email, facsimile machines, and telephones are not secure. They are portals open to scrutiny and intercept. Organizations that regularly send sensitive information through open channels may lose their propriety and technology lead.

The threat is similar for classified information. Cleared employees must understand their roles in protecting classified information from receipt to dissemination. To prevent inadvertent release via electronic transmission the federal government requires the use of encryption and decryption devices. Those who use encryption devices designate a communications security (COMSEC) custodian to account for COMSEC equipment [10]. This system involves setting up an account with the NSA and using secure telephone and facsimile machines. Classified information should never be sent over unapproved telephone or facsimile machines.

Defense Courier Service (DCS)

The DCS is an organization reporting directly to the Commander In Chief Transportation Command 11. The DCS is a network of professionals with the mission of providing international support and distribution of sensitive and classified information. This service is available to qualifying military, government and defense contractor organizations and provides continuous surveillance of the classified material aboard U.S. flagged carriers.

Appropriately cleared and approved DoD courier or escort on approved commercial air or ground transportation

TOP SECRET information can be transmitted by courier or escort when approved. TOP SECRET information should only be hand carried or escorted as a last resort and only if the information is not otherwise available or it is critical to fulfilling the contract.

SECRET

SECRET information can be disseminated using the same methods as TOP SECRET. However, they can also be disseminated by the means listed below:

United States Postal Service Registered and Express Mail

Registered and Express Mail within the US and territories is approved for SECRET. Registered mail uses a system of receipts and monitoring throughout the journey to provide the most secure method the USPS offers. With today's technology, the sender can verify a signed delivery almost immediately by logging onto the USPS website and entering the tracking number. Once delivery is confirmed with the appropriate signature, the FSO can verify with the receiver and print and file the confirmation.

Express mail can also be used for secure overnight delivery. The USPS guarantees overnight delivery where available at all times of day and night. However, the sending organization should only use USPS Express service after delivery is coordinated and the recipient is available to sign for and receive the classified delivery. When using USPS Express service, the FSO should schedule either a pickup or delivery to a USPS facility. Depositing classified material in a drop box is not authorized and provides no protection against theft, accidental loss or exposure of classified information. Also, the sender should make arrangements to deliver only to an office where an authorized person can sign for the item. According to the NISPOM "The 'Waiver of Signature and Indemnity' block on the U.S. Postal Service express mail label 11–B, will not be executed under any circumstances." The required signature ensures the item is received by a cleared person [10].

Cleared Commercial Carriers

Department of Defense contractors can use government approved commercial carriers to transport SECRET and below. The deliveries are not authorized for international travel and can only be made within the continental US or within Alaska, Hawaii and each territory with GCA providing routing information.

Commercial carrier shipments should be protected using hardened containers or other material authorized by the GCA [12]. Additionally, boxes, cars, compartments and sections should be protected with numbered seals. The numbers can help determine whether or not the containers or equipment have been opened or an attempt made to open them.

When requesting commercial carrier support, the contractor should notify the GCA of the proposed classified material to be shipped, the point of origin and the destination [12]. Once approved, they should notify the consignee and the shipping activity of the shipment and provide details of the type of shipment, number of seals, and projected time of arrival. The FSO notifies the intended recipient to expect the delivery of classified material. If the shipment does not arrive within 48 hours the receiver should notify the sender.

GSA Approved Overnight Delivery Service

SECRET and CONFIDENTIAL material can be sent using GSA approved companies. A list of these companies is available at *http://www.gsa.gov.*

These services should be used with DCSA approval. When using an overnight delivery service, the FSO of the sending organization should alert the receiving organization that classified information will be arriving via overnight service. Though overnight carriers are

192 How to Get U.S. Government Contracts and Classified Work

approved through the GSA, the carrier companies do not need to hold a facility security clearance. The carriers are only required to meet requirements of tracking shipments [7].

Every precaution should be made to ensure that the overnight delivery will not arrive during a holiday or scheduled day off. The best method is to not deliver the day prior to a weekend or federal holiday unless the receiver is operating a mail room with cleared persons and the storage capability.

Cleared Local Messenger Service

Cleared commercial messenger services can hand deliver classified information provided they have a facility clearance and cleared messengers. Once the cleared messenger service has been authorized, the FSO should coordinate the delivery with the service and the receiver. The cleared messenger should sign for a receipt when they pick up the classified package. They then require the receiver to sign a receipt acknowledging taking the classified material into their accountability.

CONFIDENTIAL

CONFIDENTIAL information can be disseminated using the same methods as SECRET and TOP SECRET. However, they can also be disseminated by the means listed below:

USPS

Confidential material can be transmitted the same as SECRET when using USPS. However, in most cases classified material can be sent using Certified Mail. The USPS Certified Mail service provides a level of security which includes tracking and delivery confirmation. As with USPS Registered Mail, the cleared facility mailing the classified items is issued a receipt and tracking number. The sender has the opportunity to verify a signed delivery almost immediately by logging onto the USPS website and entering the tracking number. Once delivery is confirmed with the appropriate signature, the confirmation can be printed and filed.

Commercial Carriers

The commercial carrier does not need to maintain a facility security clearance to transport CONFIDENTIAL material. However, the CSA or GCA must approve the shipment [9]. These commercial carriers can be hired as long as they are within US boundaries and provide a Constant Surveillance Service (CSS). In other words, the carriers be alert and document visual inspection of the classified material while en route.

Transmitting Classified Information with Couriers/Escorts

Couriers hand carry classified information during all stages of travel. Escorts accompany classified information during travel but may not be physically in the same area. While an escort may be in a passenger area, the classified information will be in a cargo area. When authorized, defense contractors can transmit classified information using cleared employees with a courier briefing. Hand carrying should be a last resort as more risks are involved and should not be used as a matter of convenience. Prior to using cleared employees, the FSO should ensure the cleared employees protect the classified material at the level.

An authorized courier has a security clearance and need to know. After the classified material is packaged, the FSO should brief the cleared employee on their responsibilities. The courier should understand that they are responsible for the classified information under their care and planning should cover pre-trip, en route, and after trip preparations.

Pre-Trip

Courier should have tickets, a travel plan, a courier letter and coordination made with involved parties. They should also inspect the classified package and ensure receipts are included, and written authorization is provided and picture identification is available [13]. A good practice is to issue courier papers that identify the cleared employee as authorized to hand carry classified material from their cleared facilities. The courier credentials should be issued only after the cleared employee has acknowledged their understanding of training. Practice runs, hands on training or using couriers with more experience is always a good practice and confidence, experience and education combine to prevent security violations.

En route

Courier should adhere to the planned route and not make deviations. If stops are necessary, they should be part of a plan with approved locations to store the classified information. The classified information must remain with the courier and should not be opened by unauthorized persons or contents discussed openly. The classified package is never to be left unattended and the courier should not allow themselves to be distracted from protecting the classified material.

If the trip involves an overnight stay, a stop should be scheduled and arrangements made for approved storage [13]. Plans should also include what to do in case of emergencies such as unintended layovers, breakdowns or other unplanned events. This approved storage should be coordinated with the GCA or DCSA. Authorized overnight storage locations include federal and government installations and other defense contractor facilities with approved classified storage capacity at the same level as or higher than the transported package. The briefing should also include delivering the classified material only to authorized persons and at the approved facilities. The courier should not store classified information in lockers, private homes, automobile trunks, hotel safes or other unauthorized areas.

A government customer may require a defense contractor to attend a classified visit or meeting at another defense contractor's cleared facility. When such arrangements are made, a contractor could also escort classified information to the meeting. Prior to departure, an inventory of the classified material should be conducted [13]. The cleared facilities where the meeting occurs may authorize the courier to report directly to the meeting without additional processing. However, the courier should be prepared to introduce the classified information according to the cleared facility's policies or per instruction from the government sponsor. Prior arrangements and coordination will prevent any delays or surprises.

After Trip

The courier should be prepared to receive a receipt from the recipient of the classified information. If they will be returning with a classified package, they should again ensure that it is prepared for delivery.

Modes of Travel

Hundreds of thousands of tons of cargo travel our roads, rails, and airspace daily. America depends on transportation to get products to customers safely and on time. When products are lost or damaged, carrier insurance will reimburse either the shipper or receiver. However, there is no insurance for damage to national security. Classified items lost, stolen or exposed during shipment pose a threat. No matter how dependable a carrier's track record, the shipper should do everything possible to transport classified information while mitigating any risk of loss or compromise.

The volume of material transported on any given day is staggering. Transportation by any means is reliable but not risk free. Vehicle accidents, traffic jams, break downs or any number of problems with land, air, rail and sea transportation can threaten the security of the classified product. Natural disasters and mechanical failure can cause delays in the reliable movement of items. Air travel also has inherent risks including: late gate departures and arrivals, crowded terminals, and maintenance problems significantly threaten the ability of an escort to keep a close eye on the cargo hold. Those escorting classified material via trains, over the road vehicles, and air carriers should be aware of inconsistencies or events during the shipment that could negatively impact the security of the item. When any event happens to cause an unscheduled delay, the escort should immediately notify shipper.

Rail

When shipping classified information by train the escort should ride in the same car, keep the package under constant surveillance and remain vigilant during stops and layovers. Experienced travelers understand the frustrations involved when others have retrieved the wrong baggage. Escorts should ensure they maintain their receipts and watch their package to prevent such mistakes from occurring as well as other attempts to pilfer or steal. Shipping classified material in a separate car poses a more difficult challenge. Coordination with railroad employees will significantly reduce the challenges while helping to strengthen security. When freight cars and passenger cars are separated, the FSO should arrange with the railroad for the freight car to be positioned immediately in front of the escort's car [14]. The biggest threat occurs during stops. When time permits, escorts should leave the train at all stops and perform a physical inspection of the protective measures (seals, locks, etc) applied to the classified items on the shipment cars.

Highway

Overnight escorts should remain alert for security violations, theft, piracy, pilferage, hi-jacking, damage or other incidences that could jeopardize the shipment and compromise the classified information. Rest and overnight stops, regulated driving hours and refueling pose additional risks to the voyage. At every stop the escort should keep the vehicle in view and remain alert to threatening actions. Highly sensitive items, urgency and threat may require a carrier to provide enough escorts to work around the clock shifts.

Air

Airlines also offer unique challenges to transporting classified material. Air carriers are experienced in flying various types of cargo to worldwide locations. Federal marshals fly prisoners, zoo keepers ship exotic animals, and doctors transport donor organs. Those transporting classified materials are also limited to the type of cargo the Federal Aviation Administration and the National Transportation Safety Board authorizes. Prior arrangements with the air carrier help them understand the unique requirements for shipping classified material and will better meet the requests of the consignor.

Passenger travel is a choreographed event. Passengers board when invited, remain in their seats during takeoff and landing and deplane when instructed. When transporting classified material, the escort should request boarding and deplaning services outside of normal operations. When layovers are expected, the escort should be the first off the plane and wait in an area where they can observe activities on and around the cargo access door. If the cargo is transshipped using another airplane, the escort should observe the process. When the plane is ready to continue the journey the escort is again the last to board. Upon reaching the final destination, the escort becomes the first to deplane.

Cleared employees traveling by commercial aircraft should conduct extensive pre planning. In addition to identification, a courier briefing, and notification to maintain accountability of the classified material at all times, travel should be coordinated with the Transportation Security Administration (TSA). For example, while traveling by automobile, the courier may only need to drive to the final destination without having to speak to anyone. The route is often direct to the destination with no interruptions. However, more vigilance is needed when traveling to and through an airport terminal.

Classified material should never be opened in transit [15]. Such a contingency should be planned with the FSO during the courier briefing. In the briefing and planning stage, the courier and FSO should understand that TSA may need to open the packaging to verify that the item is indeed a document as identified in the courier letter. If TSA requests to open the package, the courier should request to see the senior agent to quietly explain the situation. They should produce the courier paperwork and permit inspecting the package privately while not bringing attention to the fact the contents are classified.

There may be occasion to escort large, heavy, bulky or other classified material. Some classified packages cannot otherwise be inspected with an x-ray machine or other visual means without causing compromise. In such cases prior arrangements are made with the TSA or the air carrier to accommodate conveying classified material by air.

Defense contractors traveling by air could also travel with a written authorization. This authorization identifies the traveler by full name, date of birth, height, weight, type of identification used and signature. The letter also describes the classified material, all relevant travel points, name, telephone and address of the FSO and the DCSA office and expiration date of the letter. The authorization letter should provide authority for the special courier requests and the courier presents the authorization upon request.

Destruction of Classified Material

Unless permitted by the GCA, classified information must be destroyed or returned as soon as it has served its purpose. According to NISPOM, classified information can only be retained for two years unless the GCA approves an extension. Cleared contractors should develop a system to evaluate the classified information in their possession for reduction. Classified information no longer needed should be returned to the GCA or destroyed using approved methods. The FSO should create a system to help prioritize which items to evaluate. The IMS or accountability system can be used in the process to manage classified holdings and help determine what is still useful and what can be removed. The objective is to maintain only the classified material necessary to execute the classified contract. Additionally, the FSO should be able to determine that the documents were actually destroyed or returned and not lost.

The IMS can also be used to help determine classified information by status. For example, the FSO can sort classified information by contract and see how many related documents and copies exist. Items can be prioritized for return or destruction based on expired contracts, duplicate copies or other criteria as identified in the IMS.

Approved Destruction Methods

Two people are required to destroy and document the destruction of TOP SECRET information. SECRET and CONFIDENTIAL only require one person. Records and receipt of destruction should be kept on hand for two years when TOP SECRET is destroyed. However, records should also be maintained for SECRET and CONFIDENTIAL. This documentation helps determine the disposition of classified information during inspections and inventories.

Classified information can be destroyed by approved means based on its composition. For example, paper products can be shredded, burned, pulped or pulverized. The residue should be inspected to ensure that classified information is no longer legible. Shredding should only be accomplished using NSA approved equipment.

Commercial enterprises and vendors also provide destruction services. Burn facilities operate at temperatures hot enough to burn paper in bulk, computers and hard drives and other medial. However, approval through DCSA should be acquired prior to using such services. Also, classified information should be destroyed the same day as it is removed from the cleared facility and should be prepared for transmission by the same methods as dissemination described earlier.

Summary

Classified information should only be removed from the protection of a cleared facility as a last resort and when otherwise authorized and absolutely necessary. Each time SECRET or TOP SECRET classified material is introduced or removed from a cleared facility, a receipting action should take place. When directed to send classified material to another cleared location the sender should protect it from attempts to tamper, steal, or otherwise gain unauthorized access.

200 How to Get U.S. Government Contracts and Classified Work

REVIEW QUESTIONS

1. You are an FSO for a large cleared contractor organization and have just been notified by your government customer to transfer a series of compact disks classified as SECRET to another business under contractual agreement. The other business is across the country. Specific guidance is as follows: "The contractor needs the classified material at their facility to begin critical analysis and solve a pressing problem defining the success of the program."

   a. Identify authorized methods of transporting classified material at the SECRET level.

   b. Which resources will you consult for authorized methods of transmission based on your contract?

2. Your customer calls ten minutes later with a change. The contractor needs to begin work immediately.

   a. Based on the request which resources are available for shipping classified information overnight?

   b. DCSA has provided written authorization to transport classified information using approved overnight carriers. Where would you go to find a list of approved overnight carriers?

3. How would you prepare the classified compact disks for dissemination to another location? In other words, describe the process for wrapping or preparing the classified information for delivery (layers of protection, address labels and classification markings).

4. Suppose overnight carriers were not authorized for the above scenario. What methods are available through USPS?

5. If the recipient is not available to sign for the package, should the classified material be forwarded? Why or why not?

REFERENCES

1. Department of Defense, DoD 5220.22-M, National Industrial Security Operating Manual, section 5-201, February 2016
2. PART IV, National Archives and Records Administration, Information Security Oversight Office, 32 CFR Parts 2001 and 2004 Classified National Security Information, (Directive No. 1); Final Rule
3. Department of Defense, DoD 5220.22-M, National Industrial Security Operating Manual, section 5-200, February 2016
4. Executive Order 12968—Access to Classified Information, Federal Register, section 2.5, August 1995
5. Department of Defense, DoD 5220.22-M, National Industrial Security Operating Manual, section 5-401, February 2016
6. Department of Defense, DoD 5220.22-M, National Industrial Security Operating Manual, section 5-402, February 2016
7. Department of Defense, DoD 5220.22-M, National Industrial Security Operating Manual, section 5-403, February 2016
8. Department of Defense, DoD 5220.22-M, National Industrial Security Operating Manual, section 5-404, February 2016
9. Department of Defense, DoD 5220.22-M, National Industrial Security Operating Manual, section 5-409, February 2016
10. Department of Defense, DoD 5220.22-M, National Industrial Security Operating Manual, section 9-403, February 2016
11. DoD 5200.33-R, "Defense Courier Service Regulation", January 5, 1995 Assistant Secretary of Defense for Command, Control, Communication and Intelligence
12. Department of Defense, DoD 5220.22-M, National Industrial Security Operating Manual, section 5-408, February 2016
13. Department of Defense, DoD 5220.22-M, National Industrial Security Operating Manual, section 5-410, February 2016
14. Department of Defense, DoD 5220.22-M, National Industrial Security Operating Manual, section 5-413, February 2016

CHAPTER 10 TRAINING AND REPORTING

INTRODUCTION

Cleared employees provide the capability the CDCs rely on while performing on classified contracts. They are the engineers, cybersecurity experts, program members, and others who are the backbone of the company. They are also extensions of the security program. It is important to train them properly to perform on classified contracts.

Developing relationships with cleared employees creates an environment of cooperation. This environment facilitates the recruitment of all employees to protect national security. Those working in the enterprise can be the eyes, ears and muscle, acting as force multipliers, and extending the effectiveness of the security department.

FSOs should conduct initial and refresher training and file reports as required by the NISPOM. Instead of conducting training just to be compliant, the training can be performed as an effective relationship building opportunity. This education increases a cleared employee's knowledge of responsibility to protect classified material; detect attempts at espionage and other security violations; and report incidents, violations and status changes affecting personnel and facility clearances.

This chapter provides information of training and reporting requirements as outlined in the NISPOM. The reader will have access to training ideas to create a synergistic program involving all employees. This enables robust security far exceeding the capabilities of a single department. This chapter will address the following issues:

- **Training All Employees for Effective Performance** – The NISPOM requires cleared employees to attend initial and refresher training [1]. The FSO should understand the requirements and how the training objectives relate to their industry. Any FSO can quote regulations, but a good one knows how to take this annual requirement and make it applicable to the organization.

- **Adverse Information** – A report of adverse information can indicate an employee's inability to protect classified information. However, only credible and factual adverse information should be reported. As with corporate fraud and other crimes, cases of espionage often occur over a longer duration than necessary. Traditionally, those who have stolen information from their organizations have demonstrated patterns and behavior that should have raised suspicion with coworkers much earlier. Too much time at the copier, working late when unnecessary, sudden unexplained wealth and other indicators have been reported to investigators after the fact. Timely reporting is a vital link between security and employees in the protection of classified information. Adverse information should be reported immediately [2]. Reluctance to report information on themselves could stem from FSOs not adequately communicated the objective of reporting.

- **Security Violations** – Security violations occur when classified information is not protected. When violations do occur they must be reported immediately. Relationships can develop while conducting training and other interaction opportunities could lead to more willingness to report minor incidents and major violations. Investigations and interviews should be conducted to find root causes and determine whether or not a loss, compromise or suspected compromise has occurred. The results are either handled in-house or sent to DCSA depending on the findings.

FSO Training

The CSA should give initial training and briefings to the FSO [3]. The FSO is then authorized to provide the training to the cleared employees. According to NISPOM, the FSO is also required to attend the DCSA mandated FSO Program Management Course within one year of appointment [4]. DCSA provides new courses designed for FSOs of possessing and non-possessing facilities. FSOs should coordinate with their DCSA representative to determine the training that's right for their situation. The training is designed to prepare the FSO to implement and direct a NISPOM based security program in their cleared contractor facility including, but not limited to the following topics:

- Protecting classified material – The receipt, accountability, storage, dissemination and destruction of classified material. The FSO learns how to protect classified information in a cleared contractor facility.
- Required training – This instruction helps the FSO establish an ongoing training program designed to create an environment of security conscious cleared employees. The FSO learns to present effective training to cleared employees, teaching them to protect the classified material and report questionable activity and violations.
- Personnel security clearances – The FSO gains an understanding of the personnel security clearance request procedure, briefing techniques and maintenance of personnel clearances.
- Facility clearance –The FSO learns how FCLs are established and which records and activities are required to maintain the FCL.
- Foreign Ownership Control and Influence (FOCI) - Organizations analyze foreign investments, sales and ownership on a regular basis using the Certificate Pertaining to Foreign Interests (SF 328). FSOs learn to interact with management and provide guidance and direction in preventing a foreign entity from unauthorized access to or controlling work involving classified and export controlled

information [5].

- Exports compliance and international operations –FSOs receive instruction on how to prevent unauthorized disclosure of critical technology, classified and export controlled information. Companies can thrive in such an international environment provided they can execute Departments of State and Commerce licenses and agreements as required.
- Restricted areas –The restricted area is established to control temporary access to classified material. At the end of each work day, the classified material is returned to the approved classified holding area.
- Closed areas – Space is approved to store and work with classified material. This involves approved construction and limited accesses controls to prevent unauthorized disclosure during and after work hours.
- Contract security classification specification (DD Form 254) – The cleared contractor is allowed access to classified contracts based on the DD Form 254. The FSO learns how the DD Form 254 is constructed and how to provide input to better meet security requirements.
- Security classification guides (SCG) – As the DD Form 254 provides authorization to execute a classified contract, the SCG provides the "how to" instruction. All employees performing classified work consult the guide to understand what is classified and how to provide the required protection.
- Security administration and records keeping – This teaches the maintenance of facility and personnel security clearance information as well as all other accountability and IMS. The FSO is expected to provide information on personnel clearances, original documentation of their facility clearance and demonstrate classified information accountability during the DCSA annual security inspection.
- Subcontracting – When approved to subcontract classified work, the prime contractor will provide a DD Form 254 to the subcontractor.

The FSO should attend the required training at either the DCSA Academy, online or through a mobile training team. DCSA issues a certificate of training which should be filed for presentation during security audits. The FSO training should not end with this course. Career enhancing training is available through various security and management courses. More in depth online and residence training is available in each above mentioned topic. Other training certification opportunities exist in topics like special access programs, COMSEC, and intelligence protection. Other training is available in colleges, professional organizations, vendor websites, through books like this and within the security community.

Briefings Provided By the FSO

New Employees without security clearances

New employees may be hired prior to receiving their security clearances. After the security clearance is awarded at a later date, the FSO will provide the SF 312 and a briefing (discussed in more detail later). This SF 312 should be provided to newly cleared employees along with a briefing and signature. The requirement is that the form should be signed once, during the very first briefing and the FSO should not provide a newly cleared employee access to classified information or program until the employee is trained and signs the SF 312. Likewise, the employee should not be asked to sign the SF 312 until fully trained on the nature of the classified material and how to protect it. A common practice is to provide the initial security briefing prior to presenting the SF 312 for signature. Once the SF 312 is signed by all parties, the FSO will forward it to DCSA.

FSOs should dedicate more security awareness training to new employees who will have a security clearance for the first time. This is because they will be newly introduced to classified material and how to work with it. The words CONFIDENTIAL, SECRET and TOP SECRET may require further explanation. The newly cleared employee may not understand how to dial a combination or determine who to allow access to classified material. Without appropriate training, the newly cleared employees may make honest mistakes leading to security violations.

As an example of a preventable security violation, consider an FSO conducting a survey of the cleared facility's security program. He wants to get a good understanding of the security successes and challenges the company faces. He recognizes that the veteran engineers, program managers and other cleared employees have a good grasp on their responsibilities to safeguard classified material. All he has to do is provide training and resources to maintain their level of proficiency and communicate security goals and procedures on a regular basis.

Upon reviewing the security violations, the FSO noticed a trend with newly cleared employees. Though each newly cleared employee had signed a Classified Information Nondisclosure Agreement (SF 312) and an initial security briefing attendance roster, they contributed to the most incidents and violations. In one incident a newly cleared employee had failed to return a classified compact disk to the classified document holding at the end of the day. According to the preliminary investigation, the FSO attempted to contact the employee over a course of three hours. Finally at 8:00 p.m., the employee returned to work with the classified disk. His explanation involved attending a dinner and returning later to the office and finish his classified work. He had explained that as long as the disk was on his person, he had provided adequate safeguarding. In this example, both the FSO and the employee's supervisor had assumed that the employee had understood how to protect classified information. Now they can provide additional training or disciplinary action to prevent further violations.

New Employees With Extensive Classified Work Experience

Cleared facilities with new employees who have already received security clearances still have a responsibility to provide the initial security briefing. The new employees may have experience protecting classified material, but there is no way to verify the type and strength of the experience. Unique contractual requirements may have specialized performance requirements. New employees, regardless of experience level, should receive reinforcement security training on the insider threat, how to recognize and protect classified information and reporting suspicious contacts or security violations. Those with experience protecting classified information should be provided an overview of the NISP with a more contract and organization oriented briefing. They do not always need the same in depth briefing as a newly cleared employee. However, they should have a clear understanding of implementing the NISP to contract specific classified work.

The FSO is the primary security awareness trainer for the cleared contractor and DCSA provides required briefings to the FSO. Once trained, the FSO provides the training to cleared employees. The training of newly cleared employees begins with a briefing of their responsibilities to protect classified information and as outlined on the SF 312.

However, the SF 312 is not required just because an employee begins a new job at a new company. If a new employee already possesses a clearance while employed at another defense contractor or federal agency, the FSO just records the training and assumes responsibility of the cleared employee. They do not have to process another SF 312 unless there is not one on file required specifically by DCSA. An FSO can verify whether or not a cleared employee has signed an SF 312 through DCSA database.

CDC Training Requirements; Cleared Employee Training

Not only must the FSO be certified, but the cleared employees performing on classified are required to be trained as well. The training is less intensive, focusing on security responsibilities and how to be part of a security program to protect classified information. The FSO should be prepared to either teach the training or provide self-study material and capture the accomplishment in training records. Each cleared employee should participate in training.

SF-312 Briefing

Newly cleared employees must sign an SF-312, Non-Disclosure Agreement. Instead of just having them sign the box, why not give them preliminary training. What exactly is on the form and why they are signing it. Once signed, then give them the Initial Security Briefing. An SF-312 briefing is available to download at:

https://www.redbikepublishing.com/security/.

Security Awareness

All cleared employees should attend security awareness training [17]. The training reminds cleared employees to safeguard classified information and the possible criminal, civil and administrative sanctions reserved for those who violate their safeguarding responsibilities.

The NISPOM lists training topics that FSOs should train cleared employees on prior granting access to classified material. These requirements include a threat awareness briefing, the defensive security briefing, and overview of the security classification system, employee reporting obligations and requirements and the security procedures and duties applicable to the employee's job [17]. Most of the security training is left to the FSO to develop and present. This is a demanding task for anyone. Many FSOs can find prepared briefings through consultants.

Initial Security Briefings

The initial security briefing is designed to familiarize the cleared employee with the NISP as applied to the cleared facility. It also provides fundamental training of the classified work specific to the contracts under which the classified work is performed. All new cleared employees should attend this briefing regardless of whether they are receiving a clearance for the first time or bringing 30 years of related work experience [1]. As important as this initial orientation is, a truly successful program continues with on the job training.

The initial security briefing reflects how the organization protects classified material according to Presidential Executive Order 13526. The EO directs training to ensure cleared persons know how to protect classified information and the possible penalties that they can be charged with if they contribute to unauthorized disclosure [6]. The NISPOM requires that an FSO provide training to cleared employees on the following topics [1]:

- Threat awareness and Insider threat briefing – Informs the employee of active threats attempting to gain access to sensitive information and methods used to collect it. The briefing should be tailored to address the immediate threat to classified information stored in a cleared facility as well as knowledge possessed by the cleared employees. The agency threat office, DCSA and CSA can provide valuable training information.

- Defensive security briefing – Provides information to cleared employee travel to other countries. Employees should understand how foreign intelligence services might target them for recruitment or espionage attempts. The State Department, DCSA, FBI and other federal agency threat offices are good resources for training content.

- Overview of the security classification system – Covers the levels of classification, marking, safeguarding and other tasks involved with protecting classified materials.

- Employee reporting obligations – Requires employees to report suspicious contacts, adverse information, security violations and incidents. This briefing equips the cleared employee with what to report and who to report the information to.

- Security procedures and duties applicable to the cleared employee's job – Provides information on details of contracts and how they are as unique as the security programs. New employees should understand the organization specific policies as they apply to their jobs and tasks.

- Counterintelligence Awareness Briefing - Empowers employees to recognize behavior consistent with espionage and who and how to report the observed adverse behavior.

- Cybersecurity awareness training for all authorized system users - Demonstrates requirements for performing on enterprise computer systems with cyber hygiene and reducing cyber risk to the CDC. This includes performing on classified information systems.

When all individuals in the organization understand the security program and all information and tools are in place, the FSO should be able to create, implement and direct successful protection of classified information. Depending on time, resources and availability, organizations should attempt to structure this initial security briefing by experience level. For example, newly cleared employees require more in depth training than veteran security clearance holders recently hired at a defense contractor organization.

All newly cleared and all new cleared employees regardless of experience should receive initial refresher training before gaining access to classified information.

Annual refresher training

In addition to the initial security briefing, the FSO should provide annual refresher training. This training should build upon the initial briefing and the on the job training. The training covers the same topics as the initial security briefing with the addition of any new changes in the NISP since the last training event. Though the requirement is for annual refresher training, the frequency is the minimum standard. A good security program might provide constant training on a recurring basis. Whatever the frequency, the training should be documented to demonstrate each cleared employee's participation.

The changes or additional topics included in the annual refresher training should include updates to security regulations at the national level. These changes occur anytime an executive order is amended, DCSA updates regulations, or any other administrative or procedural updates affecting cleared facilities and employees. Closer to home, the additional subjects could include security requirements of new classified contracts, updated security hardware, software, alarms or procedures impacting the work force. The addition of newly constructed facilities; updated emergency procedures and local security policies and procedures; addition of classified computer processing or any other new classified work introduced to the organization are excellent topics for training [7].

Training should be captured by date, topic and employee name and the information kept on file for DCSA review. The many methods and opportunities are limitless, but some are listed below:

- Briefings
- Presentations
- Computer assisted learning
- Posters, flyers and banner
- Videos/Skits
- Newsletters
- Department updates

Derivative Classifier Training

As mentioned earlier, the government original classification authority makes classification decisions, contractors do not. Contractor personnel make derivative classification decisions when they incorporate, paraphrase, restate, or generate in new form, information that is already classified; then mark the newly developed material consistently with the classification markings that apply to the source information.

This training can help cleared contractors ensure that all personnel who perform duties as derivative classifiers meet the training requirements.

The NISPOM outlines requirements for derivative classification training to include the appropriate application of the derivative classification principles, with an emphasis on avoiding over-classification, at least once every two years. Those without this training are not authorized to perform the tasks.

Insider Threat Briefing

This training program includes the NISPOM identified Insider Threat Training requirements. The NISPOM has identified the following requirements to establish an Insider Threat Program. The program and training should include the following topics:
- Designate an Insider Threat senior official
- Provide an Insider Threat Program / Self-certify the Implementation Plan in writing
- Establish an Insider Threat Program working group
- Provide Insider Threat training
- Monitor classified network activity
- Gather, integrate, and report relevant and credible information; detect insiders posing risk to classified information; and mitigate insider threat risk
- Conduct self-inspections of Insider Threat Program

Exit Briefings

Employees should be made aware that security clearances are only issued when required and are not a right or a permanent status. Though an exit briefing is not part of the initial security briefing, the cleared employees should be aware that they will be given an exit briefings when they no longer require a clearance.

Cleared employees should be thoroughly briefed when they no longer require a clearance. A new job, loss of contract, termination, retirement and removal of access are situations where FSOs should explain the responsibility of continuing to protect the classified information. These employees should understand that they are not authorized to use the classified information they formerly had access to in future jobs, to put in resumes, for books, internet postings, etc. FSOs may be tempted to provide a canned briefing and have the employee sign the SF 312.

The exit briefing can be much more than the minimum required and conducted using information from the DD Form 254, scope of work and other contractual and job specific information to remind the employee of specifically what they had access to and that they can no longer use that information.

Reporting Requirements

Cleared employee reporting obligations should be emphasized in a cleared defense contractor organization. Each cleared employee is responsible for reporting information about themselves and fellow cleared employees that may demonstrate an inability to protect classified information. An example of such information includes illicit drug use, arrests, relations with foreign nationals, debt, foreclosure and other issues [18]. Such reporting is difficult and many may wonder why they should report adverse information on themselves or others. This requirement is found in NISPOM and based on an agreement that cleared employees make when they sign the Nondisclosure Agreement. Additionally, during the periodic review, the investigator may discover the adverse information and inquire into why it hadn't been reported earlier.

Task Oriented Training

Cleared employee training should focus on security procedures as they apply to their job. The cleared employee supervisor should follow initial training with effective security management while on the job. FSOs should provide a reminder of the SF 312 that they have signed and review the procedures for introducing and removing classified material to and from the facilities. The Industrial Security Oversight Office has created an SF 312 briefing agenda for download.

A demonstration of the procedures for working with classified material, equipment and emergency procedures specific to the company helps every cleared employee understand their role. The FSO should give new employees a good overview of the security program and the foundation they need to prepare for the on the job training with their supervisors. Additionally, the cleared employees should attend annual security awareness refresher training. The refresher training covers the topics mentioned above as well as any new changes to the NISP.

Top Secret Control Official Training (TSCO)

Certain topics should be provided during initial security briefings and annual follow up training for those cleared employees with TOP SECRET clearances. After all, the higher certification lends to tougher standards and more accountability. Full and complete training will enhance national security by empowering the holder to protect information appropriately. The key to the training is the spelling out of the TSCO duties and how they support the other cleared employees.

Performing Security Training

All training should be captured by date, topic and employee name and the information kept on file for DCSA review. The many methods and opportunities are limitless, but some are provided below:

Special Briefings

Special programs, COMSEC, couriers, and intelligence are examples of classified work that requires briefings above and beyond the initial security briefing. The briefing should educate the indoctrinated cleared employees of additional security requirements and resources available for the protection of the classified material. Because of the special handling, caveats, inventory, accountability, control and storage requirements, cleared personnel should sign acknowledgement of the additional briefing. Once the additional required briefings are conducted, the cleared persons are permitted access. Such training should be incorporated into the annual security briefing as a refresher of security policy and procedure.

Presentations

The refresher briefing is often presented to large groups and with plenty of subject matter and may occur as a lecture. While providing a large amount of information in one sitting, there may not be much interaction. Therefore presentations are the least effective. If only provided once per year, this effectiveness decreases. However, presenting to large groups is not without benefits. The meeting can be captured on a calendar and scheduled, employees can be trained simultaneously and verification of training for large audiences can easily be captured electronically or on sign-in sheets. When combined with other methods like multimedia, games, interaction and with greater frequency, presentations become more effective and help to increase security awareness and anticipation of additional training.

Computer Assisted Learning

Computers and e-mail offer additional and inexpensive training opportunities. Affordable software provides interactive training in a professional medium. Vendors in many industries also have prepackaged training slides that can be augmented for specific training needs. The multi-media presentations are interactive and very effective. For companies with small budgets, employees with basic computer skills can generate effective slide presentations with software already installed. These presentations can be tracked to provide immediate feedback of completion. The FSO can hyperlink automatic training certificates or e-mail notification at the end of the presentation for accountability and documentation purposes. They can send an updated presentation to the organization's company e-mail list on a recurring basis.

Posters, Flyers And Banners

There are great resources for delivering pinpointed security messages. Companies can brand their security specifically to the organization or mission. Government agencies have websites with downloadable brochures and posters on many topics. FSOs have hosted poster contests where instead of relying on the security department to provide all the talent, cleared employees contribute. Organically produced posters can also use the company brand and carry on the company mission statement by having the security message reflect the organizational goals and values.

Videos/Skits

Informational and dramatic videos are increasing in popularity. Many are available from government agencies while some organizations film speeches and presentations for broadcast to larger audiences. Others feature a rundown of security news and events in the Department of Defense. Mass produced videos offer a free or low cost method to provide alternate refresher security training for cleared employees.

If budget, time and talent permits, well made skits can provide a fun and entertaining message unique to the organization's mission. Using employees' talents and skills to write, act or direct provides a memorable training opportunity. The audience may be more apt to remember the message seeing familiar faces acting out situations depicting security related incidents. This method can be more enlightening than a group briefing or slide presentation. However, time, energy and resources dedicated to rehearsal, performance, cast and props add to overhead costs and lost manpower. A good and thorough return on investment (ROI) should be conducted prior to beginning any training project.

Organizations with a video department have combined live performance with their organic recording capabilities to produce high quality shows. These taped skits or plays require fewer actors and support at any given time than that of live performances. The performance can be recorded as quickly as necessary or spread out over as much time as needed. This flexibility facilitates filming with fewer work interruptions. Skits are written and performed without having large rehearsals or removing the cast from their primary jobs. The performances are made on a small scale, taped, edited and written to DVDs for dissemination or performance at a later date.

Newsletters

Newsletters provide an inexpensive form of education. Government websites, news organizations, and other media provide excellent sources for security articles. Additionally, vendors have subscription based industry specific security newsletters. Newsletters can also be locally written and e-mailed or printed and distributed to the entire organization. FSOs should also analyze national defense, crime and threat trends and statistics to provide real articles that relate directly to the organization's missions. For example, suppose a backlog of security clearance investigations is predicted to increase and the FSO is aware of the company's need to hire new employees for an upcoming contract. Additionally, several employees going through an investigation are eagerly waiting to be awarded a clearance. The FSO can publish the causes of the delays in an informative article and help the organization understand and adapt to the changes.

Caution: Newsletters should never be used as a primary source of communicating important news to management. Approved communication channels should be used to keep executives informed of security issues that will impact the organization's ability to perform classified work.

Department updates

Requests for bid, subcontracts, new contract awards, projects and mission changes affect the work requirements of federal and contractor cleared organizations. During the process of assigning a classified contract, government agencies and prime contractors analyze classified requirements. The analysis determines the type of classified work the contractor is expected to perform, the resources necessary to accomplish the mission, which part of the work is classified and how to protect the classified material from unauthorized disclosure and compromise.

Organic training resources

Defense contractors and subcontractors selected to perform on classified contracts should analyze the security requirements prior to beginning work. Those performing on the classified work receive the contract, DD form 254, security classification guide and interact with the Prime and Government customers. The cleared employees, management and the FSO identify necessary resources to receive, safeguard and perform the classified work. The analysis and dedication of resources and means to execute on classified contracts are intense and necessary form of security awareness training. Tasks associated with receiving and preparing for new classified work can be documented as security awareness training.

Reporting Security Violations

Providing required reports to the authorized persons or agency contributes to reducing the impact of the potential security violation, compromise or suspected compromise. Security incidents can be a minor infraction such as someone forgetting to sign an end of day checklist or as serious as a courier losing classified material. In either possible situation the involved cleared employees should understand to whom and what to report. The sooner the report is issued and the more details given, the more can be done to prevent or mitigate damage to national security.

Cleared employees should be trained to report events affecting the facility security clearance or personnel security clearances. These events include threats to the security of classified information or the fact that classified information has been lost or compromised. All cleared employees should know how to submit reportable information to the FSO. Additionally, FSOs have reporting channels through DCSA and the Federal Bureau of Investigation (FBI).

Reports to the FBI

Defense contractors should report to the FBI when they become aware of any of the following occasions [8]:
- Espionage – Persons attempting to obtain national defense, proprietary or other sensitive information without the appropriate permission or clearance and need to know.
- Sabotage – Persons causing damage, diversion, destruction or other activity resulting in an opponent becoming less effective. Installing computer viruses, manipulating security systems or damaging property are examples of sabotage.

- Terrorism – These are acts to create havoc and shock in order to advance goals of ideology, money, or furtherance of political agendas. Terrorists target persons and groups and gain a psychological advantage through shock and fear. Examples of terrorism and tactics abound from events of September 11, 2001, the bombings in Mumbai, India and across the world as innocent bystanders are targeted with extreme violence.
- Subversion – Acts to overthrow forms of authority. These attempts include unseating a government leader or those who aid, abet or provide relief for those who do. Subversion is exemplified through coups in other countries or through militant and paramilitary groups in the US. These groups work to overthrow the government and either cause chaos or install their own brand of authority.

The FBI is the agency trained and outfitted to address the above threats. Reports and follow-ups concerning the above issues should feed to the FBI. Written follow-ups should be reported to the DCSA with the FBI's approval [8].

Reports to DCSA

DCSA is more able to address other issues impacting a contractor's facility and personnel security clearances. FSOs should train cleared employees to submit information that adversely impacts the ability of a person or facility to protect classified information. More specifically, reports submitted to the CSA are:

Adverse Information

Adverse information indicates that a contractor or federal cleared employee may not be able to protect classified information. Adverse information topics include criteria found in the investigation/ adjudication process. Investigators research information about a subject based on 13 adjudicative criteria [9].

Once the investigation is complete, the results are adjudicated based on the whole person concept. After a clearance is granted, employees are expected to conduct themselves in a manner demonstrating continuous trustworthiness and the ability to safeguard classified material. Any activity demonstrating a violation of any of the 13 criteria could define reportable adverse information. When cleared employees display any characteristics that could imply inability to protect classified material or make them vulnerable to recruitment, they should report that information. When a cleared employee observes such behavior in another employee, they should report that as well.

Suspicious Contacts

This is any attempt by any individual to obtain unauthorized access to classified information and includes coworkers who attempt to gain unauthorized access. It could also include a foreign person attempting to recruit the services of a cleared employee to deliver classified material.

Change In Status

Agencies and contractors should report any changes in status of cleared employees. These reportable changes include: name, marital status, citizenship or termination of employment. Termination of employment involves removal of access until the employee is hired at another location requiring a security clearance. Finally, changes in citizenship and death will require removal of security clearance access and cleared employee records in the DCSA database.

Citizenship By Naturalization

When necessary, Non-U.S. employees can be granted Limited Access Authorization. In the event that these employees become naturalized U.S. Citizens, reports should be forwarded identifying the court and location where the naturalization occurred, the date naturalized, and the certificate number.

Refusal to sign the SF 312

Refusing the sign the SF 312 communicates lack of agreement to protect classified material or lack of training. Cleared employees desiring not to perform on classified work should be reported.

A Change Affecting The Contractor Facility Clearance

The defense contractor is granted a clearance based in part on their ability to safeguard classified information. As part of the procedure the company has demonstrated that it is US owned, conducting business in the US and in good standing. Changes in location, foreign control or influence, changes in key personnel status, and termination of business operations must be reported.

Changes In Storage Capability

Any changes in the storage capability must be reported. These changes include improvements or additions to the security program which raises the protection level or implement changes that deteriorate the protection level.

Inability To Protect Classified Material

Anything preventing a cleared facility from being able to protect classified information should be reported. These events include natural or man made disasters or other emergencies that could erode protection capability such as tornado, earthquake, fire, riot, or power loss. FSOs should also report vulnerabilities of security equipment such as those discovered in intrusion detection systems designed to detect and deter unauthorized access.

Unauthorized Receipt Of Classified Material

Any classified information delivered from the cleared facility to an uncleared facility or person or classified information received without

a contractual relationship should be reported.
Security Through Walking Around

An effective method of training and building rapport with other employees in the organization is to get out from behind a desk and meet them. When FSOs observe their environments they become more effective. While engaging in conversation with cleared employees, observing work habits and listening to issues, the FSO builds relationships and an understanding of how the security program is working.

Security through walking around requires a plan. A well designed and executed plan allows the FSO to enforce the security message as well as become familiar with the names and characteristics of employees, team members and executives. The FSO can simultaneously check on posters, restock pamphlets and security awareness flyers. Meeting employees also allows matching a face with the position and makes the FSO more accessible to the very people depended on to support the security programs.

The FSO should use a prioritized list of milestones that helps measure the program's effectiveness. This list could reveal effectiveness in matters of personnel, physical, IT, privacy, proprietary and, if applicable, classified information security. The FSO should build an agenda before walking through the areas. Understanding the policies in effect and the level of security success are vital to building and maintaining credibility. The FSO should know the organizational regulations and requirements and how they affect the business and team members. Answering policy questions with best guesses or flippant remarks, can contribute to the FSO losing credibility.

The FSO should anticipate feedback. There will be some who praise efforts and there will be some who criticize or question motives. Some may respond negatively to security implementing plans such as limiting access. These objections are perfect opportunities to talk about security concerns such as how access systems and door magnets prevent unwanted and unauthorized visitors while reducing energy costs. Other cleared employees may be upset with having to comply with NISPOM requirements that cause them inconvenience. This is also a great time to demonstrate how they impact the company and the benefits of compliance without quoting regulations. When faced with questions that require research, the FSO should be candid. "I don't know, but I'll get back with you," is a perfect response and the FSO should follow-up immediately.

The FSO should publicly offer praise and kudos to those deserving as soon as possible. FSOs should avoid criticism or wry comments directed toward or about an employee who expresses criticism of a program, has committed violations, or just doesn't understand security. Correcting behavior should be done in a professional manner and in private.

Investigating Security Violations

One of the tougher tasks of a security awareness program is teaching, establishing the reporting procedures and providing an environment where employees want to report activities affecting the cleared facility's or an employee's ability to protect classified material. Getting employees to understand security and report information about themselves or other employees is not easy.

The FSO is also charged with investigating security incidents. Security violations include: forgetting to set a combinations or alarms, losing classified items, receiving unauthorized classified information, transmitting classified material in an unauthorized manner, and etc. Each security incident should be investigated to determine whether or not loss, compromise or suspected compromise occurred. If loss, compromise or suspected compromise takes place, the FSO must notify DCSA [10]. If the incident did not result in loss, compromise or suspected compromise, no report is forwarded, but an internal investigation should be conducted to find root causes and improve security performance.

FSOs should analyze and review all security incidents regardless of severity or impact. Finding root causes can provide basis for improvements in the security system and reduction of vulnerabilities. Additionally, DCSA may ask to review any incidents and reports during the annual security inspection.

Anyone discovering a security violation or incident involving classified information should take positive action to protect the classified information. This protection could take the form of locking an open security container or vault, posting guard or standing by the classified material until relieved. The persons discovering the incident should report it to the FSO as soon as possible.

If an employee finds a security container or vault open or unsecured they should notify the FSO or someone identified as responsible for reacting to such violations. The person should remain in place until an authorized cleared employee relieves them. Next, the authorized cleared employee should perform an inspection of the security container to determine whether or not it has been tampered with. If there is evidence of tampering, the inspecting employee should stop the inspection and call for an authorized expert to determine the extent of the tampering. If there is no evidence of tampering or damage to the container or vault door, an exam of the contents should be conducted to determine whether or not all classified items are where they should be. The combination should be immediately changed to prevent unauthorized persons from having access if the combination has been compromised. If the security container contents include combinations to other security containers then all the affected combinations must be changed.

An FSO should initiate a preliminary inquiry once they become aware of a security violation. This preliminary inquiry is used to determine whether or not loss, compromise or suspected compromise has occurred. The FSO or designated investigator should gather facts surrounding the incident in as much detail as possible to make the final determination. Investigations are best conducted using open ended questions to discover when, where and how the incident occurred, what happened, who was involved and why it happened. The preliminary investigation also records the specific classified items involved, the level of classification and the persons and all details contributing to the violation or incident.

When interviewing witnesses or the person committing the violations, questions are better phrased: "Who else was in the building when you noticed the security container unsecured?" Or "How did you discover the lock was not engaged?" These are better questions requiring detailed answers than the following: "Were you the only one in the building when you discovered the violation?" Or "Was the drawer left open?" Which result in a "yes" or "no" response.

The detailed information provides a picture of how the incident occurred. Contributing factors may include fatigue, rescheduled deadlines, a fire drill, forgetfulness, or internal and external pressures. These factors are not researched to provide an excuse, but can be used to implement process changes, re-training of offending employees or as material for analysis and education. The primary result is to discover whether or not classified information was released, determine what happened and prevent it from happening again.

The FSO should ensure follow-up reports are conducted until all the information is collected and the investigation is concluded. Once the investigation is complete a final report is written to determine loss, compromise or suspected compromise of classified material [10]. The final report includes additional information not found in earlier reports; name of the responsible employees to include records of prior incidents; corrective actions taken against the responsible parties and reasons for reaching the conclusion. When the security violation determines that no loss, compromise or suspected compromise has occurred, the report is complete.

Depending on the severity of the violation, frequency of violations or attitude of the offending employee, graduating degrees of discipline is recommended based on company policy. The investigation should discover whether or not the violation occurred because of employee disregard of security policy, whether or not negligence was involved or whether or not the incident was deliberate. Corrective action should be taken to prevent a recurrence of the violation by the responsible employees and other employees learning from the experience. When a loss or compromise of classified material has occurred, the FSO should forward a report to DCSA.

Summary

The successful FSO should understand the incredible contribution that interaction and education lends to a winning security program. The education should be continuous, informative and increase cleared employee awareness of company policy, how to identify classified information, responsibilities to protect classified information and report required information. This begins with the cleared employee's initial security briefing and continues throughout the lifetime of their security clearance. Those working in the enterprise can be the eyes, ears and muscle extending the effectiveness of the security department.

Problems

1. As an FSO, you have just given a new employee an initial security briefing and you provide a copy of the SF 312. She refuses to sign the agreement. What should you do?

2. Name three types of adverse information and a brief description of why that information should be reported.

3. You are an FSO walking the floor and assessing the state of security in your organization. You are looking at posters, restocking pamphlets and security awareness flyers and developing rapport with employees. You discover a closed area where classified work is performed. You use your badge to scan in and notice that nobody is around. You become alarmed as closed areas must be locked and alarms set when not occupied. You also notice that classified material is in the printer bin. A moment later an engineer enters. His face turns red as he notices you standing there and he sheepishly says, "I just went to the bathroom for a second. Sorry about leaving the door unlocked."

    a. What security violations have just occurred?

    b. What is your next step to address the violations?

4. The receptionist at the front door just calls. He is clearly agitated about the bomb threat he has just received. Luckily he had a cool head and collected some information about the caller and details about the bomb. Who would a defense

contractor organization submit a bomb threat report to?

5. Security awareness training is conducted at least once per year and you maintain good records of those who attended and the subjects areas provided. However, you want to improve the training and add more intervals throughout the year. What are some training methods that you can use to increase the employee's understanding of protecting classified information?

REFERENCES

1. Department of Defense, DoD 5220.22-M, National Industrial Security Operating Manual, section 3-106, February 2016

2. Department of Defense, DoD 5220.22-M, National Industrial Security Operating Manual, section 1-302, February 2016

3. Department of Defense, DoD 5220.22-M, National Industrial Security Operating Manual, section 3-103, February 2016

4. Department of Defense, DoD 5220.22-M, National Industrial Security Operating Manual, section 3-102, February 2016

5. Department of Defense, DoD 5220.22-M, National Industrial Security Operating Manual, section 2-300, February 2016

6. The President, Executive Order 13526, Classified National Security Information—National Industrial Security Program, section 4.1(Federal Register, December 2009)

7. Department of Defense, DoD 5220.22-M, National Industrial Security Operating Manual, section 3-107, February 2016

8. Department of Defense, DoD 5220.22-M, National Industrial Security Operating Manual, section 1-301, February 2016

9. Department of Defense, DoD 5220.22-M, National Industrial Security Operating Manual, section 1-302, February 2016

10. Department of Defense, DoD 5220.22-M, National Industrial Security Operating Manual, section 1-304, February 2016

Helpful Websites

For FSO task descriptions
https://www.dcsa.mil/mc/pv/fso/
NISPOM Training and NISPOM Topics
http://www.redbikepublishing.com
For additional FSO and NIPSOM training
http://www.bennettinstitute.com

CHAPTER 11 INTERNATIONAL OPERATIONS

INTRODUCTION

The United State's economy is increasingly global. Consequently, multinational job opportunities will continue to grow as the US seeks working partners from the international community with more and lower priced resources and services.

The US government benefits from businesses engaged in the international trade and has set goals toward that possibility. Other countries offer additional talent pools, resources and technology. While inviting US industry to compete overseas, the US Government does have regulations and guidance to ensure exports are executed with controlled technology transfer and with mitigated economic and intelligence threat.

Additionally, with companies becoming more global comes the risk of foreign ownership control and influence as discussed in earlier chapters. This chapter addresses what every defense contractor should understand prior to undertaking international business opportunities. Regardless of whether or not classified work is conducted internationally, State Department, Commerce Department, GCA and DCSA rules apply. Conducting classified and defense related business in an international environment requires extreme diligence.

EXPORT LICENSES

Many companies in America produce items for international export. American made products find their way into the markets of various countries demanding US resources, products, services and training. Some of these items are available for export with few limitations or controls. These items do not affect our national defense, technology lead or prevent our technological or economic advances. Details about their production are not protected but readily available in the public domain such as: newsstands, libraries, patent offices, meetings or conferences, or as provided in technical manuals.

However, some US technology contains controlled critical military and dual-use information that cannot be exported without a license or agreement approved by the US Government. A product does not have to be physically shipped to a foreign country to constitute an export. These can occur within the US such as when sharing controlled data through conversation, viewing graphics, reading and any other methods. Exports can occur anytime a non-US person overhears a conversation or views a computer screen or printout containing controlled technical data. This information should be protected from unauthorized disclosure.

Because of the legal, ethical and civil implications associated with responsible exporting, defense contractors have assigned positions or additional duties to employees as Technology Control Officers (TCO), Exports Compliance Officers or similar titles. Employees in these positions are responsible for interpreting the International Traffic in Arms Regulation (ITAR) or the Export Administration Regulation (EAR) as it applies to the organization and the exporting mission. Defense contractors have assigned these positions internally or have hired consultants, trainers, lawyers and other professional organizations available to train and assist with export issues.

Determining Export Jurisdiction

The first step an organization should take when considering export is determining which agency has jurisdiction over the product. Depending on the technology involved, exports can fall under the jurisdiction of the State Department with the ITAR or the Commerce Department with the EAR. Defense articles are under the jurisdiction of State Department and dual use and commercial technologies fall under the Commerce Department. Other agencies exercising exports jurisdiction include the Department of Defense, Treasury, Homeland Security and Energy.

Manufacturers, exporters, and brokers of defense articles, defense services, or related technical data, as defined on the United States Munitions List (USML) (Part 121 of the ITAR) , are required to register with Director of Defense Trade Controls (DDTC). According to the DDTC website, companies desiring to export should consider which jurisdiction their product fall under [1]. If the export is certain to contain protected technology, the company should submit the products to DDTC to undergo a process to determine whether or not they fall under the guidance of ITAR, EAR or regulations of the other agencies. The affected organization is responsible for interpreting the regulations and applying the exports requirements related to their products.

Discovering jurisdiction is not always a clear task. Many jurisdictions blur as civil and military applications are not concrete and in many times overlap. When there is doubt as to whether or not the item applies to the USML, the organization can request a jurisdiction determination through the DDTC and will usually receive response within 65 days [1]. The process is used to discover the nature and function of the product to be exported and whether or not controls have been imposed by other countries. Throughout the process, the product may fall under the DDTC rules until the matter is resolved. Considerations while applying for jurisdiction determination include:

Items to export

The exporter should determine whether or not the article is commercial, dual-use or defense related. This requires a good analysis of the product and how it will be used.

Final Export Destination

The exporter should know where and how the product is to be used all the way to the final destination. If the article is to be exported to a third or fourth country, then the information must be put in the export license requests.

Final Export Customer

Businesses, countries and individuals have been excluded from export opportunities because of embargo actions or other sanctions. The contractor that wishes to export a product should determine whether or not sanctions are in place for the intended customer, organization or country. The Bureau of Industry and Security has such information on their website in the Denied Person's List.

The Intended Purpose Of The Product

How the product is to be used is extremely important in determining jurisdiction. Any product with a strictly military application will most likely go through State Department channels and dual use/commercial items will go through Commerce Department channels. There are other departments such as Transportation and Treasury that may be involved in the jurisdiction action.

Other Activities The Customer Is Involved In

Political activities, other types of business or other known practices are also important when considering jurisdiction. Exporting technical data to questionable entities could negatively affect national security.

State Department Jurisdiction

Defense Articles are made, designed, produced or modified exclusively for military purposes and do not have a predominant civil application. Organizations that export defense articles, defense services or broker sales are required to register with the DDTC. For example, a company making military weapons and demonstrates to others how to use the weapon system or provides the sale of such weapons systems is required to register [1]. One key component of the ITAR is the USML providing 21 categories of weapons, platforms and vessels falling under the control of exports[2]. A defense contractor providing goods or services should review the USML to discover how their product

applies. Find out more about State Department and exports at:
http://pmddtc.state.gov/

Commerce Department Jurisdiction

The Export Administration Regulations (EAR) addresses commercial exports and the Bureau of Industry and Security (BIS) has jurisdiction over commercial and dual use items. Companies falling under the EAR should demonstrate that their products do not impact national security and include dual use items; otherwise, they will fall under the jurisdiction of the State Department. Some items have both commercial and military application, meaning they are made for commercial use but can have military application. The Global Positioning System (GPS) and night vision technology are two examples of dual use technology. On the commercial side, millions of private cars or commercial vehicles benefit from the technology. Just punch in the address and the computer gives the directions. Also, GPS is vital to conducting rescue missions, finding lost hikers or locating aircraft, ships, cars and trucks involved in accidents. The military depends on the capability as sophisticated sensors find exact locations or guide weapon systems and vehicles. Likewise, night vision technology is used extensively in the recreation industry. However, the military also uses the technology to fight at night.

Additionally, the EAR is made up of the Commerce Control List (CCL). This list identifies 10 categories of dual use products, software or technologies that are export controlled. Each of the 10 categories has an Export Control Classification Number (ECCN). The EAR does not apply to items subject to other agencies or are otherwise available in the public domain (libraries, patent offices, etc). Discover more information about the EAR at:
http://www.access.gpo.gov/bis/index.html.

Plan Ahead

Regardless of jurisdiction, a company should always plan ahead as an export license request can take months to process. For ITAR considerations, licenses and agreements allow the export or temporary import of a defense article or service. Licenses are used for one time exports, technical proposals, certain marketing materials and overseas purchases. The State Department also approves Technical Assistance Agreements (TAA) between US and foreign entities which permit technical services or disclosing technical data. The TAAs are used during ongoing transfers, design assistance, joint ventures and assembly, depot level maintenance and other training and service contracts [3].

Protecting Technology

Those providing defense items or services have the tremendous responsibility of keeping the technology out of the wrong hands. As identified in the ITAR, unauthorized release of technical information can affect the US military's fighting capability. Licenses and agreements provide a checks and balances between the US Government and the US Company desiring to export the technology. The company identifies the technology and application and submits export requests to the State Department. The State Department reviews the application and further researches military application and how the export could affect national defense.

Without such checks and balances, other countries could gain a technological advantage. Consider the GPS and night vision technology. No other nation has the abilities as the US does to operate at all times and in all weather. The US military's technological lead creates the ability to determine, where, when and how to fight. When other nations gain unauthorized technology, they can duplicate US products and either fight like the US military or degrade US military effectiveness.

According to the ITAR, organizations are required to have permission prior to exporting technology to non-US persons [4]. The organization is responsible for understanding the permissions required as well as the exemptions and the documentation necessary to ensure compliance. The ITAR governs defense technology exports and is a broad regulation subject to interpretation by the exporting organization.

An export is simply transferring controlled technology to a foreign person either inside or outside the US. The export or transfer is conducted in many different ways and the following is a list of examples:

- Hand carrying and transferring from a US to a foreign country or person
- Through conversation while conducting tours, briefings or performing conferences
- Performing a service or demonstration
- Reading blueprints, plans using software or other computer media
- Turning over ownership of vehicles, equipment or other items identified on the US Munitions List

Technology refers to specific information one would find necessary to reproduce, develop or use an item and can be classified or unclassified. Also, the technology can be a product such as a model, blueprint, or instruction book. Technology can also be a service, instruction or some type of training.

What is a US Person?

Citizenship designation is defined differently in the ITAR and NISPOM. The ITAR addresses export of items with military application and NISPOM is concerned with protecting classified information. According to the ITAR, the definition of a US person includes those who have applied for citizenship to the US. This includes lawful permanent residents, lawful temporary residents, US citizens and nationals, and US organizations. These US persons may not be citizens, but are still authorized access to technical data without requiring export permissions [5].

NISPOM requirements prevent such US persons from having a security clearance. When access is necessary, a Limited Access Authorization (LAA) may be awarded. US persons can access technology controlled items without a license, but only US citizens with a clearance and need to know can **access classified information** [6].

Technology Transfer

Anytime an employee travels abroad with a computer, they should expect to be liberated from their computer at the host country's customs. They should also expect to have the hard drive duplicated, files read, etc. These are the contingencies for which astute technology control officers, export compliance officers and FSOs plan. Sensitive, and protected technology should not be contained within computer and related media without permissions.

Foreign governments want US Technology and aggressively seek it and defense contractors should make the information very difficult to get. However, they may spend too many resources on actions that don't address the real threat. For example, physical security efforts may focus on fortifying businesses with barriers, alarms, access control, cameras, etc. In reality technology is leaked through careless or malicious employee behavior, cyber attacks or pilfering, or actions taken due to poorly understood responsibilities and security discipline.

Export compliance officers and FSOs should develop a culture within their organizations to prevent unauthorized disclosure of economic, classified or sensitive information. Such practices include destroying sensitive waste properly, locking all desk and cabinets drawers after work, practicing extreme cyber hygiene, putting classified items in a GSA approved container and using access control to keep employees, vendors and non-US persons from accessing unauthorized areas.

Foreign Travel

Some threats an employee can face while abroad are economic and intelligence related. Economic threat is the theft of technology and commerce. The agent may be after formulas, financial gain, etc. Foreign entities may target classified or company sensitive information to gain a competitive edge.

Prior to cleared employee travel, they should be given a defensive security briefing. A defensive security briefing is for cleared employees who travel overseas and may be vulnerable to foreign entity recruiting methods. They could also be tailored for protecting export controlled information and given to all employees who travel abroad. Briefings should be constructed to make the traveler aware of their responsibilities to protect employees, product, customers and those with which they do business.

If employees bring technical data and laptop computers, export controlled information not under license or TAAs should be removed from the computer. Some companies issue special travel computers with only the information needed to conduct business, ensuring the information is authorized by license or agreement with the State or Commerce Department to prevent an exports violation.

Those conducting export operations should ensure that such actions are authorized with a license and or TAA before discussing technical data that falls under exports compliance. Employees should know the boundaries in advance before sharing any technical information with the foreign hosts. Additionally, a sanitized computer provides no threat of export violations or theft of economic or corporate data. An organization's information technology department or equivalent could provide a sanitized computer for the traveler's administrative needs. Travelers should keep technical information close at hand and prevent unauthorized disclosure of anything that could lead to export violations or the release of proprietary data.

When making corporate travel plans, a trigger mechanism should be in place to notify the FSO of an employee's need to travel on international business or pleasure. This includes plans for Canada, Mexico and Caribbean countries. The FSO can then construct a defense briefing for the specific area after researching the area to be traveled. The State Department has a great website which can inform the business and the traveler on all necessary travel documentation and what to expect while abroad.

Classified Information Disclosure

Classified information should be transferred through Government to Government channels [7]. In some situations, exports of technical data related to the agreements may be excluded from ITAR licensing agreements. It's up to the cleared contractor to ensure whether or not exemptions or licenses apply. In the case of exemptions, the contractor must ensure they are made in writing by an Authorized Exemption Official or an Exemption Certifying Official.

In the Government Security Agreement, countries sharing classified material should provide the amount of security required and identified by the owning country. For example, suppose that XYZ Contractor is working on a project and is using information that a foreign country classified as SECRET. The US government is expected to protect it in the same manner as it would protect US SECRET information. Defense contractors are expected to honor the government's agreement.

The Government Security Agreement is not meant to authorize the release of classified information or guarantee that it is transferred. It is created to identify protection measures and limit the use if it is transferred. The NISPOM requires these security agreements to be in place prior to the transfer.

In the agreement, one government agrees to provide the classified material and instructions on marking and safeguarding it and the receiving Government agrees to protect it according to the classification markings. The governments also agree to limit the use of classified products and information to what is necessary and efficient. The governments are limited with whom they can share the classified material and who has rights to the proprietary data [7].

When Classified Transfer is Authorized

Contractors do not authorize the transfer of classified material but can provide it as allowed by the US government. Classified and unclassified technical transfers should be provided by license, and use of foreign classified information, and through government to government transfer. When a defense contractor works on a contract involving foreign government classified information, the US Government agency provides an Industrial Security Agreement in an Annex of the General Security Agreement [7].

Contractors should transfer classified information only after approved by the US government. There are several ways that it can be transferred to foreign persons or released to foreign countries. The GCA provides classified information and the State Department provides the authorization. Unless exemptions apply, the authorization is granted through licensing, TAAs, and other means of permission including exemptions. Once permission is granted, the transfer can take place.

DCSA is responsible for ensuring that the contractor is providing the right level of protection, releasing it in an approved manner, and accounting for the process with the correct receipting methods. Once agreements and permissions are received, the defense contractor can release information. Unless exempted, the transfer should be executed with licenses and agreements through the State Department with input from the GCA and oversight of DCSA.

The contractor can then move appropriately to provide contractually identified classified information. Aside from government to government agreements, other methods of transfer include, but are not limited to the following venues:

- Approved classified gatherings
- Foreign visits
- Temporary exports during demonstrations
- Commercial agreements

Approved classified gatherings

The government agency owning the contract information approves meetings, conferences, seminars, exhibitions, etc where the classified information will be disclosed. The foreign visitors should be appropriately cleared, have a need to know and are approved to receive it. The defense contractors involved in these events are allowed to provide it at the direction of the agency, when licenses are provided the State Department and under the oversight of DCSA.

When the defense contractor provides classified information based on a contract, they should forward a copy of the contract and the security provisions set in place to DCSA. Additionally, the cleared contractor should maintain records identifying the source.

Visits by Non-US Persons

The defense contractor is permitted to only disclose classified and other technical information as provided by terms of licenses and agreements unless exempted. The affected contractors should make every effort to prevent foreign persons from gaining access to any other contract, technical or classified information not identified in the agreements and permissions. Some measures include locking classified information in a security container and technical or export controlled information in desks or cabinets when not attended, using access control, and segregating work areas from foreign persons. Prior to a foreign person having access to classified information, the contractor should provide a DCSA approved technology control plan (TCP) [8]. The TCP is a document demonstrating how the foreign person will be accommodated while being denied access to unauthorized information.

Temporary Exports

In the event classified material is exported to a foreign country for demonstration purposes, permission may be granted based on a temporary export. When a temporary export license is used, the classified information should remain under the complete control of the US person. Prior to gaining approval, the request should describe the nature of the demonstration, the items used during the demonstration, and how the items will be protected and stored under US government control. For example, a US person travels overseas on an approved display of a classified weapon system. While there, she will provide a live fire demonstration how the weapon performs. When the demonstration is complete, she will store the weapon at an approved location such as the US Embassy or US military facility.

Commercial Arrangements

There may be times or opportunities when a contractor can supply a classified product to a foreign country through commercial sales. These commercial sales are possible in support of a contract, international agreement or procurement requirement. However, before pursuing a foreign commercial sales opportunity, the contractor must coordinate with the GCA. Also, the defense contractor may need to obtain export permissions prior to engaging in dialog with a foreign representative that could lead to a contract.

Subcontracting

Contractors that enter into agreement to subcontract a classified work to a foreign country can only do so with approval from the government agency owning the classified information, the State Department and with coordination with the CSA. These permissions are the same as with unclassified exports authorizations; using TAAs, manufacturing licenses or some direct sales [9]. The contractor should provide contract security classification specifications (DD Form 254) as with subcontracting with a US organization. The contractor ensures that the export is permitted, the owning agency approves the transfer and DCSA has records of the transfer and an understanding of how it is to be protected and the transfer documented.

The defense contractor should maintain accountability of classified information transferred to foreign organizations and record which agency originated it. Additionally, the contractor should provide detailed security specifications and the foreign entity should agree to only use it as written in the contract. The US government owns and controls the classified information and approves the export. The foreign organization should only release, subcontract, or otherwise turn it over to a third party or foreign entity upon approved request or as directed by the contract. The foreign government should also re-mark it with their own equivalent markings. This includes any classified information generated as required in the contract.

The foreign government should agree to report all loss and compromise of US classified information if it occurs. They also should agree to return everything upon termination of the contract. All of these provisions should be provided with detailed contract language in the contract and DD Form 254.

International Transfer

International transfer of classified information should be conducted as agreed upon by all countries involved. This level of protection begins with removing the classified item from US accountability and continues through the transportation and hand-off process. Written agreements are required per NISPOM prior to any transfer. For commercial endeavors, the cleared contractor is required to write the agreement. For Government actions, the GCA is required to provide the agreement and copies to the CDC.

DCSA plays a big role as they advise the contractor on the action as well as approves the written agreements whether provided by the contractor or the GCA. DCSA appoints the US Designated Government Representative (DGR) as well as identifies the foreign DGR. They also ensure that transportation plan is adequate to protect it.

A written transportation plan is required for all classified transfers and the GCA provides the plan in support of a government action. They then provide the plans to the cleared contractor and DCSA. The cleared contractor writes transportation plans for commercial actions and DCSA approves them. Prior to any transfer, the cleared contractor should ensure a DSP-83 Non Transfer and Use Certificate is completed.

Hand Carry

A GCA can authorize a US contractor cleared employee to hand carry classified information to a foreign government representative [10]. The contractor is authorized to transfer only items marked at the SECRET level and below. The size and shape of the items should be in the courier's complete control at all times. Carrying packages too large or bulky could cause the courier to lose control of or become separated from the classified package and should be avoided. The cleared contractor should give DCSA a five working day notice prior to transferring it. DCSA should ensure that a good plan is in place. This plan includes checking that the GCA has provided written guidance for any contract or agreements with foreign governments. DCSA also makes sure that the contractor is coordinating with the transportation security administration, foreign security agencies and customs officials for the smooth transition and any other arrangements.

Prior to departing, the cleared contractor employee should be briefed, sign a one time use courier certificate and prepare a wrapped package [10]. Additionally, the classified information should be inspected by a government representative and three receipts printed. Deliveries should be double wrapped, marked and addressed. The contractor should also provide 24 hour notice to the recipient that the items will be sent. The FSO should begin a tracking system to ensure they receive documentation of the arrival. This begins when they receive a signed receipt when the courier accepts the package, and ends with a receipt when the package reaches its destination. If the FSO does not receive a final receipt within 45 days, they should notify DCSA.

While on the journey, the courier should never relinquish control during transport, layovers, and meals or at any other time. Upon arrival in the foreign country every effort should be made to ensure the classified package is not opened or inspected. However, if an inspection cannot be prevented the courier requests a written and signed explanation of such action signed by the government official. They should then report the incident to their FSO [10]. The FSO will notify the GCA and DCSA with details of the compromise included whether or not the government officials inspecting the items were from the country to which the materials are being transferred.

Though a customs officer may require an inspection, the courier should never release the package to their ultimate control. A customs search of classified material may be inevitable, but control should not be relinquished. The classified information should be turned over only to the designated foreign government representative identified on the receipts. The security manager ensures that the courier retains receipts anytime the classified material is transferred to another entity while in transit and at the final destination. Typically, the receiving government representative will inspect the classified package, compare contents with the receipt and sign a receipt for the courier.

Commercial Transfer

Prior to transferring classified information on a commercial contract, the US contractor organization should prepare a transportation plan [11]. This plan should identify how it will be transported, the names of government representatives, and identified escorts. The plan should also provide information describing how the shipment will be protected from unauthorized access throughout the journey. The plan should be turned over to DCSA for review and approval then delivered to the foreign government for review and their security implementation.

Foreign Government Information (FGI)

A US contractor also has the opportunity to receive classified information when entering into a contract with a foreign organization. When a US contractor enters into agreements with a foreign organization to receive deliveries, the CSA assumes oversight responsibility [12]. The CSA will review the contract and work with the defense contractor to provide the correct protective measures of the foreign government information. Then they evaluate the contractor's ability to protect the classified information.

As with a US contract, the foreign entity should describe the classified information, classification level, markings, and how to protect it in their contract security classification specification. When such information is not provided, the contractor can report it to DCSA for a solution or documentation. Once the contractor receives the classified material and instructions, they assume the responsibility of protecting it at the correct level. Therefore, instructions should be understood both by both DCSA and the contractor [12].

The FSO should bring the FGI into the information management system. The accountability process includes inspecting the packages, signing the receipts, documenting and bringing the classified information into the inventory log, and either maintain the original markings or re-mark the classification markings with US equivalent markings. Either is fine as long as everyone working with the classified material understands the level to store and safeguard the information. However, the front and back cover should be marked appropriately with the overall US classification and the country of origin. The markings should either be annotated: "THIS DOCUMENT CONTAINS (NAME OF COUNTRY) INFORMATION" when the originating country agrees to be identified. When the originating country is concealed the marking is: "THIS DOCUMENT CONTAINS FOREIGN GOVERNMENT INFORMATION" Additionally, when the defense contractor provides classified information to a foreign government, they should ensure that they are marked with "THIS DOCUMENT CONTAINS UNITED STATES CLASSIFIED INFORMATION". [12].

The document is then ready for storage. The contractor should protect the document at the highest level indicated in the classification marking and as described in the agreed upon classification specification. The foreign government classified items should be stored in a manner that prevents getting them mixed up with US classified information [13]. This can be done with using separate drawers of a security container or separate shelves or rooms when open storage is authorized.

Depending on the contract, classified information could easily be generated or documents could be created with derivative information. Documents should be marked to identify that they contain FGI as well as where the information originated if derived. The contractor can only use the classified items as specified in the contract. If the contractor desires to use the information in any other manner than specified, they should get approval. Contracts with third parties or other foreign entities involving the foreign country information should be requested through the GCA and DCSA. If the classified information or other technical items or services are approved for export, State Department authorization is required.

The FGI and all derivative classified information stored in US contractor facilities should be treated as US owned classified material. When moving foreign government classified information out of the facility, the security manager should transfer it using the same approved methods as apply to US classified information. For example, duplicating TOP SECRET information requires written permission from the originating government [14]. Finally, all security incidents, unauthorized disclosure, compromise and suspected compromise of foreign government classified information should be investigated and reported to DCSA immediately.

Classified Visits

In the course of business, it is not unusual for a foreign entity to request a visit to a US company. Foreign business employees may desire to visit a US contractor in furtherance of a contract. When the business is related to a classified contract, involves classified information or relates to a government to government agreed upon plant visit, the foreign entity requests the visit through their embassy. Unclassified visit requests should be sent through commercial channels and are executed through licenses with the State Department or the Commerce Department.

According to NISPOM, Government approved visits constitute an ITAR exemption. However, the cleared contractor should understand exactly what is to be released and exactly how. It is the defense contractor's responsibility to determine what constitutes the exemption and what release requires a license. The cleared contractor should maintain records of the foreign visit involving the release of classified information for one year. However, where visits are covered by ITAR licensees or agreements, records should be kept for three years.

Visit requests submitted by a foreign entity pass through their government channels to the US government for approval (Figure 11-3) [15]. The US government agency having jurisdiction over the classified contract submits the request to the US contractor for their approval. The request also includes guidance and limitations of the information and items the foreign national will be allowed to access. The contractor should review the limitations and determine whether or not they concur with the request and has the final say of whether or not the foreign national will access their facility.

For example, Country A has a contractual relationship with XYZ Contractor through the US government. Country A is able to produce sensitive electronics for a missile guidance system that XYZ Contractor is contracted to perform on. Country A draws up a visit request and submits it to their embassy for routing to the US Government channels. The US Government reviews the request and decides whether or not to grant the visit. The US Government can deny the visit, and if so, will notify the government representatives of the requesting foreign entity. If the US Government approves the request, they should provide details and access requirements specifically for Country A's visit to XYZ Contractor.

Continuing the scenario, XYZ Contractor receives the request. The program manager for the project calls a meeting with team players and includes representatives from key business units. The FSO, program manager and the contracts manager review the request. The foreign national from Country A is to be given access to only classified information related to the guidance system as contracted with the US Government. Access to other items is not authorized and XYZ Contractor should ensure that the foreign person is prevented from accessing unclassified information related to other contracts.

The FSO explains the use of the Technology Control Plan (TCP) as the required tool to prevent the visitor from seeing classified information. The advantages of the TCP includes protection of other sensitive, proprietary or privileged information in the form of blueprints, slide shows, memorandums, and classified material in conversations, computer screens or other sources. When a contractor accepts an international visit request, they assume the responsibility to protect national secrets, the company's technology and all export controlled items. The TCP controls the movement of the foreign national within the facility.

A TCP is a valuable tool written by the contractor and approved by DCSA. The contents of the TCP should be enough to ensure every employee participating in the visit understands their role in protecting the information. Additionally, the foreign person should also be alerted to their duties to protect the information as well as their responsibilities not to attempt to gain access to unauthorized information. Both employees and the foreign visitors should sign the

---

International Classified Contract Visit Request Process

1. Foreign Entity Submits Visit Request to Their Government
2. Foreign Government Submits Request to U.S. Government
3. Pentagon (Foreign Visit Section) Determines Approval
4. Pentagon Notifies Contractor of Request and Approval
5. Contractor Determines Whether or Not to Accept Request

Figure 11-3 Visit request process

---

agreements of understanding.

SUMMARY

As part of the global market, US owned technology, defense articles, and commercial items can be exported with licenses and agreements. The State Department controls the export of defense articles and services, while Commerce Department governs articles with civil or dual-use application. It is up to the defense contractor or business entity to determine the jurisdiction of an item to be exported. When jurisdiction is not easily determined, they can submit a request for determination.

Classified information can be exported to another country based on a Government to Government agreement. A defense contractor should only export classified information when approved by the GCA or other US Government entity. Defense contractors may be required to store FGI information on site. If so, they should protect it at the same US equivalent level.

PROBLEMS

1. The vice president of business development has just brought up the wonderful opportunity of selling an all weather capability the company produces for medical evacuation flights to a foreign owned company.

    a. Suppose this item needs a license prior to export. Describe the first step an organization would take in consideration of a possible export.

    b. If the item is to be delivered to a foreign company just down the street, will export requirements still apply?

2. You are travelling as an authorized courier to deliver a package that contains classified information at the CONFIDENTIAL level. Upon arrival, the foreign government customs agent wants to take custody of the package. You present your credentials and attempt to talk her out of the idea. She informs you that as a representative of the foreign government, she is authorized to accept the delivery. Is she correct? Why or why not?

3. As an FSO, you have many responsibilities including approving classified visits. A program manager enters your office and informs you that his foreign customer wants to send an employee to perform at your location on a classified project. The program manager requests that you draw up a sample visit request form that the foreign company can use to submit a visit request. Is this the proper request procedure? Why or why not?

4. In the same situation as question three, the visit has been authorized through appropriate channels. Since your cleared facility handles many classified contracts, you want to ensure the visitor does not gain access to classified and unclassified items not authorized for export. What will you produce to ensure the visitor and company employees remain in compliance with export laws?

5. Which agency has jurisdiction over commercial and dual-use items?

6. Which regulation covers commercial and dual-use items?

7. Which regulation governs the export of defense articles?

8. Your organization has an opportunity to perform a modification of a foreign government weapons platform. You will not be selling an item, but modifying the platform for a radio mount. If awarded the contract, your company will send a team to the foreign country to perform the services over the next few years. What type of request will you submit? Who is the approving agency?

References

1. Guidelines For Preparing Commodity Jurisdiction (CJ) Requests, DDTC Response Team, Downloaded Jan 2010, http://www.pmddtc.state.gov/commodity_jurisdiction/documents/cj_guidelines.pdf

2. International Traffic In Arms Regulation, 22 C.F.R Chapter I, Subchapter M Parts 120-130, Part 121.1, http://pmddtc.state.gov

3. International Traffic In Arms Regulation, 22 C.F.R Chapter I, Subchapter M Parts 120-130, Part 120.22, http://pmddtc.state.gov,

4. International Traffic In Arms Regulation, 22 C.F.R Chapter I, Subchapter M Parts 120-130, Part 120.1, http://www.redbikepublishing.com/book/itar/

5. International Traffic In Arms Regulation, 22 C.F.R Chapter I, Subchapter M Parts 120-130, Part 120.15, http://pmddtc.state.gov

6. Department of Defense, DoD 5220.22-M, National Industrial Security Operating Manual, section 2-209, February 2016

7. Department of Defense, DoD 5220.22-M, National Industrial Security Operating Manual, section 10-200, February 2016

8. Department of Defense, DoD 5220.22-M, National Industrial Security Operating Manual, section 10-508, February 2016

9. Department of Defense, DoD 5220.22-M, National Industrial Security Operating Manual, section 10-202, February 2016

10. Department of Defense, DoD 5220.22-M, National Industrial Security Operating Manual, section 10-405, February 2016

11. Department of Defense, DoD 5220.22-M, National Industrial Security Operating Manual, section 10-402, February 2016
12. Department of Defense, DoD 5220.22-M, National Industrial Security Operating Manual, section 10-300, February 2016
13. Department of Defense, DoD 5220.22-M, National Industrial Security Operating Manual, section 10-306, February 2016
14. Department of Defense, DoD 5220.22-M, National Industrial Security Operating Manual, section 10-309, February 2016
15. Department of Defense, DoD 5220.22-M, National Industrial Security Operating Manual, section 10-507, February 2016

Helpful Websites

Denied Person's List
http://www.bis.doc.gov/dpl/default.shtm

Directorate of Defense Trade Controls
http://www.pmddtc.state.gov/index.html

EAR
http://www.access.gpo.gov/bis/index.html

ITAR
http://www.pmddtc.state.gov/index.html

State Department
http://www.state.gov

Print ITAR and NISPOM
http://www.redbikepublishing.com

CHAPTER 12 PUTTING IT ALL TOGETHER

INTRODUCTION

This chapter concludes the book by helping the reader apply all the information provided in earlier chapters. They keys to successful performance lie in those providing goods and services for the classified contract. To better position security for influence and effectiveness, FSOs should understand the NISPOM, the cleared contractor's business and the cleared employees' abilities.

The FSO's ability to understand the nature of their business as it relates to the organization, separates a professional from a technician. This chapter provides information on the skill set the FSO should possess to gain credibility within their organizations. Understanding how security fits into the organizational scheme helps the FSO better implement the security program.

FSO QUALITIES

The defense contractor's cleared senior official should understand the importance of appointing the appropriate employee as FSO. In many circumstances defense contractors become aware of the requirement of the FSO appointment upon receiving a classified contract or at some point during the process. The NISPOM directs that the appointed FSO only meet two requirements, US Citizenship and a security clearance as part of the FCL [1]. However, unless the most senior officer in the cleared facility appreciates the impact of a qualified FSO, they might appoint an employee based on administrative skill and not their ability to influence a good security program. Miscalculating the role of an FSO as only an administrative position could result in appointing the person with the wrong skill set, leading to a weak and ineffective security program.

There are approximately 12,000 cleared facilities with just as many appointed FSOs. Though there are large companies with tens of thousands of employees and a mature culture, many are small enterprises with less than 50 employees. In some cases employees are appointed as FSO in addition to their primary job. This works fine when the position is held by someone who is used to the challenges of leadership. They are able to influence the culture by pushing the security culture from the top down. Where an influential, cleared management employee is appointed as FSO, the rest of the organization suddenly becomes interested in following security procedure. The opposite results arise from the appointment of a cleared employee with limited influence. The cleared contractor should be aware of the implied tasks involved with running a compliance unit.

Appointing The Wrong FSO

A lower level employee appointed as FSO may be fine when the contractor is a small organization, there are few employees and the environment is informal. However, the FSO's effectiveness may deteriorate as the company grows, more executives and managers are hired and additional business units are developed. Companies that have grown in this scenario have increased the FSO job requirements and the position has outgrown the current FSO's skill level. This could make communicating security and compliance issues challenging.

The FSOs in the above situation are technically proficient and understand their jobs very well. However, they may not possess the skills to develop healthy business relationships and communicate with other managers. This may leave them ineffective as compliance officers. Additionally, the organization charts may show the FSOs reporting to managers in non-program business units that do not understand contracting or how to manage a security program. These managers could be in overhead business units such as: safety, accounting, contracting or other administrative position several levels away from program managers and engineers the FSOs should be focused on. The FSOs could end up assigned to overhead divisions and away from those performing classified work. This could present a problem for the company as the FSO might have to address security issues through several filters before finally getting the message to the executive level.

Management should work with the FSO to keep the company in a position to maintain the facility and employee personnel security clearances. An ineffective FSO or one who is out of the decision making loop may fail in their responsibilities. Expectations for good security programs become unrealistic in this scenario as the FSOs have no input for planning or execution. Being outside of the circle of influence or decision making, the FSOs often play catch up when the company wins new contracts with increasing or new security requirements. The organization's senior officer should take into account the compliance issues of exporting technology, protecting classified information, seeking new classified contracts, maintaining an effective security environment, and the enterprise's growth potential prior to writing a job description for the appointed FSO.

Appointing the Right FSO

Primarily, the FSO should understand how to protect classified information as it relates to the cleared contract, organizational growth, enterprise goals, and NISPOM guidance. The FSO should be able to conduct a risk analysis, express the cost, benefits and impact of supporting a classified contract under the NISPOM requirements and sustain an environment of cooperation and compliance within the enterprise. Finally, they must be able to influence and compel the senior leaders to make good decisions, support compliance and integrate security into the corporate culture. After all, security violations not only cause damage to national security, but could also impact the organization with loss of contracts. The FSO is pivotal to the successful execution of classified contracts.

Large CDCs

In larger cleared contractor organizations the FSO is most likely a full time commitment held by a department manager or higher level employee. This FSO is supported by a staff of security specialists who may manage classified contract administration, safeguarding classified documents, process classified information on information systems, security clearances and other disciplines. The FSO oversees the entire security program as executed by the competent staff. In a best case scenario, they will report to the senior officer of the organization.

Small CDCs

In small businesses, the FSO may be the owner, chief officer, vice president or other senior leader picking up an additional responsibility. This is more of a situation of selecting the most knowledgeable, capable and competent cleared employee. However, the FSOs are already very busy trying to meet cost, scheduling and performance objectives. They may be able to implement and direct a security program to protect classified information, but not the day to day job functions that can pull them away from critical tasks. Jobs such as document control, visit authorization requests, security clearance requests, etc can be delegated to other competent, organized and more flexible employees.

As the small enterprise grows, more and more experienced FSOs are beginning to understand a growing company's needs and have returned to college finish their education. Colleges and universities are now offering a variety of security and management degrees perfect for meeting the growing FSO education requirements. Professional organizations also offer security certifications. Consequently, the pool of experienced and educated FSOs is growing. Cleared defense contractor executives should clearly consider the FSO job description and list the exact qualifications desired before posting the position as a job announcement.

FSOs should understand more than just the technical aspects of administering a security program. Understanding how to mark, safeguard and disseminate classified information is important. However, the FSO should reach beyond the description of implementing a security program to safeguard classified material. The position also requires assessing risks to the classified material, interpreting safeguarding requirements, communicating and incorporating a culture of compliance within the organization, and projecting the impact of classified contracts on the enterprise. To do this, the FSO should possess the vision and skills to see where the security program needs to go, how to get there and encourage a security vision from the senior executive level downward. Without the right kind of influence, the FSO is may not be able to run a program to protect classified material.

Corporate Culture

How do effective FSOs and security managers develop a culture of compliance with regulations and security programs? Quoting regulations only exasperates cleared employees and the very act does little to foster a climate of cooperation. However, developing relationships based on a good understanding of business, the company mission and influence goes a long way toward implement the successful security program.

The corporate culture of successful organizations is published organization wide and employees are well versed. Each employee should understand how they fit into the company mission and the importance of their contribution toward the enterprise's success. Though employees and business units have separate functions, they work toward the common goal of producing a product or service. Though each office has a different product, funding or budget item, each fulfills their obligation in a chain of responsibilities necessary to get the product to market. When a business unit breaks down or fails to fulfill its mission, other business units are affected. For example, if buyers do not order from suppliers, products cannot be assembled. If the human resources department does not enforce ethics rules, morale could plummet.

In the same manner, the FSO performs a vital mission of protecting classified information. Failure to safeguard classified material could result in a defense contractor losing the facility clearance and ultimately cost current and future contracts. Just as hourly workers are continuously training on performing in compliance with safety and human resources policies, security awareness should also be part of the culture. Security as an afterthought or viewed as a "necessary evil" has contributed to a loss in influence and commitment.

Though the NISPOM applies to classified projects, FSOs would be mistaken to assume that only cleared persons and cleared programs are worthy of their attention. Such philosophy dismisses the potential of all other employees and business units to assist in protecting classified information and thus frustrates the entire security effort. FSOs that ensure only cleared employees attend security awareness training miss out on the opportunity to include many others as "force multipliers" assisting in the security effort. For example, uncleared employees can help protect classified information by learning to recognize classification markings and reporting suspicious behavior or contacts.

Metrics

What is the value of security to the corporation? Security managers often work from overhead budgets. Since many security departments do not generate income, the managers have to effectively demonstrate value added programs. Security managers use metrics to effectively demonstrate how programs, security measures and functions provide a return on investment or added value.

Metrics are tools leaders use to assess the effectiveness of their programs. These metrics indicate success, failures or areas where significant improvement is needed. Metrics data is found in surveys, inspections, and reports and are used for the specific purpose of understanding how effective the program is. The other part is to understand security goals and comparing them to the results.

FSOs should make metrics development and execution a top priority. Chief security officers, chief information officers and other executive level security managers understand how to read metrics and use them to focus with pinpoint intensity on directing their programs within their companies. Security managers in lower positions can use the same skills to gain influence. Because of the nature of compliance with government regulations, the task may be easier for FSOs to accomplish.

An FSO has readily available data to determine and communicate the effectiveness of the security program. Gathering available information, creating a detailed database and performing solid analysis will help determine the program's success. Whether or not a security program is where it needs to be can be determined from information found in the following actions:

- Incidents, infractions, violations reports with compromise or suspected compromise
- Annual DCSA reviews
- Annual self-inspections
- Professional and organizational certification
- Self-reporting statistics
- Security Awareness Training
- Security budget
- Contractual requirements

The above list is not all inclusive, but contains readily available information directly affected by security or influences security decisions.

Incidents, infractions, violations and reports of compromise or suspected compromise as Metrics

These reports should be made at each occurrence and analyzed regularly. Reports indicating that compromise or suspected compromise has occurred should be forwarded to DCSA. Many other reports of minor consequences are not required to be sent outside of the organization, but are extremely helpful as indicators of the organization's security health.

Incidents, infractions and violations reports indicate lapses in judgment or worse, malicious behavior of those with access to classified information. An incident or infraction occurs when a cleared employee violates a NISPOM requirement, but no loss, compromise or suspected compromise occurs. For example, a cleared employee could lock all the security containers, but forget to fill out the end of the day checklist. Though no classified information has been compromised, they did not follow procedures based on a requirement during the end of day checks. Unless eliminated, such bad practices can contribute to more serious violations. As an example, violations occur when someone forgets to spin the combination on a security container dial. A suspected or actual compromise occurs when the investigation determines that an unauthorized person gained access to classified information.

Only security violations resulting in loss, compromise or suspected compromise are reported to the DCSA. However, even minor incidents should be investigated and documented. For example, the seemingly small infraction of forgetting to fill out the end of day security checklist could either indicate forgetfulness or a disregard of security procedures. The root cause should be investigated and the culprit warned and/or disciplined according to corporate policy.

Consider an earlier example where an FSO received notification that the administrative security container with all combinations had been left open. The FSO had been notified of an after hours security violation. She arrived on scene and interviewed the person who had called her, inventoried the contents and inspected the security container for evidence of tamper. The next day she began an investigation to determine exactly what had happened.

Results of an investigation vary depending on the situation. In the best case, the FSO conducts an investigation and determines that the security container had been left open for an hour and that nobody had access the building since. A far worse a scenario would involve conducting an inventory confirming a missing classified document. In that case an in-depth investigation to determine loss, compromise and suspected compromise would have to be conducted.

In our best case scenario, the FSO could conclude that it is a non reportable security incident. The container had been left open but no unauthorized persons had access to the container. The FSO could use the findings in the investigation to retrain the person who had not closed and locked the security containers. She could also use the information for security awareness and use it to train others in the organization on the correct procedures. She could also store the report and add information to a database to draw on it later for comparative analysis.

But what if such incidents and infractions had never been recorded? Relaxed security procedures could result in multiple incidents leading to a complicated situation of unauthorized disclosure. In such cases the report would be forwarded to DCSA. The investigation would find information revealing that such incidents had occurred frequently. The FSO may be left with concluding that the incident could have been prevented had the situation been addressed earlier. In the worst case scenario, the investigator is left to determine whether or not the relaxed security environment contributed to the security violation and suspected compromise.

Infraction, incident and violation data can be used to pinpoint security issues in specific business units or locations. For example, suppose a cleared contractor has a building dedicated to research and development and another building dedicated to modeling and simulations. The simulations operations are conducted in a closed area that allows classified work to be conducted during business hours, but it must be locked away in a security container after hours. The last person leaving the computer lab is responsible for locking the vault door and setting the alarm. The research and development area is full of cleared employees who work on large vehicles. Their labs are also closed areas and they spend most of their time assembling and testing the vehicles.

The FSO in the above scenario makes a habit of evaluating compiled security incident reports regularly, perhaps every quarter. They would never let a known incident go without investigation regardless of severity. The written reports would document a history of employees in the research and development lab leaving classified material on the printer. The FSO pulls the collected data and notices that twice in the quarter the security container drawer had been left unlocked. The FSO continues her search into root cause and notices that this is nothing new, but incidents seemed to have occurred less frequently since she had taken the job just a year earlier.

However, the research and development lab has had far fewer incidents. The nature of their business only requires mechanical work.

There is no paperwork involved other than a few classified technical manuals that they receive from the document control office and return at the end of the day. Though they have always locked the doors, the cleared employees have forgotten on several occasions to set the alarms. The FSO notices the pattern and discovers that though a root cause had been discovered during earlier investigations, the former FSO had not addressed. Then, armed with data, she is ready to compile the information into reports, graphs, training aids and other media to train the cleared employees and implement security policy.

Annual DCSA Reviews as Metrics

DCSA is responsible for determining the frequency of reviews. Inspections are typically conducted every 12 months for possessing and 18 months for non possessing facilities, but circumstances can require more or less frequent visits [2]. DCSA inspects the facility's security program for the primary purposes of ensuring classified information is protected. Additionally, the review programs are designed to improve the effectiveness of the contractor's security program. At the conclusion, the contractor is given a rating ranging from unsatisfactory to superior:

- Unsatisfactory-Indicates that the contractor has lost or is in the process of losing their ability to protect classified material. The GCA's are notified and the contractor is re-inspected to measure whether or not they have met requirements of corrective actions.
- Marginal-Indicates that a contractor is not meeting the requirements of NISPOM and has a substandard security program. The contractor will have another review to ensure they have performed required corrective actions.
- Satisfactory-Indicates that the company is generally in compliance with the NISPOM.
- Commendable-Indicates that a cleared contractors runs a successful security program and enjoys the support of management.

- Superior-Indicates consistently high security posture and minimum amount of findings or security issues. This rating is awarded to the cleared contractors demonstrating an excellent security program with complete support from management

Prior to each inspection, the FSO and cleared contractor leadership should present DCSA with a state of security briefing to introduce and go over the company security policy. Similarly, the DCSA special agent may provide an out-briefing detailing the results of the review. This out-briefing and soon to follow documentation of the inspection provides further data toward building an excellent security program.

Annual Self-Inspections As Metrics

The self-inspections offer other exceptional opportunities for FSOs to improve the security program as well as measure improvement from the previous DCSA annual audit. The self-inspection affords the opportunity to look into procedures, review documentation, and incidents, and conduct classified holding inventories. They should be conducted midway between the annual reviews and helps keep the security team focused on improvement and compliance.

Additionally, the DCSA website provides a self-inspection checklist booklet that FSOs can use to conduct their self-inspections. The self-inspection and annual review results help the defense contractor view their security program with the intent of identifying good procedures to sustain and others to improve upon. They should be conducted by anyone knowledgeable of the security program. The FSO does not necessarily need to conduct the review, but should support the self-inspection fully and the findings completely. The self-inspection can also be a team effort between employees who report to the security manager. It is not only a tool for team improvement, but also benefits the inspector with experience they may not otherwise be able to gain since it covers all areas of managing classified information, facility and personnel clearances.

Professional and Organizational Certification as Metrics

Outside agency reviews are performed to certify an organization. These reviews are thorough in an effort to discover the enterprise's business functions, policies and procedures. Depending on the inspection, each outside agency is invited to bring in experts to analyze a company's performance. The inspector visits every aspect of the organization, measuring compliance, record keeping, improvements and other performance issues and makes a determination of whether or not they are worthy of the certification.

An organizational or professional certification review is a prime opportunity for an FSO to see how the organization performs outside of the NISPOM. Not only do certification reviews inspect areas of privacy or network security, but they are especially helpful in identifying record keeping and policy issues. Though the inspectors won't have access to classified information, they may have insight to processes. They can uncover areas that may need improving as well as reinforcing organization strengths. The copy of the certification audit report provides valuable information that the FSO can apply to the security program.

Security Awareness as Metrics

Attitudes toward security awareness programs can be great indicators of the FSO's program. Comments that reflect a desire for or loathing of continuing security awareness education speaks volumes. Those who are conscious of the need to protect national security assets and classified information should understand the need for training. Refresher training is a requirement identified in the executive orders, DoD and federal agency regulations including the NISPOM [3].

When the security program is well received, the managers support training as well as weave the elements of the security message throughout their work areas. When the FSO posts flyers, sends e-mail or communicates a security message, the managers are quick to ensure their employees have access to those messages. When the FSO practices security through walking around, employees relay enthusiastic messages that indicate their understanding and contribution to protecting classified information.

Indications that the security program is not well received include resistance to training and corrective actions. E-mail go unread, phone calls go unanswered, flyers and pamphlets are unused or thrown away. Other indicators include cleared employees not knowing who the FSO is or the names of other security professionals and comments about training are negative. Cleared employees complain about the requirement and view training only as a check the block activity. When the FSO conducts a walk-through of the areas, the employees avoid the visit and provide vague answers to questions about their role in the security program.

Security Budget as Metrics

Security budget support or lack of support can either demonstrate a well received or unappreciated security program. In a functional security manager role, the intuitive FSO understands business, the company mission and how the role of protecting classified material fits. The FSO can provide risk assessment and speak intelligently of the procedures, equipment and costs associated with protecting classified information. They understand how to contract security resources to install alarms, access control and other protection measures. The FSO is also able to demonstrate an ROI for expenses.

The FSO should provide the security budget after analyzing the needs and introduce it in a manner that all business units understand. For example, if part of the budget line is to provide access control for forty doors in four different buildings the cost is understandably significant. In this example, the access controls are not required by NISPOM, but would be instrumental in protecting employees, classified information and product as addressed in a risk assessment. The budget should not be the first place to identify the need. Incorporating management involvement and support throughout the risk management process puts the company in a better position to provide the funding. Additionally, a projected ROI and due diligence research should be conducted. Sample questions and answers the FSO should be prepared to address are:

What is the benefit of access control?

Access control prevents unauthorized persons from entering the premises and gives an extra layer of protection for classified and sensitive information. The FSO should also give the risk assessment findings to support the request.

What happens if we do not implement access controls?

The organization would have to commit persons to controlling the access to the company. When considering a manager's hourly rate, this could become expensive over time. The FSO could demonstrate the cost of the access controls against the time a manager takes to ensure someone is assigned to maintain visibility of the doors (Figure 12-1).

ITEM	COST	HOURS	SALARY	SALARY SAVINGS	HVAC SAVINGS
Access Control	$28,800	750	$28/hr	$21,000	$13,000

Figure 12-1 Example of Return on Security Investment- Notice the cost reduction after installing a $28,800 access control system. Prior to installing the Access Control package, doors to the building had no access control. Employees often failed to completely close the doors upon entering or exiting. The manager performed two random checks to ensure doors had been closed to prevent unauthorized visitors. The managers also had to track down visitors and vendors who had entered without going through the visitor reception desk. The FSO realized that the door magnet and swipe card available in the access control package would realize a $21,000 cost reduction in salary paid to managers. Manager checks 300 days annually. Additionally, the organization realized a $13,000 cost reduction on heating and air conditioning.

What is the return on investment for access control?

The intangible return on investment is the prevention of damage, injury, theft, and other risks inherent to unauthorized entry. More tangible is the amount of electrical energy saved while keeping the doors closed and protecting the inside climate. In one such study an FSO estimated a reduced cost of $13,000 per year on the electric bill.

The FSO's ability to project ROI should ensure that executives understand the significance of a well supported security program. The executives will trust the counsel of a well prepared FSO. Security managers who just quote regulations or use best practices without putting much thought into the costs or talking points will quickly lose credibility. For example, a defense contractor sufficiently stores information classified at the SECRET level or below in a GSA approved container.

Providing an argument that the NISPOM requires an alarm or other supplemental protection is inaccurate and irresponsible. If an alarm is desired, it should be introduced as the result of a thorough risk assessment according to data provided from crime statistics, threat assessments, as identified in this section or as required by contract. Once the data is in, the FSO can address the issues.

Security's involvement in strategic planning provides an excellent platform allowing the FSO to contribute their best efforts. A company that enjoys the influence and experience of a competent FSO reflects a good security program. When the FSO is invited to participate in strategic planning the company demonstrates that senior leaders value the security program and want the FSO's input.

Contractual Requirements as Metrics

Classified work is identified on the DD Form 254 and the statement of work. The FSO should understand associated costs inherent to the classified work identified in the contract and the DD Form 254.

Suppose a government customer has identified the work required of XYZ Contractor in a DD Form 254. Accordingly, XYZ Contractor will receive, generate and store classified information. Because of the nature of the classified work involved, the classified material will be stored separately according to the classification level and whether or not the material is Foreign Government Information, NATO, COMSEC, etc. This requires additional storage space and security containers which are expensive, but necessary.

The company is in the perfect position to anticipate the costs involved early in the planning. The costs can be calculated accurately, budgeted, and the FSO can prepare early to accept the upcoming challenges. Prior to receiving a DD Form 254, the FSO can discuss with management their key role in assessing the requests for bid and proposal.

A company that does not enjoy the FSO's input may not be very well prepared for the upcoming classified contract. They could miscalculate costs and commit the company to decisions based on lack of information as they scramble to meet compliance requirements. This lack of knowledge may affect their ability to protect classified information and may cause more than just financial consequences.

Analyzing Metric Data

A security manager can use such metrics or data and write a white paper, report, or provide a picture graph to employees, managers and executives for several purposes. Regardless of the report media, the objective should be to improve the state of security and communicate the results to the executives and shareholders. Cleared employees can be trained on recognizing proper procedures and preventing security violations by changing their behavior. Managers can use the information to direct changes in their employees and provide better security. Executives can use the information to identify programs or projects with probable risks and use the data for strategic planning. Finally, the shareholder, tax payers, board of director members, customers, and employees have a good understanding of their return on investment.

Convergence

Involve other departments outside of security to improve the security program. Security measures are best implemented if part of the corporate culture and works best driven from the top down. Convergence is a term pairing information technology with physical security. Convergence can identify ways of introducing security to all organizational areas and business units.

Workplace Crime Prevention

In light of the continuous threat to employees, product and classified information, security professionals should study their craft and learn ways to counter the impact. Business intelligence continues to offer information technology to analyze and prevent the internal and external influences working to harm an enterprise. Not only do defense contractors protect classified information, but they could be continually focused on preventing theft, vandalism, workplace violence, fraud, and computer attacks. The FSO should continue to implement programs to protect classified information as well as techniques of identification, analysis, risk assessment, operation security and prevention to mitigate risks.

Many private and publicly traded companies have invested security staff and compliance officers to address privacy and protection issues. This staff focuses efforts to identify and prevent theft of information, technology and product. Some of the security staff focus on loss prevention, a discipline oriented toward identifying risky behavior, observing others, investigating theft, and finding methods of reducing risk.

Convergence has typically involved security and information technology resources, vigilant employees and closed circuit television (CCTV). This is a great deterrent and detection device for both the internal and external threat. Television cameras employ the use of tilt/pan/zoom and digital technology records the data for instant recall. This data can be reviewed to see the habits and patterns of suspect customers and employees.

Vandalism is a constant threat to facilities in various locations.

Empty parking lots on the weekend or late at night can attract trespassers and vandals. Family members of employees are part of workplace violence patterns and criminal trespass activities. Though rare, these events have left a heavy toll on businesses. Depending on where a product falls in the lifecycle, research and development, work in progress, shipping or in transit, expenses will fall on the company and be passed to the customer.

Security solutions to detect and prevent these events include monitoring the workplace and removing the internal threat, building security in depth to prevent the external threat, training employees, and employing loss prevention techniques. Some additional mitigating factors include traditional security methods. When needed, additional lighting, security cameras and panic alarms do wonders to give employees a peace of mind as well as help prevent violent behavior. Knowing security is in place deters the criminal element.

Fraud Detection and the FSO

Fraud, espionage and other inconspicuous corporate crime are difficult to detect. Detection can be accidental, the result of a tip, an audit (internal, external or surprise), hot line or as referred by law enforcement. Focus and discipline could be perceived as the best means to detect fraud. As with reporting adverse behavior of cleared employees, the practice can be applied to crime. Employees could participate in verifying paperwork, checking records and reporting indicators of possible criminal behavior. Unchecked fraud could impact the defense industry as many defense contractors have less than 500 employees. Large economical losses can devastate an unwitting company and incidents of fraud can continue for long occasions before detected.

Information technology and the use of business intelligence or other software used to configure data, spreadsheets or reports can be applied to detecting and preventing corporate crime and espionage. Employee and hot line tips are most effective if used correctly. Computer links could be set up on corporate sites to allow anonymous employee reporting and phones can be programmed for anonymous tips.

Most methods of fraud or crime discovery have proven to be reactionary events. Fortunately, companies have the capability to automate almost everything. Time sheets, accounting, billing, production and supply chain records are often software based. Contractors have employed access control measures such as card scanners, code readers and biometrics. This technology leaves a trail of employee activity and can used to detect suspicious behavior. Taking lessons from Chapter 8, computer keyboard activity can be limited by password protection and IS sensitive data and computer use can be restricted. Computer and related media should go through the security department before introduction or removal. This is already in place in classified closed areas, but again, convergence and successful security programs require due diligence in all enterprise areas. Aside from employee protection and assistance roles, this data can be mined to see patterns and recognize traits of abuse and fraud.

Cyber Attacks and the FSO

Cyber attacks are a huge risk to all businesses. The threat of hackers, malicious viruses, and those who hijack websites and hold financial transactions for ransom are just a few serious events of which the security manager must be aware. Technology can be stolen or destroyed, reputations can be ruined, and personal information can be stolen. These attacks can cripple an enterprise and could take months or years to recover. The FSO could help the IT department focus on these threats and provide tools to detect and combat existing and future threats.

Worms and viruses quickly destroy years of input. These threats appear innocently enough in the beginning and when the right time comes, they activate. They recreate themselves, and spread throughout networks. Cyber saboteurs continually snoop, trying to learn passwords to exploit for espionage, theft or their idea of fun. Hijackers enter a system and threaten to cripple financial transactions until payment is made; extortion in high-tech form.

Employee internet discipline is a vital countermeasure. Aside from being an issue of abuse and possible investigation, employee internet activity could cripple a company. An enemy doesn't have to break down your defenses to wreak havoc. Just like old vampire lore, all an employee has to do is invite them in. When employees visit unauthorized websites, download unauthorized software, transfer data from a home computer or forward corrupted e-mail, they can cause just as much harm. Blocking websites, allowing only company designated personnel to upload software, and screening all mobile media or preventing all media and portable storage devices are all effective countermeasures the FSO can enforce.

Unprotected systems perpetuate all the above threats. Businesses that get involved either innocently as naive contributors or as the hapless victims suffer greatly financially and productively. There is another cost that could take longer to recover from. A technically illiterate or unprotected business has no excuse when dealing with customers or partners. Embarrassing things happen when a cyber crime investigation leads to a witless company that inadvertently released sensitive information.

There are many existing security methods available to help companies take the offense against such attack. As the in the above examples, this effort takes the coordination, input and involvement of all business units and departments in the organization. This cannot be given to the security department alone to handle. However, such actions should be accountable to one department.

Threat recognition works best when tracking such statistics as where the threat is coming from, how often the defenses are probed, what the threat is using to probe the defenses and what times of day are the threats are most active. The FSO and key managers should look at their organizations through the eyes of the perpetrator and identify what makes their business so tempting to target. Additional information concerning threat analysis and identification can be found with DCSA, military counter-intelligence, FBI, law enforcement organizations and government customers.

Currently there is a new partnership between the Department of Defense and CDCs that where applied appropriately will develop metrics for the prevention of cyberattacks. This partnership requires all defence contractors (including cleared defense contractors) to develop the Cybersecurity Maturity Model Certification (CMMC).

The CMMC will review and combine various cybersecurity standards and best practices and map these controls and processes across several maturity levels that range from basic cyber hygiene to advanced. For a given CMMC level, the associated controls and processes, when implemented, will reduce risk against a specific set of cyber threats. The FSO can assist with helping the CDC implement the appropriate CMMC level in an affordable and effective manner.

Preparing for Growth

Business for defense contractors is growing fast. How do defense contractors structure and align to meet the growth? Additional contracts can easily require cleared facilities to have closed areas, additional classified storage, different classified media and other unique protection and storage requirements. Analysis of growth and personnel requirements can help security managers stay on top of all upcoming events.

Growth for the FSO involves not only the number of cleared employees, contract and storage requirements in a possessing facility. Meeting legitimate growth is another area where an FSO is involved in strategic planning. New contracts with varying classified work requirements, new facility or alternate locations with physical security needs and an increase in classified storage or volume are all concerns an FSO should be able to address. Such growth affects the security department and input from the FSO benefits the entire organization.

When classified contract requirements necessitate the need for additional security personnel, the FSO should be prepared to hire based on identified employee characteristics. Just as the senior executive should identify an FSO's desired traits such as growth and management potential, technical competence, and skills, the same should be taken into account while preparing to hire additional security help. Potential security professionals should not only be U.S. citizens with security clearances, but demonstrate competence in the tasks they are asked to do and a desire to perform. They should also have the ability to grasp and teach concepts of security.

If available, hiring a security specialist who has worked in the career field for other defense contractors is a good option. They already possess the skills and the hiring manager will just have to ensure they have the ability to fit in with the company. However, another option may be to hire someone who lacks the skills, but has the desire and ability to perform well with a little training. In either case, because of the complexity and differences in contracts, no two organizations work the same way. Two defense contractor companies working under NISPOM can remain in compliance while having different operating procedures. Hiring a person with a desire to learn, formal education and a perfect match for the company culture would be desirable even though they lack technical competence. The nuances of security can be taught on the job and at formal training.

As early as possible, FSOs and security specialists should work toward establishing operating procedures and a job performance description. New employees can become successful faster with formalized training. This training should be unique to the organization and is made with milestones that eventually allow new employees to work unsupervised. The new employee can enroll in government provided on-line and residence training, lessons provided by company personnel or on the job training directly under their manager's supervision. With a good training or certification plan in place, much of the employee's success can be measured within the first 90 days.

FSOs and Cost Reduction

Process Streamlining and Reduction in Supplies

Consider an FSO's leadership dilemma in the next example. During his first few months at XYZ Contractor, his security employees expressed opinions that engineers working on classified projects needed extra reminders of classification levels. To compensate, the security employees applied additional classification markings beyond the required markings already provided on the top and bottom of the front and back cover of classified documents.

The FSO understood that Federal regulations required applying risk management to reduce wasteful and redundant operations. He reviewed the NISPOM and document marking references to ensure he understood the requirements. He also re-read the DD Forms 254 and related SCGs for all classified contracts to identify any unique marking or storage requirements. He used his IMS inventory software to pull up information about how many classified documents the company received and generated. He also pulled past purchasing requests for security supplies.

His research revealed that the company purchased over $3,000 worth of unnecessary label making supplies annually. Additionally, the document custodian's process bottleneck occurred during the application of markings. Whether receiving documents from outside of the organization or as newly created, his staff added the unnecessary additional markings even though they were already clearly marked. The additional markings cluttered the document, covered valuable information and provided unnecessary redundant work and ineffective security measures. Often, the engineers waited far too long to access the classified material as it went through the preparation process.

After careful evaluation and retraining his employees, the FSO ended the practice of additional markings. He led the employees to improve security and reduce the hourly and material costs associated with over marking the documents. He also demonstrated his fiscal responsibility in a detailed budget amendment showing a significant cost reduction.

Overhead Cost Reduction

The security staff, FSO and other parts of the enterprise not directly paid for directly through a contract is referred to as overhead. These employees charge their salaries, services and support to the company. Overhead includes other career fields such as human resources, contracts management, accounting, safety and others who do not charge their time to a contract. Overhead expenses come out of a company's budget. These positions do not earn money for the company. In fact, they spend money on salaries, supplies, equipment, software and other items necessary to support the enterprise. Industrial security specialist charging to overhead spend money and resources protecting classified information. Supplies and equipment take up valuable space, generate waste related costs and expenses when maintained unnecessarily. Personnel in the security department require salary, benefits, training and health care. FSOs should learn to prioritize security efforts and streamline performance and equipment costs.

Security Equipment Cost Reduction

If required, other expenses include construction costs for closed areas, SCIFs, vaults and areas for classified meetings. Security containers and other GSA approved security devices are expensive and must be maintained. FSOs and security specialists working with multiple security containers, vaults and personnel should consider how to reduce expenses while maintaining the appropriate level of security.

Security Services

Cleared employees are needed for the safeguarding, processing and disseminating of classified information. Conducting inquiries, staffing classified document repositories, maintaining personnel and facility clearance and changing security container combinations are part of the day to day functions of a security specialist. Other services include sending classified information by USPS or authorized overnight carrier. This could constitute a large part of the budget the FSO should be projecting. USPS Registered and other required mailing service costs add up proportionally as the volume of mail increases.

Process And Bottom Line

Since overhead does take from an organization's top line, it is important for managers to understand how best to reduce expenditures when at all possible. The FSO should understand how to reduce costs without decreasing security effectiveness. Those who have accelerated their careers have done so after being recognized for reducing costs without sacrificing national security.

Successful programs designed to engineer out waste work well with services to reduce costs, eliminate waste and perform more effectively. This requires a dynamic change in thinking led by strong leadership. The predominant thinking should not be to provide security at all costs. Consider a few tasks routinely conducted by industrial security specialists in two different disciplines. The first is in personnel security and the second is in document control.

Cost Reduction and Personnel Security

The personnel security specialist maintains records on employees who are being processed for a security clearance or who already have security clearances. Information in the file includes employment data, the SF 312 Classified Information Nondisclosure Agreement and security training records. These records are thick with information that included a copy of the SF 86 Questionnaire for National Security Positions as well as paper copies on any information about the security clearances and the cleared person.

In recent years, changes in privacy laws and the development of new security clearance online databases have led to fewer paper files required to be stored on site. Prior to the DoD's implementation of their database, copies of security clearance status, SF 86, signature pages, and many other files had to be maintained. Paper files were dense and required room for storage.

Databases automated the personnel security system. The national database proved a reliable method for keeping up with and tracking the security clearances and status. Records are updated online and most transactions can take place without the exchange of paperwork and the online systems eliminated the need for bulky personnel files. Other personnel actions such as submitting and receiving visit requests were also executed with more confidentiality as personal information is better protected on the secure server, and without wasteful paperwork.

Cost Reduction and Document Control

FSOs can also reduce costs during classified document storage and inventory. Knowing what type of classified information is stored and how it is stored can lead to effective product management. For a possessing facility, a new classified contract can lead to more classified information and storage requirements. The FSO would need to know what type of storage would be necessary. For example, an increase in classified information on DVDs or CDs requires different storage shelving than that of paper documents. Two hundred DVDs can be stored in a smaller area than as many 150 page documents. A competent IMS database or software can help an FSO identify these types of trends. The FSO can research such information by pulling up records of the number and type of documents received, stored, and disseminated or destroyed.

Additionally, good software can work with barcodes and scanners. When the FSO logs in classified information, they can also input bar code information. When the FSO stores, issues, destroys or disseminates classified information, they can scan the barcode. The information is then entered into the IMS and the classified information status is updated. Such scanning identifies documents by bar code, document number, and other vital information.

Barcode inventory is used regularly in retail and other inventory applications. Manual inventory is costly. However, when inventory is conducted with simultaneous daily operations, it can be time saving and purposeful. When used correctly, barcode inventory can allow the custodians to free valuable time, save the company overtime and other expenses, and maintain the same or better level of security and required inventory events.

FSOs can recognize wasteful movement and processes in their security departments. They can draw on security experiences and transferable skills from other jobs to make positive changes and reduce expenses. FSOs should effectively lead and train employees in such changes in processes and demonstrate cost reduction to management. Defense contractors and Federal agencies regularly reward employees who take the initiative to identify wasteful processes and recommend solutions. Additionally, figuring the security return on investment (ROI) adds to the cost reductions.

Consider the installation of access control such as card readers. Though not required, they may be necessary to prevent unauthorized persons from entering a facility. An FSO should be able to demonstrate reduced costs through compared heating and cooling bills before and after the installation of access controls systems. For example, suppose a cleared contractor has three warehouses with ten doors each that remain open at all times. Unauthorized persons have entered on several occasions and employees have practiced little discipline in keeping the doors closed. The new FSO performs a risk and cost analysis pointing to a need for an access control system.

The FSO should provide a sound business plan to demonstrate to shareholders the benefits of a more secure work environment. In the past, management has attempted to maintain closed doors by recommending that supervisors check the doors several times daily. The FSO schedules time with his immediate vice president to inspect the procedure. Soon the vice-president notices the lack of discipline, possible liability with unauthorized visitors and waste of process with frequents supervisor door checks. Shortly thereafter, management authorizes the installation of the access control system. The FSO keeps management informed of results and how installation contributed to reducing costs. By keeping the doors closed, the access control system cost was made up from saving in air conditioning costs over the period of a year (Figure 13-1).

ITEM	COST	HOURS	SALARY	SALARY SAVINGS	HVAC SAVINGS
Access Control	$28,800	750	28	$21,000	$13,000
High Security Locks	$4,200	5	28	$140	
Crash Bars	$500	NA	NA	$0	
Door locks	$2,000	NA	NA	$0	
2 Cameras	$1,345	5	28	$140	

Figure 13-1 Example of Return on Security Investment- Notice the cost reduction after installing a $28,800 access control system. Prior to installing the Access Control package, doors to the building had no access control. Employees often failed to completely close the doors upon entering or exiting, leaving and others could enter unhindered. As a result, managers performed two random checks to ensure doors had been closed to prevent unauthorized visitors. The managers also had to track down visitors and vendors who had entered without going through the visitor reception desk. The FSO realized that the door magnet and swipe card available in the access control package would result in a $21,000 cost reduction in salary paid to managers since managers performed checks 300 days annually.

Summary

There is a large distinction between being a security technician and a professional. Security technicians work on individual tasks and are focused on task completion. Security professionals should not only be technically proficient, but should understand how security fits into the company culture. To better guide the organization's security program, the FSO should understand the organization's primary mission. Understanding the goals, mission and culture and how to implement the security program helps the FSO establish credibility and integrate into the company culture.

The FSO has many tools to help improve organization's security posture. These tools provide metrics that can be used to relate to executives and senior managers who understand evaluations, ratings and assessments. FSOs who translate security needs and requirements based on facts, risk management and compliance help executives make good decisions.

Problems

1. A facility security officer has many milestone tools available for finding solid facts about their security program. Name two of the tools the FSO can use to gather information about their security program's posture.

2. After conducting a preliminary investigation on a security incident, the FSO concludes that though a security violation had occurred, there was no compromise or suspected compromise. What can the FSO do with the results and discoveries made during the investigation?

3. DCSA conducts an annual security review to determine a defense contractor's ability to protect classified information. What are the four ratings a defense contractor is eligible for? Which rating makes the contractor eligible to compete for the Cogswell award and what is required of a contractor to get that rating?

REFERENCES

1. Department of Defense, DoD 5220.22-M, National Industrial Security Operating Manual, section 1-201, February 2006
2. Department of Defense, DoD 5220.22-M, National Industrial Security Operating Manual, section 1-207, February 2006
3. Department of Defense, DoD 5220.22-M, National Industrial Security Operating Manual, section 3-107, February 2006

HELPFUL WEBSITES:

FSO training Certification

http://www.dcsa.mil
https://www.bennettinstitute.com

FSO newsletter
https://www.redbikepublishing.com/contact

Cyber Maturity Model Certification
http://www.acq.osd.mil/cmmc/

Self Inspection Handbook for NISP Contractors
https://www.redbikepublishing.com
https://www.dcsa.mil

APPENDIX A

How to prepare for a Defense Counterintelligence and Security Agency (DCSA) Inspection

DCSA performs annual reviews to ensure cleared contractors are protecting classified information according to the national industrial security program Operating Manual. DCSA conducts the reviews every 12 months for possessing facilities and every 18 months for non-possessing facilities. However, other factors could affect the frequency. DCSA will send a notice prior to inspection. Initial notification could be by phone, mail or email and followed up in writing.

The inspection should be an exercise of what DCSA, the FSO and cleared employees already understand about the security program. The relationship will be a reflection of what the FSO has established with employees and DCSA as identified in this book. Such relationships create an environment where all elements take ownership of the program and DCSA representative is aware of program effectiveness throughout the year. The inspection should be a wrap-up of what everyone already understands about the program. In a best case scenario, there should be no long hours focused on passing the inspection. In other words, the inspection should be just another great security day.

Prior to the inspection, DCSA should send a request for information. Requested information includes information about the facility and personnel security clearances. The questionnaire is detailed and will take some time to gather the requested information. Most information can be researched using the Joint Personnel Adjudication System database. For example, be prepared to disclose number of cleared employees by clearance level, number of classified documents on site by classification, organizational changes that affect the facility clearance level and etc.

Depending on which parts of NISPOM apply to your company, prepare the following for presentation (see the NISPOM questionnaire covered in Chapter 2). Some FSOs create a folder for the DCSA representative to help the inspection flow smoothly. The folders include useful information about the security program to help the FSO answer questions and demonstrate program effectiveness. Though DCSA has not yet released inspection criteria, the DCSA Self Inspection Handbook available on the DCSA website, is a good resource to base DCSA reviews on. Items to consider include, but are not limited to the following:

1. Original and current facility security clearance documentation
   - Sponsorship Letter
   - DCSA FL 381-R Cleared Facility Letter-Provided by DCSA acknowledging organization as cleared facility
   - DD FORM 441- Department of Defense Security Agreement
   - STANDARD FORM 328 Certificate Pertaining to Foreign Interests
   - Key Management Personnel List
2. Personnel security clearance information
   - PCL Information
   - Personnel clearance information
   - Current Outgoing Classified Visit Request Authorizations
   - Consultants
   - Number of Non-US Citizens
3. Copies of DCSA and self inspection results. Address any issues or findings.
   - Last year's DCSA Inspection
   - Self-Inspection
   - Implementations made after inspections
4. Provide list of all DD Form 254 Department of Defense Contract Security Classification Specifications

This will remind the DCSA representative of the security requirements and how your organization is poised to meet and exceed those requirements. Your risk assessment matrix should also be included to demonstrate security focus as related to current threats, NISPOM and DD Form 254 requirements.

- Contracts Information
- DD Form 254 Information
- Current Classified Contracts List (DD 254s)
- Prime and Subcontractors

5. Security Incidents/Violations
- Preliminary investigations
- Mismarked documents
- Unauthorized disclosure

6. Reports to DCSA
- Adverse Information
- Suspicious Contacts Report
- List suspicious contacts reported to DCSA

7. Demonstrate Security Program Awareness

8. Proof of (documentation and proof of attendance):
- Initial security briefings
- Annual Security Awareness Training
- COMSEC, NATO, and other access briefings
- Location and type of posters
- Handouts available
- Automated or other email notices
- Security training websites for employees
- Certifications of training for FSO and security specialists
- Upcoming training dates

9. Locations of where classified information is stored (Security Containers and Closed areas)
- Location
- Type
- Record of combination changes

10. Classified processing
- Copies of certifications and accreditations
- List of IS
- Copy of SSP

11. Paper trail/receipts of classified documents received, copied,

transmitted, downgraded, declassified and destroyed.

12. International Operations
- List of Export Licenses
- Technology Control Plan
- Defensive Security Briefings

While preparing for the inspection, send reminders to all employees to help them recall the security program, the name of the FSO and key terms they need to know. Cleared employees may be interviewed as part of the review. They should understand and be able to answer questions concerning foreign travel, required briefings, reports, access, need to know and the ever popular adverse information.

On the review day, prepare a warm reception for the DCSA Special Agent. Prepare a briefing and ensure senior managers and Key Management Personnel attend. This will give a good impression of company involvement.

APPENDIX B
Definitions

Access-The ability and opportunity to gain knowledge of classified information.

Adverse Information-Any information that adversely reflects on the integrity or character of a cleared employee, that suggests that his or her ability to safeguard classified information may be impaired, or that his or her access to classified information clearly may not be in the interest of national security.

Authorized Person-A person who has a need-to-know for classified information in the performance of official duties and who has been granted a PCL at the required level.

Classified Contract-Any contract requiring access to classified information by a contractor or his or her employees in the performance of the contract. (A contract may be a classified contract even though the contract document is not classified.) The requirements prescribed for a "classified contract" also are applicable to all phases of pre-contract activity, including solicitations (bids, quotations, and proposals), pre-contract negotiations, post-contract activity, or other GCA program or project which requires access to classified information by a contractor.

Classified Information-Official information that has been determined, pursuant to reference (b) or any predecessor order, to require protection against unauthorized disclosure in the interest of national security and which has been so designated.

Classified Visit-A visit during which a visitor will require, or is expected to require, access to classified information.

Cleared Commercial Carrier-A carrier authorized by law, regulatory body, or regulation to transport SECRET material and has been granted a SECRET facility clearance.

Cleared Employees-All contractor employees granted PCLs and all employees being processed for PCLs.

Closed Area-An area that meets the requirements of NISPOM for safeguarding classified material that, because of its size, nature, or operational necessity, cannot be adequately protected by the normal safeguards or stored during nonworking hours in approved containers.

Cognizant Security Agency (CSA)-Agencies of the Executive Branch that have been authorized by reference (a) to establish an industrial security program to safeguard classified information under the jurisdiction of those agencies when disclosed or released to U.S. Industry. These agencies are: The Department of Defense, DOE, CIA, and NRC.

Cognizant Security Office (CSO)-The organizational entity delegated by the Head of a CSA to administer industrial security on behalf of the CSA.

Compromise-An unauthorized disclosure of classified information.

CONFIDENTIAL-The classification level applied to information, the unauthorized disclosure of which reasonable could be expected to cause damage to the national security that the original classification authority is able to identify or describe.

Constant Surveillance Service-A transportation protective service provided by a commercial carrier qualified to transport CONFIDENTIAL shipments. The service requires constant surveillance of the shipment at all times by a qualified carrier representative; however, an FCL is not required for the carrier. The carrier providing the service must maintain a signature and tally record for the shipment.

Contractor-Any industrial, educational, commercial, or other entity that has been granted an FCL by a CSA.

Courier-A cleared employee, designated by the contractor, whose principal duty is to transmit classified material to its destination. The classified material remains in the personal possession of the courier except for authorized overnight storage.

Declassification-The determination that classified information no longer requires, in the interest of national security, any degree of protection against unauthorized disclosure, together with removal or cancellation of the classification designation.

Derivative Classification-The incorporating, paraphrasing, restating, or generating in new form information that is already classified, and marking the newly developed material consistent with the classification markings that apply to the source information. Derivative classification includes the classification of information based on classification guidance.

Escort-A cleared person, designated by the contractor, who accompanies a shipment of classified material to its destination. The classified material does not remain in the personal possession of the escort but the conveyance in which the material is transported remains under the constant observation and control of the escort.

Facility (Security) Clearance (FCL)-An administrative determination that, from a security viewpoint, a company is eligible for access to classified information of a certain category (and all lower categories).

Foreign Government Information (FGI)-Information that is:

Provided to the U.S. by a foreign government or governments, an international organization of governments, or any element thereof with the expectation, expressed or implied, that the information, the source of the information, or both, are to be held in confidence; or

Produced by the U.S. pursuant to, or as a result of, a joint arrangement with a foreign government or governments, an international organization of governments, or any element thereof, requiring that the information, the arrangement, or both are to be held in confidence.

Freight Forwarder- Any agent or facility designated to receive, process, and transship U.S. material to foreign recipients. In the context of the NISPOM, an agent or facility cleared specifically to perform these functions for the transfer of U.S. classified material to foreign recipients.

Government Contracting Activity (GCA)-An element of an agency designated by the agency head and delegated broad authority regarding acquisition functions.

Handcarrier-A cleared employee, designated by the contractor, who occasionally handcarries classified material to its destination in connection with a classified visit or meeting. The classified material remains in the personal possession of the handcarrier except for authorized overnight storage.

Industrial Security-That portion of information security concerned with the protection of classified information in the custody of U.S. industry.

Information System (IS)-An assembly of computer hardware, software, and firmware configured for the purpose of automating the functions of calculating, computing, sequencing, storing, retrieving, displaying, communicating, or otherwise manipulating data, information and textual material.

Limited Access Authorization (LAA)-Security access authorization to CONFIDENTIAL or SECRET information granted to non-U.S. citizens requiring such limited access in the course of their regular duties.

Material-Any product or substance on or in which information is embodied.

Multiple Facility Organization (MFO)-A legal entity (single proprietorship, partnership, association, trust, or corporation) composed of two or more contractors.

Need to Know-A determination made by an authorized holder of classified information that a prospective recipient has a requirement for access to, knowledge, or possession of the classified information to perform tasks or services essential to the fulfillment of a classified contract or program.

Original Classification Authority-Government Officials who have been designated in writing to make an initial determination that information requires, in the interest of national security, protection against unauthorized disclosure, together with a classification designation signifying the level of protection required.

Personnel (Security) Clearance (PCL)-An administrative determination that an individual is eligible, from a security point of view, for access to classified information of the same or lower category as the level of the personnel clearance being granted.

Prime Contractor-The contractor who receives a prime contract from a GCA.

Protective Security Service-A transportation protective service provided by a cleared commercial carrier qualified by the SDDC to transport SECRET shipments.

Restricted Area-A controlled access area established to safeguard classified material, that because of its size or nature, cannot be adequately protected during working hours by the usual safeguards, but that is capable of being stored during non-working hours in an approved repository or secured by other methods approved by the CSA.

SECRET-The classification level applied to information, the unauthorized disclosure of which reasonably could be expected to cause serious damage to the national security that the original classification authority is able to identify or describe.

Security Classification Guide-A document issued by an authorized original classifier that identifies the elements of information regarding a specific subject that must be classified and prescribes the level and duration of classification and appropriate declassification instructions. (Classification guides are provided to contractors by the Contract Security Classification Specification.)

Security in Depth-A determination made by the CSA that a contractor's security program consists of layered and complementary security controls sufficient to deter and detect unauthorized entry and movement within the facility.

Security Violation-Failure to comply with the policy and procedures established by the NISPOM that reasonably could result in the loss or compromise of classified information.

Standard Practice Procedures (SPP)-A document prepared by a contractor that implements the applicable requirements of the NISPOM for the contractor's operations and involvement with classified information at the contractor's facility.

Subcontract-Any contract entered into by a contractor to furnish supplies or services for performance of a prime contract or a subcontract. For purposes of NISPOM, a subcontract is any contract, subcontract, purchase order, lease agreement, service agreement, request for quotation (RFQ), request for proposal (RFP), invitation for bid (IFB), or other agreement or procurement action between contractors that requires or will require access to classified information to fulfill the performance requirements of a prime contract.

Subcontractor-A supplier, distributor, vendor, or firm that furnishes supplies or services to or for a prime contractor or another subcontractor, who enters into a contract with a prime contractor. For purposes of this NISPOM, each subcontractor shall be considered as a prime contractor in relation to its subcontractors.

TOP SECRET-The classification level applied to information, the unauthorized disclosure of which reasonable could be expected to cause exceptionally grave damage to the national security that the original classification authority is able to identify or describe.

Unauthorized Person-A person not authorized to have access to specific classified information in accordance with the requirements of the NISPOM.

US Person-Any form of business enterprise or entity organized, chartered or incorporated under the laws of the United States or its territories and any person who is a citizen or national of the United States.

APPENDIX C

BL Bill of Lading
CAGE Commercial and Government Entity
CIA Central Intelligence Agency
CM Configuration Management
COMSEC Communications Security
CSA Cognizant Security Agency
CSO Cognizant Security Office
DAA Designated Accrediting/Approving Authority
DGR Designated Government Representative
DNI Director of National Intelligence
DoD Department of Defense
DoE Department of Energy
DCSA Defense Counterintelligence and Security Agency
EAA Export Administration Act
FBI Federal Bureau of Investigation
FCL Facility (Security) Clearance
FGI Foreign Government Information
FOCI Foreign Ownership, Control or Influence
FSO Facility Security Officer
GCA Government Contracting Activity
GSA General Services Administration
IS Information System
ISOO Information Security Oversight Office
ISSM Information System Security Manager
ISSO Information System Security Officer
ITAR International Traffic in Arms Regulations
LAA Limited Access Authorization
MFO Multiple Facility Organization

NACLC National Agency Check with Local Agency Check and Credit Check
NISP National Industrial Security Program
NISPOM National Industrial Security Program Operating Manual
NSA National Security Agency
OADR Originating Agency's Determination Required
PCL Personnel (Security) Clearance
RFP Request for Proposal
RFQ Request for Quotation
SCI Sensitive Compartmented Information
SCIF Sensitive Compartmented Information Facility
SSBI Single Scope Background Investigation
SSP Systems Security Plan
TCO Technology Control Officer
TCP Technology Control Plan
TP Transportation Plan

Index

F

facility clearance. *See* Facility Security Clearance
Facility (Security) Clearance 291, 295
Facility Security Officer 20, 21
FBI 32, 71, 80, 220, 221, 295
FCL 9, 43, 66, 67, 69, 79, 205, 255, 63
Federal Bureau of Investigation 32, 71, 160, 220
FGI 30, 109, 246, 247, 250, 291, 295
FOCI 57, 65, 69, 205, 295. *See also* Facility Security Clearance
Foreign Government Information 30, 91, 92, 246, 270, 291, 295
Foreign Ownership Control or Influence 65
FOR OFFICIAL USE ONLY 91
Freight Forwarder 291
FSO 20, 21, 22, 23, 25, 35, 36, 40, 43, 44, 45, 46, 47, 49, 50, 51, 52, 53, 54,
  55, 56, 58, 59, 67, 68, 70, 71, 72, 79, 80, 81, 82, 83, 84, 85, 86, 89, 90,
  91, 93, 94, 95, 96, 97, 98, 99, 100, 101, 103, 104, 105, 106, 107, 108,
  110, 111, 126, 127, 140, 141, 142, 144, 150, 151, 152, 153, 154, 155,
  156, 157, 158, 182, 183, 184, 185, 186, 187, 190, 191, 192, 193, 196,
  197, 198, 199, 200, 204, 205, 206, 207, 208, 209, 211, 212, 215, 245,
  217, 219, 220, 224, 225, 226, 227, 228, 245, 246, 247, 249, 250, 251,
  255, 256, 257, 258, 207, 259, 260, 261, 262, 263, 264, 265, 266, 267,
  268, 269, 270, 271, 272, 273, 274, 275, 276, 277, 278, 279, 280, 281,
  282, 283, 207, 212

G

GCA 10, 43, 65, 68, 69, 81, 82, 85, 87, 88, 89, 90, 91, 92, 93, 94, 130, 131,
  133, 181, 182, 188, 191, 193, 194, 198, 231, 241, 243, 244, 245, 246,
  247, 248, 250, 251, 264, 289, 291, 293, 295. *See also* Facility Security
  Clearance
Government Contracting Activity 8, 81, 89, 188, 291, 295
GSA 51, 52, 53, 82, 103, 109, 117, 147, 151, 152, 153, 191, 192, 269, 278,
  295. *See also* Facility Security Clearance
GSA Approved Overnight Delivery Service 191

H

Handcarrier 292

I

identification 87, 94, 106, 111, 119, 126, 127, 140, 194, 197, 198, 106, 271
Identification Marking 119
IMS 108, 146, 181, 182, 183, 186, 198, 199, 277, 106, 280

Questionnaire for National Security Positions 70, 279

R

Rail 196
receipt 90, 97, 102, 103, 104, 106, 107, 108, 109, 110, 111, 127, 182, 183,
        185, 186, 187, 192, 195, 199, 205, 223, 245, 246
reporting 24, 37, 45, 47, 49, 57, 77, 105, 133, 189, 203, 204, 209, 215, 220,
        221, 225, 226, 256, 260, 261, 272
restricted area 150, 158, 206
Restricted Area 293
RFP 81, 294, 296
RFQ 81, 294, 296
risk assessment. *See* Facility Security Clearance
Risk Assessment 51

S

SCG 36, 66, 67, 82, 83, 87, 92, 94, 107, 126, 127, 128, 133, 157, 206
SCI 25, 71, 91, 92, 95, 96, 296
SCIF 50, 91, 296. *See also* Facility Security Clearance
SECRET 9, 27, 28, 29, 30, 34, 37, 40, 48, 50, 51, 52, 84, 71, 85, 86, 90, 93,
        97, 101, 102, 105, 106, 107, 108, 112, 113, 114, 115, 116, 145, 119,
        120, 121, 122, 123, 124, 125, 126, 127, 129, 130, 131, 135, 144, 145,
        146, 147, 151, 152, 157, 181, 186, 187, 188, 189, 190, 191, 192, 199,
        200, 207, 240, 244, 245, 248, 269, 290, 292, 293, 76
security awareness training 20, 23, 45, 55, 56, 207, 220, 221, 260
security classification guide 33, 35, 37
Security Classification Guide 35, 82, 134, 293
Security Containers 152
Security in Depth 293
security plan 46, 49, 68
Security Violation 293
Sensitive Compartmented Information Facility 50, 91
SF 86 70, 71, 72, 76, 77, 279
SF 312 38, 207, 209, 214, 215, 223, 279, 228, 207
SF 328. *See* Facility Security Clearance
SSBI 70, 71, 90, 76, 76
SSP 287, 296
Standard Form 86. *See* Facility Security Clearance
Standard Practice Procedures 293
Subcontract 293
Subcontractor 294
Subject and Title Marking 119

T

TCO 232, 296
TCP 242, 249, 296
threat awareness briefing 210
TOP SECRET 9, 27, 28, 29, 34, 48, 50, 84, 71, 85, 86, 90, 97, 101, 102, 105,
    108, 113, 116, 145, 119, 120, 122, 127, 131, 144, 145, 146, 147, 151,
    152, 181, 188, 189, 190, 192, 199, 207, 248, 76
TP 296
training 19, 20, 22, 23, 24, 28, 29, 32, 40, 45, 55, 56, 57, 83, 90, 105, 106,
    114, 118, 121, 123, 124, 129, 130, 131, 132, 160, 194, 203, 204, 205,
    207, 208, 209, 210, 211, 212, 267, 215, 216, 217, 218, 219, 220, 223,
    224, 227, 229, 232, 236, 237, 260, 212, 264, 213, 266, 267, 276, 278
transmission 38, 98, 100, 101, 127, 146, 182, 187, 189, 199, 200
Transportation Plan 296
TS 71, 121, 122

U

unauthorized access 54, 101, 151, 157, 199, 205, 222, 223, 246
unauthorized disclosure 20, 21, 25, 27, 28, 29, 32, 38, 39, 45, 65, 67, 68, 69,
    98, 101, 102, 104, 106, 111, 117, 126, 128, 139, 144, 145, 183, 206,
    211, 219, 232, 238, 239, 248, 263
Unauthorized Person 294
uncleared facilities. *See* Facility Security Clearance
Uncleared Facilities 62
United States Munitions List 233
USML 234
US Person 237, 294
USPS 107, 188, 190, 192, 200, 278

V

violation 85, 102, 103, 141, 153, 208, 220, 222, 226, 227, 239, 262, 263, 283

W

Working Papers 146, 147

CONCLUSION

This concludes our book and I hope you have found it informative and useful. I also hope that I have delivered on my promise of helping you prepare to bid on and perform on classified contracts.

ABOUT THE AUTHOR

Jeffrey W. Bennett, ISOC, ISP, SAPPC, SFPC is a security expert with experience in the Army, U.S. Government and as a Facility Security Officer (FSO). He holds DoD Certifications including SAPPC, SFPC, ISOC and the ISP certificate number 117.

Jeff is enthusiastic about protecting our nation's secrets. He believes that integrity, influence and credibility are paramount qualities required of security professionals. His primary goal is to show Cleared Defense Contractors how to bring about security awareness, build influence within the organization and to make a difference where they work.

He speaks, writes, consults and provides products to help professionals better protect sensitive and classified information. Jeff is the author of many books including: *Insider's Guide to Security Clearances, ISP and ISOC Master Exam Prep, Get Rich in a Niche-Insider's Guide to Self Publishing* and several novels.

Contact Jeff:
editor@redbikepublishing.com
Hear Jeff's Podcast at:
https://www.redbikepublishing.com/dodsecure

Join NISPOM and ISP Cert training at:
https://bennettinstitute.com

Red Bike Publishing

Our company is registered as a government contractor company with the CCR and VetBiz (DUNS 826859691). Specifically we are a service disabled veteran owned small business. Red Bike Publishing provides high quality books and training @ www.redbikepublishing.com.

Additional Resources:

An additional study resource includes the *Self Inspection Handbook For NISP Contractors* with Change 2, May 18, 2016. Available at the DCSA website and at Red Bike Publishing https://www.redbikepublishing.com

Books

This book, other security and NISP books and training are also available at our website. Helpful books include those part of the Security Clearances and Cleared Defense Contractor series by Red Bike Publishing:

Security Clearances and Cleared Defense Contractor (Series)

1. *Insider's Guide to Security Clearances*
2. *How to Get U.S. Government Contracts and Classified Work*
3. *National Industrial Security Program Operating Manual (NISPOM)*
4. *Self Inspection Guidebook for NISP Contractors*
5. *ISP and ISOC Master Exam Prep*
6. *International Traffic In Arms Regulation (ITAR)*

Training

Training topics include the follow either stand alone or as an FSO Certification Bundle https://www.redbikepublishing.com/fsocertification/:

- SF-312 Non Disclosure Briefing
- Insider Threat Training
- Derivative Classifier Training
- Security Awareness Training

Bennett Institute https://www.bennettinstitute.com

NISPOM Fundamentals Course-Training that discusses each chapter of the NISPOM in depth; more than 8 hours of recorded training

- Alternatively, you can take course one chapter or topic at a time
- Great study material. Each course provides completion certificates that can be used to earn CEUs for recertification.
- We also have a complimentary course available called Certification Test Tips

A special word of thanks and a favor to ask

Thank you for buying my book. I really appreciate you being a reader and hope you find it helpful. If you have any questions, please feel free to contact me.

I would really love to hear your feedback and your input would help to make the next version of this book and my future books better. Please leave me a helpful review on Amazon letting me know what you thought of the book.

I would also ask that you let a friend know about our book as well. Thanks so much and best of success to you!!

Jeffrey W. Bennett

Sign up for our reader newsletter:
https://www.redbikepublishing.com/contact
Like us on Facebook.

Our page is DoD Security at:
https://www.facebook.com/DoD-Security

If you want more information about Red Bike Publishing, check out our video.
https://www.redbikepublishing.com/security/

Made in the USA
Columbia, SC
18 October 2024

44601454R10170